YOUR 15-MON...
COMPLETE AND IND...

ARIES
March 21 - April 20

1988
SUPER HOROSCOPE

ARROW BOOKS LIMITED
62-65 Chandos Place
London WC2N 4NW

CONTENTS

NOTE TO THE CUSP-BORN iii
HISTORY AND USES OF ASTROLOGY 1
HOW TO USE THESE PREDICTIONS 20
THE MOON 21
MOON TABLES, 1988
  Time Conversions 28
  Moon Tables... 29
  Planting Guide, 1988................................ 33
  Fishing Guide, 1988................................. 34
  Influence Over Daily Affairs 34
  Influence Over Health and Plants 35
THE SIGNS OF THE ZODIAC
  Dominant Characteristics........................... 37
  Key Words 62
  The Elements and the Qualities.................... 63
  How to Approximate Your Rising Sign 71
THE PLANETS OF THE SOLAR SYSTEM............. 76
FAMOUS PERSONALITIES 86
ARIES: 1988
  Character Analysis 89
  Love and Marriage 96
  Yearly Forecast 124
  Daily Forecast 128
  October, November, December, 1987 227

THE PUBLISHERS REGRET THAT THEY CANNOT ANSWER INDIVIDUAL LETTERS REQUESTING PERSONAL HOROSCOPE INFORMATION.

FIRST PUBLISHED IN GREAT BRITAIN BY ARROW BOOKS 1987
© GROSSET & DUNLAP, INC., 1974, 1978, 1979, 1980, 1981, 1982
© CHARTER COMMUNICATIONS, INC., 1983, 1984, 1985
COPYRIGHT © 1986, 1987 THE BERKLEY PUBLISHING GROUP

PRINTED IN GREAT BRITAIN BY
GUERNSEY PRESS CO. LTD
GUERNSEY C.I.
ISBN 0 09 948850 7

NOTE TO THE CUSP-BORN

First find the year of your birth, and then find the sign under which you were born according to your day of birth. Thus, you can determine if you are a true Aries (or Pisces or Taurus), according to the variations of the dates of the Zodiac. (See also page 7.)

Are you *really* an Aries? If your birthday falls during the fourth week of March, at the beginning of Aries, will you still retain the traits of Pisces, the sign of the Zodiac before Aries? And what if you were born late in April—are you more Taurus than Aries? Many people born at the edge, or cusp, of a sign have difficulty determining exactly what sign they are. If you are one of these people, here's how you can figure it out, once and for all.

Consult the following table. It will tell you the precise days on which the Sun entered and left your sign for the year of your birth. If you were born at the beginning or end of Aries, yours is a lifetime reflecting a process of subtle transformation. Your life on Earth will symbolize a significant change in consciousness, for you are either about to enter a whole new way of living or are leaving one behind.

If your birthday falls at the end of March, you may want to read the horoscope book for Pisces as well as Aries, for Pisces holds the keys to many of your hidden uncertainties, past guilts, weaknesses, sorrows, unspoken wishes, and your cosmic unfoldment.

You are eager to start living, and possess, in a way, the secret of eternal youth. Obstacles enrage you but never beat you, for you usually feel you have sacrificed more than your share. In some way (after waiting) you will assert yourself and your right to make your own decisions.

However, you are often drawn back through Pisces into a sense of responsibility, a duty to others, a selflessness that at times eats away at your confidence and undermines your character. Honor and the vitality of life are your gifts.

If you were born late in April, you may want to read the horoscope book for Taurus as well as Aries. The investment could be revealing and profitable, for Taurus is often your means of putting your talents to practical use and turning your ideas into actual, tangible rewards.

You are headstrong and determined; you have a sense of independence and fight that nothing can destroy. Sometimes you can vacillate and be worried and negative, but you never give up. You have the earthy sense of all your needs to meet responsibilities, do your duties, build, acquire, and collect. You are attracted to all you possess, and the more you possess, the more permanent your life. You are thus less able to simply pick up and go back to zero; what you start you must try to finish.

DATES SUN ENTERS ARIES
(LEAVES PISCES)

March 20 every year from 1900 to 2000, except for the following:

March 21:				
1901	1911	1923	1938	1955
02	13	26	39	59
03	14	27	42	63
05	15	30	43	67
06	18	31	46	71
07	19	34	47	75
09	22	35	51	79
10				

DATES SUN LEAVES ARIES
(ENTERS TAURUS)

April 20 every year from 1900 to 2000, except for the following:

April 19:			April 21:
1948	1972	1988	1903
52	76	89	07
56	80	92	11
60	81	93	19
64	84	96	
68	85	97	

HISTORY AND USES
OF ASTROLOGY

Does astrology have a place in the fast-moving, ultra-scientific world we live in today? Can it be justified in a sophisticated society whose outriders are already preparing to step off the moon into the deep space of the planets themselves? Or is it just a hangover of ancient superstition, a psychological dummy for neurotics and dreamers of every historical age?

These are the kind of questions that any inquiring person can be expected to ask when they approach a subject like astrology which goes beyond, but never excludes, the materialistic side of life.

The simple, single answer is that astrology works. It works for tens of millions of people in the western world alone. In the United States there are 10 million followers and in Europe, an estimated 25 million. America has more than 4000 practicing astrologers, Europe nearly three times as many. Even down-under Australia has its hundreds of thousands of adherents. The importance of such vast numbers of people from diverse backgrounds and cultures is recognized by the world's biggest newspapers and magazines who probably devote more of their space to this subject in a year than to any other. In the eastern countries, astrology has enormous followings, again, because it has been proved to work. In countries like India, brides and grooms for centuries have been chosen on the basis of astrological compatibility. The low divorce rate there, despite today's heavy westernizing influence, is attributed largely to this practice.

In the western world, astrology today is more vital than ever before; more practicable because it needs a sophisticated society like ours to understand and develop its contribution to the full; more valid because science itself is confirming the precepts of astrological knowledge with every new exciting step. The ordinary person who daily applies astrology intelligently does not have to wonder whether it is true nor believe in it blindly. He can see it working for himself. And, if he can use it—and this book is designed to help the reader to do just that—he can make living a far richer experience, and become a more developed personality and a better person.

Astrology is the science of relationships. It is not just a study of planetary influences on man and his environment. It is the study of man himself.

We are at the center of our personal universe, of all our relationships. And our happiness or sadness depends on how we act, how we relate to the people and things that surround us. The emotions that we generate have a distinct affect—for better or worse—on the world around us. Our friends and our enemies will confirm this. Just look in the mirror the next time you are angry. In other words, each of us is a kind of sun or planet or star and our influence on our personal universe, whether loving, helpful or destructive, varies with our changing moods, expressed through our individual character.

And to an extent that includes the entire galaxy, this is true of the planetary bodies. Their radiations affect each other, including the earth and all the things on it. And in comparatively recent years, giant constellations called "quasars" have been discovered. These exist far beyond the night stars that we can observe, and science says these quasars are emitting radiating influences more powerful and different than ever recorded on earth. Their effect on man from an astrological point of view is under deep study. Compared with these inter-stellar forces, our personal "radiations" are negligible on the planetary scale. But ours are just as potent in the way they affect our moods, and our ability to control them. To this extent they determine much of the happiness and satisfaction in our lives. For instance, if we were bound and gagged and had to hold some strong emotion within us without being able to move, we would soon start to feel very uncomfortable. We are obviously pretty powerful radiators inside, in our own way. But usually, we are able to throw off our emotion in some sort of action—we have a good cry, walk it off, or tell someone our troubles—before it can build up too far and make us physically ill. Astrology helps us to understand the universal forces working on us, and through this understanding, we can become more properly adjusted to our surroundings and find ourselves coping where others may flounder.

Closely related to our emotions is the "other side" of our personal universe, our physical welfare. Our body, of course, is largely influenced by things around us over which we have very little control. The phone rings, we hear it. The train runs late. We snag our stocking or cut our face shaving. Our body is under a constant bombardment of events that influence our lives to varying degrees.

The question that arises from all this is, what makes each of us act so that we have to involve other people and keep the ball of activity and evolution rolling? This is the question that both science and astrology are involved with. The scientists have attacked it from different angles: anthropology, the study of human evolution as body, mind and response to environment; anatomy, the study of bodily structure; psychology, the science of the human mind; and so on. These studies have produced very impressive classifications and valuable information, but because the approach to the problem is fragmented, so is the result. They remain "branches" of science. Science generally studies effects. It keeps turning up wonderful answers but no lasting solutions. Astrology, on the other hand approaches the question from the broader viewpoint. Astrology began its inquiry with the totality of human experience and saw it as an effect. It then looked to find the cause, or at least the prime movers, and during thousands of years of observation of man and his *universal* environment, came up with the extraordinary principle of planetary influence—or astrology, which, from the Greek, means the science of the stars.

Modern science, as we shall see, has confirmed much of astrology's foundations—most of it unintentionally, some of it reluctantly, but still, indisputably.

It is not difficult to imagine that there must be a connection between outer space and the earth. Even today, scientists are not too sure how our earth was created, but it is generally agreed that it is only a tiny part of the universe. And as a part of the universe, people on earth see and feel the influence of heavenly bodies in almost every aspect of our existence. There is no doubt that the sun has the greatest influence on life on this planet. Without it there would be no life, for without it there would be no warmth, no division into day and night, no cycles of time or season at all. This is clear and easy to see. The influence of the moon, on the other hand, is more subtle, though no less definite.

There are many ways in which the influence of the moon manifests itself here on earth, both on human and animal life. It is a well-known fact, for instance, that the large movements of water on our planet—that is the ebb and flow of the tides—are caused by the moon's gravitational pull. Since this is so, it follows that these water movements do not occur only in the oceans, but that all bodies of water are affected, even down to the tiniest puddle.

The human body, too, which consists of about 70 percent water, falls within the scope of this lunar influence. For example the menstrual cycle of most women corresponds to the lunar month; the period of pregnancy in humans is 273 days, or equal to nine lunar months. Similarly, many illnesses reach a crisis at the change of the moon, and statistics in many countries have shown that the crime rate is highest at the time of the full moon. Even human sexual desire has been associated with the phases of the moon. But, it is in the movement of the tides that we get the clearest demonstration of planetary influence, and the irresistible correspondence between the so-called metaphysical and the physical.

Tide tables are prepared years in advance by calculating the future positions of the moon. Science has known for a long time that the moon is the main cause of tidal action. But only in the last few years has it begun to realize the possible extent of this influence on mankind. To begin with, the ocean tides do not rise and fall as we might imagine from our personal observations of them. The moon as it orbits around the earth, sets up a circular wave of attraction which pulls the oceans of the world after it, broadly in an east to west direction. This influence is like a phantom wave crest, a loop of power stretching from pole to pole which passes over and around the earth like an invisible shadow. It travels with equal effect across the land masses and, as scientists were recently amazed to observe, caused oysters placed in the dark in the middle of the United States where there is no sea, to open their shells to receive the non-existent tide. If the land-locked oysters react to this invisible signal, what effect does it have on us who not so long ago in evolutionary time, came out of the sea and still have its salt in our blood and sweat?

Less well known is the fact that the moon is also the primary force behind the circulation of blood in human beings and animals, and the movement of sap in trees and plants. Agriculturists have established that the moon has a distinct influence on crops, which explains why for centuries people have planted according to moon cycles. The habits of many animals, too, are directed by the movement of the moon. Migratory birds, for instance, depart only at or near the time of the full moon. Just as certain fish, eels in particular, move only in accordance with certain phases of the moon.

Know Thyself—Why?

In today's fast-changing world, everyone still longs to know what the future holds. It is the one thing that everyone has in common: rich and poor, famous and infamous, all are deeply concerned about tomorrow.

But the key to the future, as every historian knows, lies in the past. This is as true of individual people as it is of nations. You cannot understand your future without first understanding your past, which is simply another way of saying that you must first of all know yourself.

The motto "know thyself" seems obvious enough nowadays, but it was originally put forward as the foundation of wisdom by the ancient Greek philosophers. It was then adopted by the "mystery religions" of the ancient Middle East, Greece and Rome, and is still used in all genuine schools of mind training or mystical discipline, both in those of the East, based on yoga, and those of the West. So it is universally accepted now, and has been through the ages.

But how do you go about discovering what sort of person you are? The first step is usually classification into some sort of system of types. Astrology did this long before the birth of Christ. Psychology has also done it. So has modern medicine, in its way.

One system classifies men according to the source of the impulses they respond to most readily: the muscles, leading to direct bodily action; the digestive organs, resulting in emotion, or the brain and nerves. Another such system says that character is determined by the endocrine glands, and gives us labels like "pituitary," "thyroid" and "hyperthyroid" types. These different systems are neither contradictory nor mutually exclusive. In fact, they are very often different ways of saying the same thing.

Very popular and useful classifications were devised by Dr. C. G. Jung, the eminent disciple of Freud. Jung observed among the different faculties of the mind, four which have a predominant influence on character. These four faculties exist in all of us without exception, but not in perfect balance. So when we say, for instance, that a man is a "thinking type," it means that in any situation he tries to be rational. It follows that emotion, which some say is the opposite of thinking, will be his weakest function. This type can be sensible and reasonable, or calculating and unsympathetic. The emotional type, on the other hand, can often be recognized by exaggerated language—everything is either marvelous or terrible—and in extreme cases they even invent dramas and quarrels out of nothing just to make life more interesting.

The other two faculties are intuition and physical sensation. The sensation type does not only care for food and drink, nice clothes and furniture; he is also interested in all forms of physical experience. Many scientists are sensation types as are athletes and naturelovers. Like sensation, intuition is a form of perception and we all possess it. But it works through that part of the mind which is not under conscious control—consequently it sees meanings and connections which are not obvious to thought or emotion. Inventors and original thinkers are always intuitive, but so, too, are superstitious people who see meanings where none exist.

Thus, sensation tells us what is going on in the world, feeling (that is, emotion) tells us how important it is to ourselves, thinking enables us to interpret it and work out what we should do about it, and intuition tells us what it means to ourselves and others. All four faculties are essential, and all are present in every one of us. But some people are guided chiefly by one, others by another.

Besides these four types, Jung observed a division into extrovert and introvert, which cuts across them. By and large, the introvert is one who finds truth inside himself rather than outside. He is not, therefore, ideally suited to a religion or a political party which tells him what to believe. Original thinkers are almost necessarily introverts. The extrovert, on the other hand, finds truth coming to him from outside. He believes in experts and authorities, and wants to think that nature and the laws of nature really exists, that they are what they appear to be and not just generalities made by men.

A disadvantage of all these systems of classification, is that one cannot tell very easily where to place oneself. Some people are reluctant to admit that they act to please their emotions. So they deceive themselves for years by trying to belong to whichever type they think is the "best." Of course, there is no best; each has its faults and each has its good points.

The advantage of the signs of the Zodiac is that they simplify classification. Not only that, but your date of birth is personal—it is unarguably yours. What better way to know yourself than by going back as far as possible to the very moment of your birth? And this is precisely what your horoscope is all about.

What Is a Horoscope?

If you had been able to take a picture of the heavens at the moment of your birth, that photograph would be your horoscope. Lacking such a snapshot, it is still possible to recreate the picture—and this is at the basis of the astrologer's art. In other words, your horoscope is a representation of the skies with the planets in the exact positions they occupied at the time you were born.

This information, of course, is not enough for the astrologer. He has to have a background of significance to put the photograph on. You will get the idea if you imagine two balls—one inside the other. The inner one is transparent. In the center of both is the astrologer, able to look up, down and around in all directions. The outer sphere is the Zodiac which is divided into twelve approximately equal segments, like the segments of an orange. The inner ball is our photograph. It is transparent except for the images of the planets. Looking out from the center, the astrologer sees the planets in various segments of the Zodiac. These twelve segments are known as the signs or houses.

The position of the planets when each of us is born is always different. So the photograph is always different. But the Zodiac and its signs are fixed.

Now, where in all this are you, the subject of the horoscope?

You, or your character, is largely determined by the sign the sun is in. So that is where the astrologer looks first in your horoscope.

There are twelve signs in the Zodiac and the sun spends approximately one month in each. As the sun's motion is almost perfectly regular, the astrologers have been able to fix the dates governing each sign. There are not many people who do not know which sign of the Zodiac they were born under or who have not been amazed at some time or other at the accuracy of the description of their own character. Here are the twelve signs, the ancient zodiacal symbol, and their dates for the year 1988.*

ARIES	Ram	March 20–April 19
TAURUS	Bull	April 19–May 20
GEMINI	Twins	May 20–June 20
CANCER	Crab	June 20–July 22
LEO	Lion	July 22–August 22
VIRGO	Virgin	August 22–September 22
LIBRA	Scales	September 22–October 23
SCORPIO	Scorpion	October 23–November 21
SAGITTARIUS	Archer	November 21–December 21
CAPRICORN	Sea-Goat	December 21–January 20
AQUARIUS	Water-Bearer	January 20–February 19
PISCES	Fish	February 19–March 20

The time of birth—apart from the date—is important in advanced astrology because the planets travel at such great speed that the patterns they form change from minute to minute. For this reason, each person's horoscope is his and his alone. Further on we will see that the practicing astrologer has ways of determining and reading these minute time changes which dictate the finger character differences in us all.

However, it is still possible to draw significant conclusions and make meaningful predictions based simply on the sign of the Zodiac a person is born under. In a horoscope, the signs do not necessarily correspond with the divisions of the houses. It could be that a house begins half way across a sign. It is the interpretation of such combinations of different influences that distinguishes the professional astrologer from the student and the follower.

However, to gain a workable understanding of astrology, it is not necessary to go into great detail. In fact, the beginner is likely to find himself confused if he attempts to absorb too much too quickly. It should be remembered that this is a science and to become proficient at it, and especially to grasp the tremendous scope of possibilities in man and his affairs and direct them into a worthwhile reading, takes a great deal of study and experience.

*These dates are fluid and change with the motion of the Earth from year to year.

If you do intend to pursue it seriously you will have to learn to figure the exact moment of birth against the degrees of longitude and latitude of the planets at that precise time. This involves adapting local time to Greenwich Mean Time (G.M.T.), reference to tables of houses to establish the Ascendant, as well as making calculations from Ephemeris—the tables of the planets' positions.

After reading this introduction, try drawing up a rough horoscope to get the "feel" of reading some elementary characteristics and natal influences.

Draw a circle with twelve equal segments. Write in counterclockwise the names of the signs—Aries, Taurus, Gemini etc.—one for each segment. Look up an ephemeris for the year of the person's birth and note down the sign each planet was in on the birthday. Do not worry about the number of degrees (although if a planet is on the edge of a sign its position obviously should be considered). Write the name of the planet in the segment/sign on your chart. Write the number 1 in the sign where the sun is. This is the first house. Number the rest of the houses, counterclockwise till you finish at 12. Now you can investigate the probable basic expectation of experience of the person concerned. This is done first of all by seeing what planet or planets is/are in what sign and house. (See also page 72.)

The 12 houses control these functions:

1st.	Individuality, body appearance, general outlook on life	(Personality house)
2nd.	Finance, business	(Money house)
3rd.	Relatives, education, correspondence	(Relatives house)
4th.	Family, neighbors	(Home house)
5th.	Pleasure, children, attempts, entertainment	(Pleasure house)
6th.	Health, employees	(Health house)
7th.	Marriage, partnerships	(Marriage house)
8th.	Death, secret deals, difficulties	(Death house)
9th.	Travel, intellectual affairs	(Travel house)
10th.	Ambition, social standing	(Business and Honor house)
11th.	Friendship, social life, luck	(Friends house)
12th.	Troubles, illness, loss	(Trouble house)

The characteristics of the planets modify the influence of the Sun according to their natures and strengths.

Sun: Source of life. Basic temperament according to sun sign. The will.
Moon: Superficial nature. Moods. Changeable. Adaptive. Mother.
Mercury: Communication. Intellect. Reasoning power. Curiosity. Short travels.
Venus: Love. Delight. Art. Beautiful possessions.
Mars: Energy. Initiative. War. Anger. Destruction. Impulse.
Jupiter: Good. Generous. Expansive. Opportunities. Protection.
Saturn: Jupiter's opposite. Contraction. Servant. Delay. Hardwork. Cold. Privation. Research. Lasting rewards after long struggle.
Uranus: Fashion. Electricity. Revolution. Sudden changes. Modern science.
Neptune: Sensationalism. Mass emotion. Devastation. Delusion.
Pluto: Creates and destroys. Lust for power. Strong obsessions.

Superimpose the characteristics of the planets on the functions of the house in which they appear. Express the result through the character of the birth (sun) sign, and you will get the basic idea of how astrology works.

Of course, many other considerations have been taken into account in producing the carefully worked out predictions in this book: The aspects of the planets to each other; their strength according to position and sign; whether they are in a house of exaltation or decline; whether they are natural enemies or not; whether a planet occupies his own sign; the position of a planet in relation to its own house or sign; whether the planet is male, female or neuter; whether the sign is a fire, earth, water or air sign. These are only a few of the colors on the astrologer's pallet which he must mix with the inspiration of the artist and the accuracy of the mathematician.

The Problem of Love

Love, of course, is never a problem. The problem lies in recognizing the difference between infatuation, emotion, sex and, sometimes, the downright deceit of the other person. Mankind, with its record of broken marriages, despair and disillusionment, is obviously not very good at making these distinctions.

Can astrology help?

Yes. In the same way that advance knowledge can usually help in any human situation. And there is probably no situation as human, as poignant, as pathetic and universal, as the failure of man's love.

Love, of course, is not just between man and woman. It involves love of children, parents, home and so on. But the big problems usually involve the choice of partner.

Astrology has established degrees of compatibility that exist between people born under the various signs of the Zodiac. Because people are individuals, there are numerous variations and modifications and the astrologer, when approached on mate and marriage matters makes allowances for them. But the fact remains that some groups of people are suited for each other and some are not and astrology has expressed this in terms of characteristics which all can study and use as a personal guide.

No matter how much enjoyment and pleasure we find in the different aspects of each other's character, if it is not an overall compatibility, the chances of our finding fulfillment or enduring happiness in each other are pretty hopeless. And astrology can help us to find someone compatible.

History of Astrology

The origins of astrology have been lost far back in history, but we do know that reference is made to it as far back as the first written records of the human race. It is not hard to see why. Even in primitive times, people must have looked for an explanation for the various happenings in their lives. They must have wanted to know why people were different from one to another. And in their search they turned to the regular movements of the sun, moon and stars to see if they could provide an answer.

It is interesting to note that as soon as man learned to use his tools in any type of design, or his mind in any kind of calculation, he turned his attention to the heavens. Ancient cave dwellings reveal dim crescents and circles representative of the sun and moon, rulers of day and night. Mesopotamia and the civilization of Chaldea, in itself the foundation of those of Babylonia and Assyria, show a complete picture of astronomical observation and well-developed astrological interpretation.

Humanity has a natural instinct for order. The study of anthropology reveals that primitive people—even as far back as prehistoric times—were striving to achieve a certain order in their lives. They tried to organize the apparent chaos of the universe. They had the desire to attach meaning to things. This demand for order has persisted throughout the history of man. So that observing the regularity of the heavenly bodies made it logical that primitive peoples should turn heavenwards in their search for an understanding of the world in which they found themselves so random and alone.

And they did find a significance in the movements of the stars. Shepherds tending their flocks, for instance, observed that when the cluster of stars now known as the constellation Aries was in sight, it was the time of fertility and they associated it with the Ram. And they noticed that the growth of plants and plant life corresponded with different phases of the moon, so that certain times were favorable for the planting of crops, and other times were not. In this way, there grew up a tradition of seasons and causes connected with the passage of the sun through the twelve signs of the Zodiac.

Astrology was valued so highly that the king was kept informed of the daily and monthly changes in the heavenly bodies, and the results of astrological studies regarding events of the future. Head astrologers were clearly men of great rank and position, and the office was said to be a hereditary one.

Omens were taken, not only from eclipses and conjunctions of the moon or sun with one of the planets, but also from storms and earthquakes. In the eastern civilizations, particularly, the reverence inspired by astrology appears to have remained unbroken since the very earliest days. In ancient China, astrology, astronomy and religion went hand in hand. The astrologer, who was also an astronomer, was part of the official government service and had his own corner in the Imperial Palace. The duties of the Imperial astrologer, whose office was one of the most important in the land, were clearly defined, as this extract from early records shows:

"This exalted gentleman must concern himself with the stars in the heavens, keeping a record of the changes and movements of the Planets, the Sun and the Moon, in order to examine the movements of the terrestial world with the object of prognosticating good and bad fortune. He divides the territories of the nine regions of the empire in accordance with their dependence on particular celestial bodies. All the fiefs and principalities are connected with the stars and from this their prosperity or misfortune should be ascertained. He makes prognostications according to the twelve years of the Jupiter cycle of good and evil of the terrestial world. From the colors of the five kinds of clouds, he determines the coming of floods or droughts, abundance or famine. From the twelve winds, he draws conclusions about the state of harmony of heaven and earth, and takes note of good and bad signs that result from their accord or disaccord. In general, he concerns himself with five kinds of phenomena so as to warn the Emperor to come to the aid of the government and to allow for variations in the ceremonies according to their circumstances."

The Chinese were also keen observers of the fixed stars, giving them such unusual names as Ghost Vehicle, Sun of Imperial Concubine, Imperial Prince, Pivot of Heaven, Twinkling Brilliance or Weaving Girl. But, great astrologers though they may have been, the Chinese lacked one aspect of mathematics that the Greeks applied to astrology—deductive geometry. Deductive geometry was the basis of much classical astrology in and after the time of the Greeks, and this explains the different methods of prognostication used in the East and West.

Down through the ages the astrologer's art has depended, not so much on the uncovering of new facts, though this is important, as on the interpretation of the facts already known. This is the essence of his skill. Obviously one cannot always tell how people will react (and this underlines the very important difference between astrology and predestination which will be discussed later on) but one can be prepared, be forewarned, to know what to expect.

But why should the signs of the zodiac have any effect at all on the formation of human character? It is easy to see why people thought they did, and even now we constantly use astrological expressions in our everyday speech. The thoughts of "lucky star," "ill-fated," "star-crossed," "mooning around," are interwoven into the very structure of our language.

In the same way that the earth has been created by influences from outside, there remains an indisputable togetherness in the working of the universe. The world, after all, is a coherent structure, for if it were not, it would be quite without order and we would never know what to expect. A dog could turn into an apple, or an elephant sprout wings and fly at any moment without so much as a by your leave. But nature, as we know, functions according to laws, not whims, and the laws of nature are certainly not subject to capricious exceptions.

This means that no part of the universe is ever arbitrarily cut off from any other part. Everything is therefore to some extent linked with everything else. The moon draws an imperceptible tide on every puddle; tiny and trivial events can be effected by outside forces (such as the fall of a feather by the faintest puff of wind). And so it is fair to think that the local events at any moment reflect to a very small extent the evolution of the world as a whole.

From this principle follows the possibility of divination, and also knowledge of events at a distance, provided one's mind were always as perfectly undisturbed, as ideally smooth, as a mirror or unruffled lake. Provided, in other words, that one did not confuse the picture with hopes, guesses, and expectations. When people try to foretell the future by cards or crystal ball gazing they find it much easier to confuse the picture with expectations than to reflect it clearly.

But the present does contain a good deal of the future to which it leads—not all, but a good deal. The diver halfway between bridge and water is going to make a splash; the train whizzing towards the station will pass through it unless interfered with; the burglar breaking a pane of glass has exposed himself to the possibility of a prison sentence. Yet this is not a doctrine of determinism, as was emphasized earlier. Clearly, there are forces already at work in the present, and any one of them could alter the situation in some way. Equally, a change of decision could alter the whole situation as well. So the future depends, not on an irresistible force, but on a small act of free will.

An individual's age, physique, and position on the earth's surface are remote consequences of his birth. Birth counts as the original cause for all that happens subsequently. The horoscope, in this case, means "this person represents the further evolution of the state of the universe pictured in this chart." Such a chart can apply equally to man or woman, dog, ship or even limited company.

If the evolution of an idea, or of a person, is to be understood as a totality, it must continue to evolve from its own beginnings, which is to say, in the terms in which it began. The brown-eyed person will be faithful to brown eyes all his life; the traitor is being faithful to some complex of ideas which has long been evolving in him; and the person born at sunset will always express, as he evolves, the psychological implications or analogies of the moment when the sun sinks out of sight.

This is the doctrine that an idea must continue to evolve in terms of its origin. It is a completely non-materialist doctrine, though it never fails to apply to material objects. And it implies, too, that the individual will continue to evolve in terms of his moment of origin, and therefore possibly of the sign of the Zodiac rising on the eastern horizon at his birth. It also implies that the signs of the Zodiac themselves will evolve in the collective mind of the human race in the same terms that they were first devised and not in the terms in which modern astrologers consciously think they ought to work.

For the human race, like every other kind of animal, has a collective mind, as Professor Jung discovered in his investigation of dreams. If no such collective mind existed, no infant could ever learn anything, for communication would be impossible. Furthermore, it is absurd to suggest that the conscious mind could be older than the "unconscious," for an infant's nervous system functions correctly before it has discovered the difference between "myself" and "something else" or discovered what eyes and hands are for. Indeed, the involuntary muscles function correctly even before birth, and will never be under conscious control. They are part of what we call the "unconscious" which is not really "unconscious" at all. To the contrary, it is totally aware of itself and everything else; it is merely that part of the mind that cannot be controlled by conscious effort.

And human experience, though it varies in detail with every individual, is basically the same for each one of us, consisting of sky and earth, day and night, waking and sleeping, man and woman, birth and death. So there is bound to be in the mind of the human race a very large number of inescapable ideas, which are called our natural archetypes.

There are also, however, artificial or cultural archetypes which are not universal or applicable to everyone, but are nevertheless inescapable within the limits of a given culture. Examples of these are the cross in Christianity, and the notion of "escape from the wheel of rebirth" in India. There was a time when these ideas did not exist. And there was a time, too, when the scheme of the Zodiac did not exist. One would not expect the Zodiac to have any influence on remote and primitive peoples, for example, who have never heard of it. If the Zodiac is only an archetype, their horoscopes probably would not work and it would not matter which sign they were born under.

But where the Zodiac is known, and the idea of it has become worked into the collective mind, then there it could well appear to have an influence, even if it has no physical existence. For ideas do not have a physical existence, anyway. No physical basis has yet been discovered for the telepathy that controls an anthill; young swallows migrate before, not after, their parents; and the weaverbird builds its intricate nest without being taught. Materialists suppose, but cannot prove, that "instinct" (as it is called, for no one knows how it works) is controlled by nucleic acid in the chromosomes. This is not a genuine explanation, though, for it only pushes the mystery one stage further back.

Does this mean, then, that the human race, in whose civilization the idea of the twelve signs of the Zodiac has long been embedded, is divided into only twelve types? Can we honestly believe that it is really as simple as that? If so, there must be pretty wide ranges of variation within each type. And if, to explain the variation, we call in heredity and environment, experiences in early childhood, the thyroid and other glands, and also the four functions of the mind mentioned at the beginning of this introduction, and extroversion and introversion, then one begins to wonder if the original classification was worth making at all. No sensible person believes that his favorite system explains everything. But even so, he will not find it much use at all if it does not even save him the trouble of bothering with the others.

Under the Jungian system, everyone has not only a dominant or principal function, but also a secondary or subsidiary one, so that the four can be arranged in order of potency. In the intuitive type, sensation is always the most inefficient function, but the second most inefficient function can be either thinking (which tends to make original thinkers such as Jung himself) or else feeling (which tends to make artistic people). Therefore, allowing for introversion and extroversion, there are at least four kinds of intuitive types, and sixteen types in all. Furthermore, one can see how the sixteen types merge into each other, so that there are no unrealistic or unconvincingly rigid divisions.

In the same way, if we were to put every person under only one sign of the Zodiac, the system becomes too rigid and unlike life. Besides, it was never intended to be used like that. It may be convenient to have only twelve types, but we know that in practice there is every possible gradation between aggressiveness and timidity, or between conscientiousness and laziness. How, then, do we account for this?

The Tyrant and the Saint

Just as the thinking type of man is also influenced to some extent by sensation and intuition, but not very much by emotion, so a person born under Leo can be influenced to some extent by one or two (but not more) of the other signs. For instance, famous persons born under the sign of Gemini include Henry VIII, whom nothing and no-one could have induced to abdicate, and Edward VIII, who did just that. Obviously, then, the sign Gemini does not fully explain the complete character of either of them.

Again, under the opposite sign, Sagittarius, were both Stalin, who was totally consumed with the notion of power, and Charles V, who freely gave up an empire because he preferred to go into a monastery. And we find under Scorpio, many uncompromising characters such as Luther, de Gaulle, Indira Gandhi and Montgomery, but also Petain, a successful commander whose name later became synonymous with collaboration.

A single sign is therefore obviously inadequate to explain the differences between people; it can only explain resemblances, such as the combativeness of the Scorpio group, or the far-reaching devotion of Charles V and Stalin to their respective ideals—the Christian heaven and the Communist utopia.

But very few people are born under one sign only. As well as the month of birth, as was mentioned earlier, the day matters, and, even more, the hour, which ought, if possible, to be noted to the nearest minute. Without this, it is impossible to have an actual horoscope, for the word horoscope means literally, "a consideration of the hour."

The month of birth tells you only which sign of the Zodiac was occupied by the sun. The day and hour tell you what sign was occupied by the moon. And the minute tells you which sign was rising on the eastern horizon. This is called the Ascendant, and it is supposed to be the most important thing in the whole horoscope.

If you were born at midnight, the sun is then in an important position, although invisible. But at one o'clock in the morning the sun is not important, so the moment of birth will not matter much. The important thing then will be the Ascendant, and possibly one or two of the planets. At a given day and hour, say, dawn on January 1st, or 9:00 p.m. on the longest day, the Ascendant will always be the same at any given place. But the moon and planets alter from day to day, at different speeds and have to be looked up in an astronomical table.

The sun is said to signify one's heart, that is to say, one's deepest desires and inmost nature. This is quite different from the moon, which, as we have seen, signifies one's superficial way of behaving. When the ancient Romans referred to the Emperor Augustus as a Capricornian, they meant that he had the moon in Capricorn; they did not pay much attention to the sun, although he was born at sunrise. Or, to take another example, a modern astrologer would call Disraeli a Scorpion because he had Scorpio rising, but most people would call him Sagittarian because he had the sun there. The Romans would have called him Leo because his moon was in Leo.

The sun, as has already been pointed out, is important if one is born near sunrise, sunset, noon or midnight, but is otherwise not reckoned as the principal influence. So if one does not seem to fit one's birth month, it is always worthwhile reading the other signs, for one may have been born at a time when any of them were rising or occupied by the moon. It also seems to be the case that the influence of the sun develops as life goes on, so that the month of birth is easier to guess in people over the age of forty. The young are supposed to be influenced mainly by their Ascendant which characterizes the body and physical personality as a whole.

It should be clearly understood that it is nonsense to assume that all people born at a certain time will exhibit the same characteristics, or that they will even behave in the same manner. It is quite obvious that, from the very moment of its birth, a child is subject to the effects of its environment, and that this in turn will influence its character and heritage to a decisive extent. Also to be taken into account are education and economic conditions, which play a very important part in the formation of one's character as well.

However, it is clearly established that people born under one sign of the Zodiac do have certain basic traits in their character which are different from those born under other signs. It is obvious to every thinking person that certain events produce different reactions in various people. For instance, if a man slips on a banana skin and falls heavily on the pavement, one passer-by may laugh and find this extremely amusing, while another may just walk on, thinking: "What a fool falling down like that. He should look where he is going." A third might also walk away saying to himself: "It's none of my business—I'm glad it wasn't me." A fourth might walk past and think: "I'm sorry for that man, but I haven't the time to be bothered with helping him." And a fifth might stop to help the fallen man to his feet, comfort him and take him home. Here is just one event which could produce entirely different reactions in different people. And, obviously, there are many more. One that comes to mind immediately is the violently opposed views to events such as wars, industrial strikes, and so on. The fact that people have different attitudes to the same event is simply another way of saying that they have different characters. And this is not something that can be put down to background, for people of the same race, religion, or class, very often express quite different reactions to happenings or events. Similarly, it is often the case that members of the same family, where there is clearly uniform background of economic and social standing, education, race and religion, often argue bitterly among themselves over political and social issues.

People have, in general, certain character traits and qualities which, according to their environment, develop in either a positive or a negative manner. Therefore, selfishness (inherent selfishness, that is) might emerge as unselfishness; kindness and consideration as cruelty and lack of consideration towards others. In the same way, a naturally constructive person, may, through frustration, become destructive, and so on. The latent characteristics with which people are born can, therefore, through environment and good or bad training, become something that would appear to be its opposite, and so give the lie to the astrologer's description of their character. But this is not the case. The true character is still there, but it is buried deep beneath these external superficialities.

Careful study of the character traits of different signs can be immeasurable help, and can render beneficial service to the intelligent person. Undoubtedly, the reader will already have discovered that, while he is able to get on very well with some people, he just "cannot stand" others. The causes sometimes seem inexplicable. At times there is intense dislike, at other times immediate sympathy. And there is, too, the phenomenon of love at first sight, which is also apparently inexplicable. People appear to be either sympathetic or unsympathetic towards each other for no apparent reason.

Now if we look at this in the light of the Zodiac, we find that people born under different signs are either compatible or incompatible with each other. In other words, there are good and bad interrelating factors among the various signs. This does not, of course, mean that humanity can be divided into groups of hostile camps. It would be quite wrong to be hostile or indifferent toward people who happen to be born under an incompatible sign. There is no reason why everybody should not, or cannot, learn to control and adjust their feelings and actions, especially after they are aware of the positive qualities of other people by studying their character analyses, among other things.

Every person born under a certain sign has both positive and negative qualities, which are developed more or less according to his free will. Nobody is entirely good or entirely bad, and it is up to each one of us to learn to control himself on the one hand, and at the same time to endeavor to learn about himself and others.

It cannot be repeated often enough that, though the intrinsic nature of man and his basic character traits are born in him, nevertheless it is his own free will that determines whether he will make really good use of his talents and abilities—whether, in other words, he will overcome his vices or allow them to rule him. Most of us are born with at least a streak of laziness, irritability, or some other fault in our nature, and it is up to each one of us to see that we exert sufficient willpower to control our failings so that they do not harm ourselves or others.

Astrology can reveal our inclinations and tendencies. Our weaknesses should not be viewed as shortcomings that are impossible to change. The horoscope of a man may show him to have criminal leanings, for instance, but this does not mean he will definitely become a criminal.

The ordinary man usually finds it difficult to know himself. He is often bewildered. Astrology can frequently tell him more about himself than the different schools of psychology are able to do. Knowing his failings and shortcomings, he will do his best to overcome them, and make himself a better and more useful member of society and a helpmate to his family and friends. It can also save him a great deal of unhappiness and remorse.

And yet it may seem absurd that an ancient philosophy, something that is known as a "pseudo-science," could be a prop to the men and women of the twentieth century. But below the materialistic surface of modern life, there are hidden streams of feeling and thought. Symbology is reappearing as a study worthy of the scholar; the psychosomatic factor in illness has passed from the writings of the crank to those of the specialist; spiritual healing in all its forms is no longer a pious hope but an accepted phenomenon. And it is into this context that we consider astrology, in the sense that it is an analysis of human types.

Astrology and medicine had a long journey together, and only parted company a couple of centuries ago. There still remain in medical language such astrological terms as "saturnine," "choleric," and "mercurial," used in the diagnosis of physical tendencies. The herbalist, for long the handyman of the medical profession, has been dominated by astrology since the days of the Greeks. Certain herbs traditionally respond to certain planetary influences, and diseases must therefore be treated to ensure harmony between the medicine and the disease.

No one expects the most eccentric of modern doctors to go back to the practices of his predecessors. We have come a long way since the time when phases of the moon were studied in illness. Those days were a medical nightmare, with epidemics that were beyond control, and an explanation of the Black Death sought in conjunction with the planets. Nowadays, astrological diagnosis of disease has literally no parallel in modern life. And yet, age-old symbols of types and of the vulnerability of, say, the Saturnian to chronic diseases or the choleric to apoplexy and blood pressure and so on, are still applicable.

But the stars are expected to foretell and not only to diagnose. The astrological forecaster has a counterpart on a highly conventional level in the shape of the weather prophet, racing tipster and stock market forecaster, to name just three examples. All in their own way are aiming at the same result. They attempt to look a little further into the pattern of life and also try to determine future patterns accurately.

Astrological forecasting has been remarkably accurate, but often it is wide of the mark. The brave man who cares to predict world events takes dangerous chances. Individual forecasting is less clear cut; it can be a help or a disillusionment. Then welcome to the nagging question: if it is possible to foreknow, is it right to foretell? A complex point of ethics on which it is hard to pronounce judgment. The doctor faces the same dilemma if he finds that symptoms of a mortal disease are present in his patient and that he can only prognosticate a steady decline. How much to tell an individual in a crisis is a problem that has perplexed many distinguished scholars. Honest and conscientious astrologers in this modern world, where so many people are seeking guidance, face the same problem.

The ancient cults, the symbols of old religions, are eclipsed for the moment. They may return with their old force within a decade or two. But at present the outlook is dark. Human beings badly need assurance, as they did in the past, that all is not chaos. Somewhere, somehow, there is a pattern that must be worked out. As to the why and wherefore, the astrologer is not expected to give judgment. He is just someone who, by dint of talent and training, can gaze into the future.

Five hundred years ago it was customary to call in a learned man who was an astrologer who was probably also a doctor and a philosopher. By his knowledge of astrology, his study of planetary influences, he felt himself qualified to guide those in distress. The world has moved forward at a fantastic rate since then, and in this twentieth century speed has been the keyword everywhere. Tensions have increased, the spur of ambition has been applied indiscriminately. People are uncertain of themselves. At first sight it seems fantastic in the light of modern thinking that they turn to the most ancient of all studies, and get someone to calculate a horoscope for them. But is it *really* so fantastic if you take a second look? For astrology is concerned with tomorrow, with survival. And in a world such as ours, those two things are the keywords of the time in which we live.

HOW TO USE
THESE PREDICTIONS

A person reading the predictions in this book should understand that they are produced from the daily position of the planets for a group of people and are not, of course, individually specialized. To get the full benefit of them he should relate the predictions to his own character and circumstances, co-ordinate them, and draw his own conclusions from them.

If he is a serious observer of his own life he should find a definite pattern emerge that will be a helpful and reliable guide.

The point is that we always retain our free will. The stars indicate certain directional tendencies but we are not compelled to follow. We can do or not do, and wisdom must make the choice.

We all have our good and bad days. Sometimes they extend into cycles of weeks. It is therefore advisable to study daily predictions in a span ranging from the day before to several days ahead; also to re-read the monthly predictions for similar cycles.

Daily predictions should be taken very generally. The word "difficult" does not necessarily indicate a whole day of obstruction or inconvenience. It is a warning to you to be cautious. Your caution will often see you around the difficulty before you are involved. This is the correct use of astrology.

In another section, detailed information is given about the influence of the moon as it passes through the various signs of the Zodiac. It includes instructions on how to use the Moon Tables. This information should be used in conjunction with the daily forecasts to give a fuller picture of the astrological trends.

THE MOON

Moon is the nearest planet to the earth. It exerts more observable influence on us from day to day than any other planet. The effect is very personal, very intimate, and if we are not aware of how it works it can make us quite unstable in our ideas. And the annoying thing is that at these times we often see our own instability but can do nothing about it. A knowledge of what can be expected may help considerably. We can then be prepared to stand strong against the moon's negative influences and use its positive ones to help us to get ahead. Who has not heard of going with the tide?

Moon reflects, has no light of its own. It reflects the sun—the life giver—in the form of vital movement. Moon controls the tides, the blood rhythm, the movement of sap in trees and plants. Its nature is inconstancy and change so it signifies our moods, our superficial behavior—walking, talking and especially thinking. Being a true reflector of other forces, moon is cold, watery like the surface of a still lake, brilliant and scintillating at times, but easily ruffled and disturbed by the winds of change.

The moon takes 28½ days to circle the earth and the Zodiac. It spends just over 2¼ days in each sign. During that time it reflects the qualities, energies and characteristics of the sign and, to a degree, the planet which rules the sign. While the moon in its transit occupies a sign incompatible with our own birth sign, we can expect to feel a vague uneasiness, perhaps a touch of irritableness. We should not be discouraged nor let the feeling get us down, or, worse still, allow ourselves to take the discomfort out on others. Try to remember that the moon has to change signs within 55 hours and, provided you are not physically ill, your mood will probably change with it. It is amazing how frequently depression lifts with the shift in the moon's position. And, of course, when the moon is transiting a sign compatible or sympathetic to yours you will probably feel some sort of stimulation or just plain happy to be alive.

In the horoscope, the moon is such a powerful indicator that competent astrologers often use the sign it occupied at birth as the birth sign of the person. This is done particularly when the sun is on the cusp, or edge, of two signs. Most experienced astrologers, however, coordinate both sun and moon signs by reading and confirming from one to the other and secure a far more accurate and personalized analysis.

For these reasons, the moon tables which follow this section (see pages 28–35) are of great importance to the individual. They show the days and the exact times the moon will enter each sign of the Zodiac for the year. Remember, you have to adjust the indicated times to local time. The corrections, already calculated for most of the main cities, are at the beginning of the tables. What follows now is a guide to the influences that will be reflected to the earth by the moon while it transits each of the twelve signs. The influence is at its peak about 26 hours after the moon enters a sign.

MOON IN ARIES

This is a time for action, for reaching out beyond the usual self-imposed limitations and faint-hearted cautions. If you have plans in your head or on your desk, put them into practice. New ventures, applications, new jobs, new starts of any kind—all have a good chance of success. This is the period when original and dynamic impulses are being reflected onto the earth. The energies are extremely vital and favor the pursuit of pleasure and adventure in practically every form. Sick people should feel an improvement. Those who are well will probably find themselves exuding confidence and optimism. People fond of physical exercise should find their bodies growing with tone and well-being. Boldness, strength, determination should characterize most of your activities with a readiness to face up to old challenges. Yesterday's problems may seem petty and exaggerated—so deal with them. Strike out alone. Self-reliance will attract others to you. This is a good time for making friends. Business and marriage partners are more likely to be impressed with the man and woman of action. Opposition will be overcome or thrown aside with much less effort than usual. CAUTION: Be dominant but not domineering.

MOON IN TAURUS

The spontaneous, action-packed person of yesterday gives way to the cautious, diligent, hardworking "thinker." In this period ideas will probably be concentrated on ways of improving finances. A great deal of time may be spent figuring out and going over schemes and plans. It is the right time to be careful with detail. People will find themselves working longer than usual at their desks. Or devoting more time to serious thought about the future. A strong desire to put order into business and financial arrangements may cause extra work. Loved ones may complain of being neglected and may fail to appreciate that your efforts are for their ultimate benefit. Your desire for system may extend to criticism of arrangements in the home and lead to minor upsets. Health may be affected through overwork. Try to secure a reasonable amount of rest and relaxation, although the tendency will be to "keep going" despite good advice. Work done conscientiously in this period should result in a solid contribution to your future security. CAUTION: Try not to be as serious with people as the work you are engaged in.

MOON IN GEMINI

The humdrum of routine and too much work should suddenly end. You are likely to find yourself in an expansive, quicksilver world of change and self-expression. Urges to write, to paint, to experience the freedom of some sort of artistic outpouring, may be very strong. Take full advantage of them. You may find yourself finishing something you began and put aside long ago. Or embarking on something new which could easily be prompted by a chance meeting, a new acquaintance, or even an advertisement. There may be a yearning for a change of scenery, the feeling to visit another country (not too far away), or at least to get away for a few days. This may result in short, quick journeys. Or, if you are planning a single visit, there may be some unexpected changes or detours on the way. Familiar activities will seem to give little satisfaction unless they contain a fresh element of excitement or expectation. The inclination will be towards untried pursuits, particularly those that allow you to express your inner nature. The accent is on new faces, new places. CAUTION: Do not be too quick to commit yourself emotionally.

MOON IN CANCER

Feelings of uncertainty and vague insecurity are likely to cause problems while the moon is in Cancer. Thoughts may turn frequently to the warmth of the home and the comfort of loved ones. Nostalgic impulses could cause you to bring out old photographs and letters and reflect on the days when your life seemed to be much more rewarding and less demanding. The love and understanding of parents and family may be important, and, if it is not forthcoming you may have to fight against a bit of self-pity. The cordiality of friends and the thought of good times with them that are sure to be repeated will help to restore you to a happier frame of mind. The feeling to be alone may follow minor setbacks or rebuffs at this time, but solitude is unlikely to help. Better to get on the telephone or visit someone. This period often causes peculiar dreams and up-surges of imaginative thinking which can be very helpful to authors of occult and mystical works. Preoccupation with the more person-al world of simple human needs should overshadow any material strivings. CAUTION: Do not spend too much time thinking—seek the company of loved ones or close friends.

MOON IN LEO

New horizons of exciting and rather extravagant activity open up. This is the time for exhilarating entertainment, glamorous and lavish parties, and expensive shopping sprees. Any merrymaking that relies upon your generosity as a host has every chance of being a spectacular success. You should find yourself right in the center of the fun, either as the life of the party or simply as a person whom happy people like to be with. Romance thrives in this heady at-mosphere and friendships are likely to explode unexpectedly into serious attachments. Children and younger people should be at-tracted to you and you may find yourself organizing a picnic or a visit to a fun-fair, the cinema or the seaside. The sunny company and vitality of youthful companions should help you to find some unsuspected energy. In career, you could find an opening for pro-motion or advancement. This should be the time to make a direct approach. The period favors those engaged in original research. CAUTION: Bask in popularity but not in flattery.

MOON IN VIRGO

Off comes the party cap and out steps the busy, practical worker. He wants to get his personal affairs straight, to rearrange them, if necessary, for more efficiency, so he will have more time for more work. He clears up his correspondence, pays outstanding bills, makes numerous phone calls. He is likely to make inquiries, or sign up for some new insurance and put money into gilt-edged invest-ment. Thoughts probably revolve around the need for future secur-ity—to tie up loose ends and clear the decks. There may be a ten-dency to be "finicky," to interfere in the routine of others, particu-larly friends and family members. The motive may be a genuine desire to help with suggestions for updating or streamlining their affairs, but these will probably not be welcomed. Sympathy may be felt for less fortunate sections of the community and a flurry of some sort of voluntary service is likely. This may be accompanied by strong feelings of responsibility on several fronts and health may suffer from extra efforts made. CAUTION: Everyone may not want your help or advice.

MOON IN LIBRA

These are days of harmony and agreement and you should find yourself at peace with most others. Relationships tend to be smooth and sweet-flowing. Friends may become closer and bonds deepen in mutual understanding. Hopes will be shared. Progress by cooperation could be the secret of success in every sphere. In business, established partnerships may flourish and new ones get off to a good start. Acquaintances could discover similar interests that lead to congenial discussions and rewarding exchanges of some sort. Love, as a unifying force, reaches its optimum. Marriage partners should find accord. Those who wed at this time face the prospect of a happy union. Cooperation and tolerance are felt to be stronger than dissension and impatience. The argumentative are not quite so loud in their bellowings, nor as inflexible in their attitudes. In the home, there should be a greater recognition of the other point of view and a readiness to put the wishes of the group before selfish insistence. This is a favorable time to join an art group. CAUTION: Do not be too independent—let others help you if they want to.

MOON IN SCORPIO

Driving impulses to make money and to economize are likely to cause upsets all round. No area of expenditure is likely to be spared the axe, including the household budget. This is a time when the desire to cut down on extravagance can become near fanatical. Care must be exercised to try to keep the aim in reasonable perspective. Others may not feel the same urgent need to save and may retaliate. There is a danger that possessions of sentimental value will be sold to realize cash for investment. Buying and selling of stock for quick profit is also likely. The attention may turn to having a good clean up round the home and at the office. Neglected jobs could suddenly be done with great bursts of energy. The desire for solitude may intervene. Self-searching thoughts could disturb. The sense of invisible and mysterious energies at work could cause some excitability. The reassurance of loves ones may help. CAUTION: Be kind to the people you love.

MOON IN SAGITTARIUS

These are days when you are likely to be stirred and elevated by discussions and reflections of a religious and philosophical nature. Ideas of far-away places may cause unusual response and excitement. A decision may be made to visit someone overseas, perhaps a person whose influence was important to your earlier character development. There could be a strong resolution to get away from present intellectual patterns, to learn new subjects and to meet more interesting people. The superficial may be rejected in all its forms. An impatience with old ideas and unimaginative contacts could lead to a change of companions and interests. There may be an upsurge of religious feeling and metaphysical inquiry. Even a new insight into the significance of astrology and other occult studies is likely under the curious stimulus of the moon in Sagittarius. Physically, you may express this need for fundamental change by spending more time outdoors: sports, gardening or going for long walks. CAUTION: Try to channel any restlessness into worthwhile study.

MOON IN CAPRICORN

Life in these hours may seem to pivot around the importance of gaining prestige and honor in the career, as well as maintaining a spotless reputation. Ambitious urges may be excessive and could be accompanied by quite acquisitive drives for money. Effort should be directed along strictly ethical lines where there is no possibility of reproach or scandal. All endeavors are likely to be characterized by great earnestness, and an air of authority and purpose which should impress those who are looking for leadership or reliability. The desire to conform to accepted standards may extend to sharp criticism of family members. Frivolity and unconventional actions are unlikely to amuse while the moon is in Capricorn. Moderation and seriousness are the orders of the day. Achievement and recognition in this period could come through community work or organizing for the benefit of some amateur group. CAUTION: Dignity and esteem are not always self-awarded.

MOON IN AQUARIUS

Moon in Aquarius is in the second last sign of the Zodiac where ideas can become disturbingly fine and subtle. The result is often a mental "no-man's land" where imagination cannot be trusted with the same certitude as other times. The dangers for the individual are the extremes of optimism and pessimism. Unless the imgination is held in check, situations are likely to be misread, and rosy conclusions drawn where they do not exist. Consequences for the unwary can be costly in career and business. Best to think twice and not speak or act until you think again. Pessimism can be a cruel self-inflicted penalty for delusion at this time. Between the two extremes are strange areas of self-deception which, for example, can make the selfish person think he is actually being generous. Eerie dreams which resemble the reality and even seem to continue into the waking state are also possible. CAUTION: Look for the fact and not just for the image in your mind.

MOON IN PISCES

Everything seems to come to the surface now. Memory may be crystal clear, throwing up long-forgotten information which could be valuable in the career or business. Flashes of clairvoyance and intuition are possible along with sudden realizations of one's own nature, which may be used for self-improvement. A talent, never before suspected, may be discovered. Qualities not evident before in friends and marriage partners are likely to be noticed. As this is a period in which the truth seems to emerge, the discovery of false characteristics is likely to lead to disenchantment or a shift in attachments. However, where qualities are realized it should lead to happiness and deeper feeling. Surprise solutions could bob up for old problems. There may be a public announcement of the solving of a crime or mystery. People with secrets may find someone has "guessed" correctly. The secrets of the soul or the inner self also tend to reveal themselves. Religious and philosophical groups may make some interesting discoveries. CAUTION: Not a time for activities that depend on secrecy.

MOON TABLES

TIME CORRECTIONS FOR
GREENWICH MOON TABLES

London, Glasgow, Dublin, Dakar..Same time

Vienna, Prague, Rome, Kinshasa, Frankfurt,
Stockholm, Brussels, Amsterdam, Warsaw,
Zurich...Add 1 hour

Bucharest, Istanbul, Beirut, Cairo, Johannesburg,
Athens, Cape Town, Helsinki, Tel Aviv............................Add 2 hours

Dhahran, Baghdad, Moscow, Leningrad, Nairobi,
Addis Ababa, Zanzibar...Add 3 hours

Delhi, Calcutta, Bombay, Colombo...............................Add 5 ½ hours

Rangoon..Add 6 ½ hours

Saigon, Bangkok, Chungking...Add 7 hours

Canton, Manila, Hong Kong, Shanghai, Peking...............Add 8 hours

Tokyo, Pusan, Seoul, Vladivostok, Yokohama...................Add 9 hours

Sydney, Melbourne, Guam, Port Moresby.........................Add 10 hours

Azores, Reykjavik...Deduct 1 hour

Rio de Janeiro, Montevideo, Buenos Aires,
Sao Paulo, Recife...Deduct 3 hours

LaPaz, San Juan, Santiago, Bermuda, Caracas,
Halifax..Deduct 4 hours

New York, Washington, Boston, Detroit, Lima,
Havana, Miami, Bogota...Deduct 5 hours

Mexico, Chicago, New Orleans, Houston.........................Deduct 6 hours

San Francisco, Seattle, Los Angeles, Hollywood,
Ketchikan, Juneau..Deduct 8 hours

Honolulu, Fairbanks, Anchorage, Papeete.......................Deduct 10 hours

1988 MOON TABLES—GREENWICH TIME

JANUARY		FEBRUARY		MARCH	
Day Moon Enters		**Day Moon Enters**		**Day Moon Enters**	
1. Gemini		1. Leo	6:31 pm	1. Leo	
2. Gemini		2. Leo		2. Virgo	1:26 pm
3. Cancer	0:30 am	3. Leo		3. Virgo	
4. Cancer		4. Virgo	7:10 am	4. Virgo	
5. Leo	Noon	5. Virgo		5. Libra	1:29 am
6. Leo		6. Libra	7:27 pm	6. Libra	
7. Leo		7. Libra		7. Scorpio	0:35 pm
8. Virgo	0:37 am	8. Libra		8. Scorpio	
9. Virgo		9. Scorpio	6:38 am	9. Sagitt.	8:59 pm
10. Libra	1:12 pm	10. Scorpio		10. Sagitt.	
11. Libra		11. Sagitt.	2:19 pm	11. Sagitt.	
12. Scorpio	11:21 pm	12. Sagitt.		12. Capric.	2:35 am
13. Scorpio		13. Capric.	6:20 pm	13. Capric.	
14. Scorpio		14. Capric.		14. Aquar.	5:06 am
15. Sagitt.	5:28 am	15. Aquar.	7:22 pm	15. Aquar.	
16. Sagitt.		16. Aquar.		16. Pisces	5:30 am
17. Capric.	8:20 am	17. Pisces	6:43 pm	17. Pisces	
18. Capric.		18. Pisces		18. Aries	5:30 am
19. Aquar.	8:08 am	19. Aries	6:39 pm	19. Aries	
20. Aquar.		20. Aries		20. Taurus	6:56 am
21. Pisces	7:58 am	21. Taurus	8:56 pm	21. Taurus	
22. Pisces		22. Taurus		22. Gemini	10:58 am
23. Aries	8:32 am	23. Taurus		23. Gemini	
24. Aries		24. Gemini	2:42 am	24. Cancer	7:36 pm
25. Taurus	0:54 pm	25. Gemini		25. Cancer	
26. Taurus		26. Cancer	0:36 pm	26. Cancer	
27. Gemini	7:53 pm	27. Cancer		27. Leo	7:23 am
28. Gemini		28. Cancer		28. Leo	
29. Gemini		29. Leo	0:50 am	29. Virgo	8:13 pm
30. Cancer	6:39 am			30. Virgo	
31. Cancer				31. Virgo	

Summer time to be considered where applicable.

1988 MOON TABLES—GREENWICH TIME

APRIL Day Moon Enters		MAY Day Moon Enters		JUNE Day Moon Enters	
1. Libra	8:12 am	1. Scorpio	1:24 am	1. Capric.	8:51 pm
2. Libra		2. Scorpio		2. Capric.	
3. Scorpio	6:28 pm	3. Sagitt.	8:40 am	3. Aquar.	11:48 pm
4. Scorpio		4. Sagitt.		4. Aquar.	
5. Scorpio		5. Capric.	1:55 pm	5. Aquar.	
6. Sagitt.	2:28 am	6. Capric.		6. Pisces	2:16 am
7. Sagitt.		7. Aquar.	6:08 pm	7. Pisces	
8. Capric.	8:38 am	8. Aquar.		8. Aries	5:16 am
9. Capric.		9. Pisces	8:50 pm	9. Aries	
10. Aquar.	0:41 pm	10. Pisces		10. Taurus	9:12 am
11. Aquar.		11. Aries	11:20 pm	11. Taurus	
12. Pisces	2:46 pm	12. Aries		12. Gemini	2:22 pm
13. Pisces		13. Aries		13. Gemini	
14. Aries	3:39 pm	14. Taurus	2:22 am	14. Cancer	9:42 pm
15. Aries		15. Taurus		15. Cancer	
16. Taurus	5:26 pm	16. Gemini	6:24 am	16. Cancer	
17. Taurus		17. Gemini		17. Leo	7:10 am
18. Gemini	8:48 pm	18. Cancer	0:46 pm	18. Leo	
19. Gemini		19. Cancer		19. Virgo	7:04 pm
20. Gemini		20. Leo	10:54 pm	20. Virgo	
21. Cancer	4:04 am	21. Leo		21. Virgo	
22. Cancer		22. Leo		22. Libra	7:59 am
23. Leo	2:51 pm	23. Virgo	11:12 am	23. Libra	
24. Leo		24. Virgo		24. Scorpio	6:59 pm
25. Leo		25. Libra	11:55 pm	25. Scorpio	
26. Virgo	3:44 am	26. Libra		26. Scorpio	
27. Virgo		27. Libra		27. Sagitt.	2:21 am
28. Libra	3:55 pm	28. Scorpio	10:03 am	28. Sagitt.	
29. Libra		29. Scorpio		29. Capric.	6:06 am
30. Libra		30. Sagitt.	4:44 pm	30. Capric.	
		31. Sagitt.			

Summer time to be considered where applicable.

1988 MOON TABLES—GREENWICH TIME

JULY	AUGUST	SEPTEMBER
Day Moon Enters	Day Moon Enters	Day Moon Enters
1. Aquar. 7:38 am	1. Aries 5:48 pm	1. Taurus
2. Aquar.	2. Aries	2. Gemini 8:08 am
3. Pisces 8:52 am	3. Taurus 8:12 pm	3. Gemini
4. Pisces	4. Taurus	4. Cancer 3:50 pm
5. Aries 10:41 am	5. Taurus	5. Cancer
6. Aries	6. Gemini 1:34 am	6. Cancer
7. Taurus 2:31 pm	7. Gemini	7. Leo 2:32 am
8. Taurus	8. Cancer 10:07 am	8. Leo
9. Gemini 8:17 pm	9. Cancer	9. Virgo 3:02 pm
10. Gemini	10. Leo 8:57 pm	10. Virgo
11. Gemini	11. Leo	11. Virgo
12. Cancer 4:29 am	12. Leo	12. Libra 3:32 am
13. Cancer	13. Virgo 8:37 am	13. Libra
14. Leo 2:25 pm	14. Virgo	14. Scorpio 3:25 pm
15. Leo	15. Libra 9:26 pm	15. Scorpio
16. Leo	16. Libra	16. Scorpio
17. Virgo 2:24 am	17. Libra	17. Sagitt. 2:01 am
18. Virgo	18. Scorpio 9:37 am	18. Sagitt.
19. Libra 3:04 pm	19. Scorpio	19. Capric. 9:40 am
20. Libra	20. Sagitt. 7:49 pm	20. Capric.
21. Libra	21. Sagitt.	21. Aquar. 2:09 pm
22. Scorpio 3:01 am	22. Sagitt.	22. Aquar.
23. Scorpio	23. Capric. 1:45 am	23. Pisces 2:45 pm
24. Sagitt. Noon	24. Capric.	24. Pisces
25. Sagitt.	25. Aquar. 4:20 am	25. Aries 2:33 pm
26. Capric. 4:15 pm	26. Aquar.	26. Aries
27. Capric.	27. Pisces 4:14 am	27. Taurus 2:30 pm
28. Aquar. 5:58 pm	28. Pisces	28. Taurus
29. Aquar.	29. Aries 3:45 am	29. Gemini 5:01 pm
30. Pisces 5:45 pm	30. Aries	30. Gemini
31. Pisces	31. Taurus 4:30 am	

Summer time to be considered where applicable.

1988 MOON TABLES—GREENWICH TIME

OCTOBER		NOVEMBER		DECEMBER	
Day Moon Enters		Day Moon Enters		Day Moon Enters	
1. Cancer	10:43 pm	1. Leo		1. Virgo	
2. Cancer		2. Leo		2. Virgo	
3. Cancer		3. Virgo	4:25 am	3. Libra	1:13 am
4. Leo	9:00 am	4. Virgo		4. Libra	
5. Leo		5. Libra	5:15 pm	5. Scorpio	0:47 pm
6. Virgo	9:22 pm	6. Libra		6. Scorpio	
7. Virgo		7. Libra		7. Sagitt.	10:10 pm
8. Virgo		8. Scorpio	4:39 am	8. Sagitt.	
9. Libra	10:00 am	9. Scorpio		9. Sagitt.	
10. Libra		10. Sagitt.	1:53 pm	10. Capric.	4:14 am
11. Scorpio	9:34 pm	11. Sagitt.		11. Capric.	
12. Scorpio		12. Capric.	9:23 pm	12. Aquar.	9:04 am
13. Scorpio		13. Capric.		13. Aquar.	
14. Sagitt.	7:35 am	14. Capric.		14. Pisces	0:10 pm
15. Sagitt.		15. Aquar.	2:46 am	15. Pisces	
16. Capric.	3:38 pm	16. Aquar.		16. Aries	2:53 pm
17. Capric.		17. Pisces	6:37 am	17. Aries	
18. Aquar.	9:07 pm	18. Pisces		18. Taurus	5:50 pm
19. Aquar.		19. Aries	8:50 am	19. Taurus	
20. Pisces	11:56 pm	20. Aries		20. Gemini	9:48 pm
21. Pisces		21. Taurus	10:41 am	21. Gemini	
22. Pisces		22. Taurus		22. Gemini	
23. Aries	0:49 am	23. Gemini	1:13 pm	23. Cancer	2:42 am
24. Aries		24. Gemini		24. Cancer	
25. Taurus	1:22 am	25. Cancer	5:36 pm	25. Leo	10:08 am
26. Taurus		26. Cancer		26. Leo	
27. Gemini	3:07 am	27. Cancer		27. Virgo	8:36 pm
28. Gemini		28. Leo	1:04 am	28. Virgo	
29. Cancer	7:42 am	29. Leo		29. Virgo	
30. Cancer		30. Virgo	0:12 pm	30. Libra	8:58 am
31. Leo	4:25 pm			31. Libra	

Summer time to be considered where applicable.

1988 PHASES OF THE MOON—GREENWICH TIME

New Moon	First Quarter	Full Moon	Last Quarter
(1987)	(1987)	Jan. 4	Jan. 12
Jan. 19	Jan. 25	Feb. 2	Feb. 10
Feb. 17	Feb. 24	Mar. 3	Mar. 11
Mar. 18	Mar. 25	Apr. 1	Apr. 9
Apr. 16	Apr. 23	May 1	May 9
May 15	May 23	May 31	June 7
June 14	June 22	June 29	July 6
July 13	July 22	July 29	Aug. 4
Aug. 12	Aug. 20	Aug. 27	Sep. 3
Sep. 11	Sep. 19	Sep. 25	Oct. 2
Oct. 10	Oct. 18	Oct. 25	Nov. 1
Nov. 9	Nov. 16	Nov. 23	Dec. 1
Dec. 9	Dec. 16	Dec. 23	Dec. 31

1988 PLANTING GUIDE

	Aboveground Crops	Root Crops	Pruning	Weeds Pests
January	3-21-22-26-30-31	4-11-12-13-14-17-18	4-13-14	6-7-8-9-15-16
February	18-22-23-27-28	7-8-9-10-14	9-10	3-4-5-12-16
March	20-21-25-26	5-6-7-8-12-13-16-17	8-16-17	4-10-11-14-15
April	1-17-21-22-29-30	2-3-4-5-8-9-13	4-5-13	6-7-11-15
May	1-19-20-26-27-28-29	2-6-10-11-14-15	2-10-11	3-4-8-12-13
June	15-16-22-23-24-25-26	2-3-6-7-10-11-30	6-7	4-5-8-9-13
July	20-21-22-23-27	3-4-8-12-13-31	3-4-12-13-31	1-2-6-10-11-29
August	16-17-18-19-23-24	4-5-9-28-31	9-28	2-6-7-11-29-30
September	12-13-14-15-16-19-20-24	1-5-6-28	5-6	2-3-7-8-9-10-26-30
October	11-12-13-17-21-22	2-3-9-25-26-29-30	2-3-29-30	1-4-5-6-7-27-28
November	13-14-17-18-21-22	6-7-8-26-27	8-26-27	1-2-3-4-24-28-29-30
December	10-11-15-19	3-4-5-6-7-23-24-30-31	6-7-23-24	1-2-8-26-27-28-29

1988 FISHING GUIDE

	Good	Best
January	1-2-5-6-7-19-25	3-4-12-30-31
February	1-2-3-4-5-17-24-29	10
March	1-2-3-4-11-18-30-31	5-6-25
April	16-23-28	1-2-3-4-5-9-29-30
May	3-4-9-23-30-31	1-2-15-28-29
June	1-14-27-28	2-3-7-22-26-29-30
July	1-2-6-26-28-29-30	13-22-27-31
August	1-12-20-25-26-29-30	4-24-27-28
September	3-11-22-23-25-26-27	19-24-28
October	18-23-24-27-28	2-10-22-25-26
November	1-16-20-21-23-24-25	9-22-26
December	1-9-16-20-21-22-25-26	23-24-31

MOON'S INFLUENCE OVER DAILY AFFAIRS

The Moon makes a complete transit of the Zodiac every 27 days 7 hours and 43 minutes. In making this transit the Moon forms different aspects with the planets and consequently has favorable or unfavorable bearings on affairs and events for persons according to the sign of the Zodiac under which they were born.

Whereas the Sun exclusively represents fire, the Moon rules water. The action of the Moon may be described as fluctuating, variable, absorbent and receptive. It is well known that the attraction to the Moon in combination with the movement of the Earth is responsible for the tides. The Moon has a similar effect on men. A clever navigator will make use of the tides to bring his ship to the intended destination. You also can reach your "destination" better by making use of your tides.

When the Moon is in conjunction with the Sun it is called a New Moon; when the Moon and Sun are in opposition it is called a Full Moon. From New Moon to Full Moon, first and second quarter—which takes about two weeks—the Moon is increasing or waxing. From Full Moon to New Moon, third and fourth quarter, the Moon is said to be decreasing or waning. The Moon Table indicates the New Moon and Full Moon and the quarters.

ACTIVITY	MOON IN
Business	
buying and selling	Sagittarius, Aries, Gemini, Virgo
new, requiring public support	1st and 2nd quarter
meant to be kept quiet	3rd and 4th quarter
Investigation	3rd and 4th quarter
Signing documents	1st & 2nd quarter, Cancer, Scorpio, Pisces
Advertising	2nd quarter, Sagittarius
Journeys and trips	1st & 2nd quarter, Gemini, Virgo
Renting offices, etc.	Taurus, Leo, Scorpio, Aquarius
Painting of house/apartment	3rd & 4th quarter, Taurus, Scorpio, Aquarius
Decorating	Gemini, Libra, Aquarius
Buying clothes and accessories	Taurus, Virgo
Beauty salon or barber shop visit	1st & 2nd quarter, Taurus, Leo, Libra, Scorpio, Aquarius
Weddings	1st & 2nd quarter

MOON'S INFLUENCE OVER YOUR HEALTH

ARIES	Head, brain, face, upper jaw
TAURUS	Throat, neck, lower jaw
GEMINI	Hands, arms, lungs, shoulders, nervous system
CANCER	Esophagus, stomach, breasts, womb, liver
LEO	Heart, spine
VIRGO	Intestines, liver
LIBRA	Kidneys, lower back
SCORPIO	Sex and eliminative organs
SAGITTARIUS	Hips, thighs, liver
CAPRICORN	Skin, bones, beeth, knees
AQUARIUS	Circulatory system, lower legs
PISCES	Feet, tone of being

Try to avoid work being done on that part of the body when the Moon is in the sign governing that part.

MOON'S INFLUENCE OVER PLANTS

Centuries ago it was established that seeds planted when the Moon is in certain signs and phases called "fruitful" will produce more than seeds planted when the Moon is in a Barren sign.

FRUITFUL SIGNS	*BARREN SIGNS*	*DRY SIGNS*
Taurus	Aries	Aries
Cancer	Gemini	Gemini
Libra	Leo	Sagittarius
Scorpio	Virgo	Aquarius
Capricorn	Sagittarius	
Pisces	Aquarius	

ACTIVITY	MOON IN
Mow lawn, trim plans	Fruitful sign, 1st & 2nd quarter
Plant flowers	Fruitful sign, 2nd quarter; best in Cancer and Libra
Prune	Fruitful sign, 3rd & 4th quarter
Destroy pests; spray	Barren sign, 4th quarter
Harvest potatoes, root crops	Dry sign, 3rd & 4th quarter; Taurus, Leo, and Aquarius

THE SIGNS: DOMINANT CHARACTERISTICS

March 21–April 20

The Positive Side of Aries

The Arien has many positive points to his character. People born under this first sign of the Zodiac are often quite strong and enthusiastic. On the whole, they are forward-looking people who are not easily discouraged by temporary setbacks. They know what they want out of life and they go out after it. Their personalities are strong. Others are usually quite impressed by the Arien's way of doing things. Quite often they are sources of inspiration for others traveling the same route. Aries men and women have a special zest for life that is often contagious; for others, they are often the example of how life should be lived.

The Aries person usually has a quick and active mind. He is imaginative and inventive. He enjoys keeping busy and active. He generally gets along well with all kinds of people. He is interested in mankind, as a whole. He likes to be challenged. Some would say he thrives on opposition, for it is when he is set against that he often does his best. Getting over or around obstacles is a challenge he generally enjoys. All in all, the Arien is quite positive and young-thinking. He likes to keep abreast of new things that are happening in the world. Ariens are often fond of speed. They like things to be done quickly and this sometimes aggravates their slower colleagues and associates.

The Aries man or woman always seems to remain young. Their whole approach to life is youthful and optimistic. They never say die, no matter what the odds. They may have an occasional setback, but it is not long before they are back on their feet again.

The Negative Side of Aries

Everybody has his less positive qualities—and Aries is no exception. Sometimes the Aries man or woman is not very tactful in communicating with others; in his hurry to get things done he is apt to

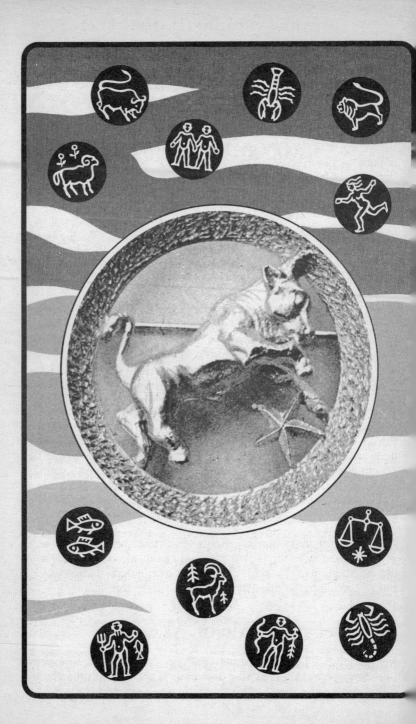

be a little callous or inconsiderate. Sensitive people are likely to find him somewhat sharp-tongued in some situations. Often in his eagerness to achieve his aims, he misses the mark altogether. At times the Arien is too impulsive. He can occasionally be stubborn and refuse to listen to reason. If things do not move quickly enough to suit the Aries man or woman, he or she is apt to become rather nervous or irritable. The uncultivated Arien is not unfamiliar with moments of doubt and fear. He is capable of being destructive if he does not get his way. He can overcome some of his emotional problems by steadily trying to express himself as he really is, but this requires effort.

April 21–May 20

The Positive Side of Taurus

The Taurus person is known for his ability to concentrate and for his tenacity. These are perhaps his strongest qualities. The Taurus man or woman generally has very little trouble in getting along with others; it's his nature to be helpful toward people in need. He can always be depended on by his friends, especially those in trouble.

The Taurean generally achieves what he wants through his ability to persevere. He never leaves anything unfinished but works on something until it has been completed. People can usually take him at his word; he is honest and forthright in most of his dealings. The Taurus person has a good chance to make a success of his life because of his many positive qualities. The Taurean who aims high seldom falls short of his mark. He learns well by experience. He is thorough and does not believe in short-cuts of any kind. The Taurean's thoroughness pays off in the end, for through his deliberateness he learns how to rely on himself and what he has learned. The Taurus person tries to get along with others, as a rule. He is not overly critical and likes people to be themselves. He is a tolerant person and enjoys peace and harmony—especially in his home life.

The Taurean is usually cautious in all that he does. He is not a person who believes in taking unnecessary risks. Before adopting any one line of action, he will weigh all of the pros and cons. The

Taurus person is steadfast. Once his mind is made up it seldom changes. The person born under this sign usually is a good family person—reliable and loving.

The Negative Side of Taurus

Sometimes the Taurus man or woman is a bit too stubborn. He won't listen to other points of view if his mind is set on something. To others, this can be quite annoying. The Taurean also does not like to be told what to do. He becomes rather angry if others think him not too bright. He does not like to be told he is wrong, even when he is. He dislikes being contradicted.

Some people who are born under this sign are very suspicious of others—even of those persons close to them. They find it difficult to trust people fully. They are often afraid of being deceived or taken advantage of. The Taurean often finds it difficult to forget or forgive. His love of material things sometimes makes him rather avaricious and petty.

May 21–June 20

The Positive Side of Gemini

The person born under this sign of the Heavenly Twins is usually quite bright and quick-witted. Some of them are capable of doing many different things. The Gemini person very often has many different interests. He keeps an open mind and is always anxious to learn new things.

The Geminian is often an analytical person. He is a person who enjoys making use of his intellect. He is governed more by his mind than by his emotions. He is a person who is not confined to one view; he can often understand both sides to a problem or question. He knows how to reason; how to make rapid decisions if need be.

He is an adaptable person and can make himself at home almost anywhere. There are all kinds of situations he can adapt to. He is a person who seldom doubts himself; he is sure of his talents and his

ability to think and reason. The Geminian is generally most satisfied when he is in a situation where he can make use of his intellect. Never short of imagination, he often has strong talents for invention. He is rather a modern person when it comes to life; the Geminian almost always moves along with the times—perhaps that is why he remains so youthful throughout most of his life.

Literature and art appeal to the person born under this sign. Creativity in almost any form will interest and intrigue the Gemini man or woman.

The Geminian is often quite charming. A good talker, he often is the center of attraction at any gathering. People find it easy to like a person born under this sign because he can appear easygoing and usually has a good sense of humor.

The Negative Side of Gemini

Sometimes the Gemini person tries to do too many things at one time—and as a result, winds up finishing nothing. Some Geminians are easily distracted and find it rather difficult to concentrate on one thing for too long a time. Sometimes they give in to trifling fancies and find it rather boring to become too serious about any one thing. Some of them are never dependable, no matter what they promise.

Although the Gemini man or woman often appears to be well-versed on many subjects, this is sometimes just a veneer. His knowledge may be only superficial, but because he speaks so well he gives people the impression of erudition. Some Geminians are sharp-tongued and inconsiderate; they think only of themselves and their own pleasure.

June 21–July 20

The Positive Side of Cancer

The Cancerians's most positive point is his understanding nature. On the whole, he is a loving and sympathetic person. He would never go out of his way to hurt anyone. The Cancer man or woman

is often very kind and tender; they give what they can to others. They hate to see others suffering and will do what they can to help someone in less fortunate circumstances than themselves. They are often very concerned about the world. Their interest in people generally goes beyond that of just their own families and close friends; they have a deep sense of brotherhood and respect humanitarian values. The Cancerian means what he says, as a rule; he is honest about his feelings.

The Cancer man or woman is a person who knows the art of patience. When something seems difficult, he is willing to wait until the situation becomes manageable again. He is a person who knows how to bide his time. The Cancerian knows how to concentrate on one thing at a time. When he has made his mind up he generally sticks with what he does, seeing it through to the end.

The Cancerian is a person who loves his home. He enjoys being surrounded by familiar things and the people he loves. Of all the signs, Cancer is the most maternal. Even the men born under this sign often have a motherly or protective quality about them. They like to take care of people in their family—to see that they are well loved and well provided for. They are usually loyal and faithful. Family ties mean a lot to the Cancer man or woman. Parents and in-laws are respected and loved. The Cancerian has a strong sense of tradition. He is very sensitive to the moods of others.

The Negative Side of Cancer

Sometimes the Cancerian finds it rather hard to face life. It becomes too much for him. He can be a little timid and retiring, when things don't go too well. When unfortunate things happen, he is apt to just shrug and say, "Whatever will be will be." He can be fatalistic to a fault. The uncultivated Cancerian is a bit lazy. He doesn't have very much ambition. Anything that seems a bit difficult he'll gladly leave to others. He may be lacking in initiative. Too sensitive, when he feels he's been injured, he'll crawl back into his shell and nurse his imaginary wounds. The Cancer woman often is given to crying when the smallest thing goes wrong.

Some Cancerians find it difficult to enjoy themselves in environments outside their homes. They make heavy demands on others, and need to be constantly reassured that they are loved.

July 21–August 21

The Positive Side of Leo

Often Leos make good leaders. They seem to be good organizers and administrators. Usually they are quite popular with others. Whatever group it is that he belongs to, the Leo man is almost sure to be or become the leader.

The Leo person is generous most of the time. It is his best characteristic. He or she likes to give gifts and presents. In making others happy, the Leo person becomes happy himself. He likes to splurge when spending money on others. In some instances it may seem that the Leo's generosity knows no boundaries. A hospitable person, the Leo man or woman is very fond of welcoming people to his house and entertaining them. He is never short of company.

The Leo person has plenty of energy and drive. He enjoys working toward some specific goal. When he applies himself correctly, he gets what he wants most often. The Leo person is almost never unsure of himself. He has plenty of confidence and aplomb. He is a person who is direct in almost everything he does. He has a quick mind and can make a decision in a very short time.

He usually sets a good example for others because of his ambitious manner and positive ways. He knows how to stick to something once he's started. Although the Leo person may be good at making a joke, he is not superficial or glib. He is a loving person, kind and thoughtful.

There is generally nothing small or petty about the Leo man or woman. He does what he can for those who are deserving. He is a person others can rely upon at all times. He means what he says. An honest person, generally speaking, he is a friend that others value.

The Negative Side of Leo

Leo, however, does have his faults. At times, he can be just a bit too arrogant. He thinks that no one deserves a leadership position except him. Only he is capable of doing things well. His opinion of himself is often much too high. Because of his conceit, he is sometimes rather unpopular with a good many people. Some Leos are too materialistic; they can only think in terms of money and profit.

Some Leos enjoy lording it over others—at home or at their place of business. What is more, they feel they have the right to. Egocentric to an impossible degree, this sort of Leo cares little about how others think or feel. He can be rude and cutting.

August 22–September 22

The Positive Side of Virgo

The person born under the sign of Virgo is generally a busy person. He knows how to arrange and organize things. He is a good planner. Above all, he is practical and is not afraid of hard work.

The person born under this sign, Virgo, knows how to attain what he desires. He sticks with something until it is finished. He never shirks his duties, and can always be depended upon. The Virgo person can be thoroughly trusted at all times.

The man or woman born under this sign tries to do everything to perfection. He doesn't believe in doing anything half-way. He always aims for the top. He is the sort of a person who is constantly striving to better himself—not because he wants more money or glory, but because it gives him a feeling of accomplishment.

The Virgo man or woman is a very observant person. He is sensitive to how others feel, and can see things below the surface of a situation. He usually puts this talent to constructive use.

It is not difficult for the Virgoan to be open and earnest. He believes in putting his cards on the table. He is never secretive or under-handed. He's as good as his word. The Virgo person is generally plain-spoken and down-to-earth. He has no trouble in expressing himself.

The Virgo person likes to keep up to date on new developments in his particular field. Well-informed, generally, he sometimes has a keen interest in the arts or literature. What he knows, he knows well. His ability to use his critical faculties is well-developed and sometimes startles others because of its accuracy.

The Virgoan adheres to a moderate way of life; he avoids excesses. He is a responsible person and enjoys being of service.

The Negative Side of Virgo

Sometimes a Virgo person is too critical. He thinks that only he can do something the way it should be done. Whatever anyone else does is inferior. He can be rather annoying in the way he quibbles over insignificant details. In telling others how things should be done, he can be rather tactless and mean.

Some Virgos seem rather emotionless and cool. They feel emo-

tional involvement is beneath them. They are sometimes too tidy, too neat. With money they can be rather miserly. Some try to force their opinions and ideas on others.

September 23–October 22

The Positive Side of Libra

Librans love harmony. It is one of their most outstanding character traits. They are interested in achieving balance; they admire beauty and grace in things as well as in people. Generally speaking, they are kind and considerate people. Librans are usually very sympathetic. They go out of their way not to hurt another person's feelings. They are outgoing and do what they can to help those in need.

People born under the sign of Libra almost always make good friends. They are loyal and amiable. They enjoy the company of others. Many of them are rather moderate in their views; they believe in keeping an open mind, however, and weighing both sides of an issue fairly before making a decision.

Alert and often intelligent, the Libran, always fair-minded, tries to put himself in the position of the other person. They are against injustice; quite often they take up for the underdog. In most of their social dealings, they try to be tactful and kind. They dislike discord and bickering, and most Libras strive for peace and harmony in all their relationships.

The Libra man or woman has a keen sense of beauty. They appreciate handsome furnishings and clothes. Many of them are artistically inclined. Their taste is usually impeccable. They know how to use color. Their homes are almost always attractively arranged and inviting. They enjoy entertaining people and see to it that their guests always feel at home and welcome.

The Libran gets along with almost everyone. He is well-liked and socially much in demand.

The Negative Side of Libra

Some people born under this sign tend to be rather insincere. So eager are they to achieve harmony in all relationships that they will even go so far as to lie. Many of them are escapists. They find facing

the truth an ordeal and prefer living in a world of make-believe.

In a serious argument, some Librans give in rather easily even when they know they are right. Arguing, even about something they believe in, is too unsettling for some of them.

Librans sometimes care too much for material things. They enjoy possessions and luxuries. Some are vain and tend to be jealous.

October 23–November 22

The Positive Side of Scorpio

The Scorpio man or woman generally knows what he or she wants out of life. He is a determined person. He sees something through to the end. The Scorpion is quite sincere, and seldom says anything he doesn't mean. When he sets a goal for himself he tries to go about achieving it in a very direct way.

The Scorpion is brave and courageous. They are not afraid of hard work. Obstacles do not frighten them. They forge ahead until they achieve what they set out for. The Scorpio man or woman has a strong will.

Although the Scorpion may seem rather fixed and determined, inside he is often quite tender and loving. He can care very much for others. He believes in sincerity in all relationships. His feelings about someone tend to last; they are profound and not superficial.

The Scorpio person is someone who adheres to his principles no matter what happens. He will not be deterred from a path he believes to be right.

Because of his many positive strengths, the Scorpion can often achieve happiness for himself and for those that he loves.

He is a constructive person by nature. He often has a deep understanding of people and of life, in general. He is perceptive and unafraid. Obstacles often seem to spur him on. He is a positive person who enjoys winning. He has many strengths and resources; challenge of any sort often brings out the best in him.

The Negative Side of Scorpio

The Scorpio person is sometimes hypersensitive. Often he imagines injury when there is none. He feels that others do not bother to

recognize him for his true worth. Sometimes he is given to excessive boasting in order to compensate for what he feels is neglect

The Scorpio person can be rather proud and arrogant. They can be rather sly when they put their minds to it and they enjoy outwitting persons or institutions noted for their cleverness.

Their tactics for getting what they want are sometimes devious and ruthless. They don't care too much about what others may think. If they feel others have done them an injustice, they will do their best to seek revenge. The Scorpion often has a sudden, violent temper; and this person's interest in sex is sometimes quite unbalanced or excessive.

November 23–December 20

The Positive Side of Sagittarius

People born under this sign are often honest and forthright. Their approach to life is earnest and open. The Sagittarian is often quite adult in his way of seeing things. They are broadminded and tolerant people. When dealing with others the person born under the sign of Sagittarius is almost always open and forthright. He doesn't believe in deceit or pretension. His standards are high. People who associate with the Sagittarian, generally admire and respect him.

The Sagittarian trusts others easily and expects them to trust him. He is never suspicious or envious and almost always thinks well of others. People always enjoy his company because he is so friendly and easy-going. The Sagittarius man or woman is often good-humored. He can always be depended upon by his friends, family, and co-workers.

The person born under this sign of the Zodiac likes a good joke every now and then; he is keen on fun and this makes him very popular with others.

A lively person, he enjoys sports and outdoor life. The Sagittarian is fond of animals. Intelligent and interesting, he can begin an animated conversation with ease. He likes exchanging ideas and discussing various views.

He is not selfish or proud. If someone proposes an idea or plan that is better than his, he will immediately adopt it. Imaginative yet practical, he knows how to put ideas into practice.

He enjoys sport and game, and it doesn't matter if he wins or loses. He is a forgiving person, and never sulks over something that has not worked out in his favor.

He is seldom critical, and is almost always generous.

The Negative Side of Sagittarius

Some Sagittarians are restless. They take foolish risks and seldom learn from the mistakes they make. They don't have heads for money and are often mismanaging their finances. Some of them devote much of their time to gambling.

Some are too outspoken and tactless, always putting their feet in their mouths. They hurt others carelessly by being honest at the wrong time. Sometimes they make promises which they don't keep. They don't stick close enough to their plans and go from one failure to another. They are undisciplined and waste a lot of energy.

December 21–January 19

The Positive Side of Capricorn

The person born under the sign of Capricorn is usually very stable and patient. He sticks to whatever tasks he has and sees them through. He can always be relied upon and he is not averse to work.

An honest person, the Capricornian is generally serious about whatever he does. He does not take his duties lightly. He is a practical person and believes in keeping his feet on the ground.

Quite often the person born under this sign is ambitious and knows how to get what he wants out of life. He forges ahead and never gives up his goal. When he is determined about something, he almost always wins. He is a good worker—a hard worker. Although things may not come easy to him, he will not complain, but continue working until his chores are finished.

He is usually good at business matters and knows the value of money. He is not a spendthrift and knows how to put something away for a rainy day; he dislikes waste and unnecessary loss.

The Capricornian knows how to make use of his self-control. He

can apply himself to almost anything once he puts his mind to it. His ability to concentrate sometimes astounds others. He is diligent and does well when involved in detail work.

The Capricorn man or woman is charitable, generally speaking, and will do what is possible to help others less fortunate. As a friend, he is loyal and trustworthy. He never shirks his duties or responsibilities. He is self-reliant and never expects too much of the other fellow. He does what he can on his own. If someone does him a good turn, then he will do his best to return the favor.

The Negative Side of Capricorn

Like everyone, the Capricornian, too, has his faults. At times, he can be over-critical of others. He expects others to live up to his own high standards. He thinks highly of himself and tends to look down on others.

His interest in material things may be exaggerated. The Capricorn man or woman thinks too much about getting on in the world and having something to show for it. He may even be a little greedy.

He sometimes thinks he knows what's best for everyone. He is too bossy. He is always trying to organize and correct others. He may be a little narrow in his thinking.

January 20–February 18

The Positive Side of Aquarius

The Aquarius man or woman is usually very honest and forthright. These are his two greatest qualities. His standards for himself are generally very high. He can always be relied upon by others. His word is his bond.

The Aquarian is perhaps the most tolerant of all the Zodiac personalities. He respects other people's beliefs and feels that everyone is entitled to his own approach to life.

He would never do anything to injure another's feelings. He is never unkind or cruel. Always considerate of others, the Aquarian is always willing to help a person in need. He feels a very strong tie between himself and all the other members of mankind.

The person born under this sign is almost always an individualist. He does not believe in teaming up with the masses, but prefers going his own way. His ideas about life and mankind are often quite advanced. There is a saying to the effect that the average Aquarian is fifty years ahead of his time.

He is broadminded. The problems of the world concern him greatly. He is interested in helping others no matter what part of the globe they live in. He is truly a humanitarian sort. He likes to be of service to others.

Giving, considerate, and without prejudice, Aquarians have no trouble getting along with others.

The Negative Side of Aquarius

The Aquarian may be too much of a dreamer. He makes plans but seldom carries them out. He is rather unrealistic. His imagination has a tendency to run away with him. Because many of his plans are impractical, he is always in some sort of a dither.

Others may not approve of him at all times because of his unconventional behavior. He may be a bit eccentric. Sometimes he is so busy with his own thoughts, that he loses touch with the realities of existence.

Some Aquarians feel they are more clever and intelligent than others. They seldom admit to their own faults, even when they are quite apparent. Some become rather fanatic in their views. Their criticism of others is sometimes destructive and negative.

February 19–March 20

The Positive Side of Pisces

The Piscean can often understand the problems of others quite easily. He has a sympathetic nature. Kindly, he is often dedicated in the way he goes about helping others. The sick and the troubled often turn to him for advice and assistance.

He is very broadminded and does not criticize others for their faults. He knows how to accept people for what they are. On the whole, he is a trustworthy and earnest person. He is loyal to his

friends and will do what he can to help them in time of need. Generous and good-natured, he is a lover of peace; he is often willing to help others solve their differences. People who have taken a wrong turn in life often interest him and he will do what he can to persuade them to rehabilitate themselves.

He has a strong intuitive sense and most of the time he knows how to make it work for him; the Piscean is unusually perceptive and often knows what is bothering someone before that person, himself, is aware of it. The Pisces man or woman is an idealistic person, basically, and is interested in making the world a better place in which to live. The Piscean believes that everyone should help each other. He is willing to do more than his share in order to achieve cooperation with others.

The person born under this sign often is talented in music or art. He is a receptive person; he is able to take the ups and downs of life with philosophic calm.

The Negative Side of Pisces

Some Pisceans are often depressed; their outlook on life is rather glum. They may feel that they have been given a bad deal in life and that others are always taking unfair advantage of them. The Piscean sometimes feel that the world is a cold and cruel place. He is easily discouraged. He may even withdraw from the harshness of reality into a secret shell of his own where he dreams and idles away a good deal of his time.

The Piscean can be rather lazy. He lets things happen without giving the least bit of resistance. He drifts along, whether on the high road or on the low. He is rather short on willpower.

Some Pisces people seek escape through drugs or alcohol. When temptation comes along they find it hard to resist. In matters of sex, they can be rather permissive.

THE SIGNS AND
THEIR KEY WORDS

		POSITIVE	NEGATIVE
ARIES	self	courage, initiative, pioneer instinct	brash rudeness, selfish impetuosity
TAURUS	money	endurance, loyalty, wealth	obstinacy, gluttony
GEMINI	mind	versatility	capriciousness, unreliability
CANCER	family	sympathy, homing instinct	clannishness, childishness
LEO	children	love, authority, integrity	egotism, force
VIRGO	work	purity, industry, analysis	fault-finding, cynicism
LIBRA	marriage	harmony, justice	vacillation, superficiality
SCORPIO	sex	survival, regeneration	vengeance, discord
SAGITTARIUS	travel	optimism, higher learning	lawlessness
CAPRICORN	career	depth	narrowness, gloom
AQUARIUS	friends	human fellowship, genius	perverse unpredictability
PISCES	confine-ment	spiritual love, universality	diffusion, escapism

THE ELEMENTS AND QUALITIES OF THE SIGNS

ELEMENT	SIGN	QUALITY	SIGN
FIRE..................	ARIES LEO SAGITTARIUS	CARDINAL.........	ARIES LIBRA CANCER CAPRICORN
EARTH...............	TAURUS VIRGO CAPRICORN	FIXED................	TAURUS LEO SCORPIO AQUARIUS
AIR.....................	GEMINI LIBRA AQUARIUS		
WATER..............	CANCER SCORPIO PISCES	MUTABLE.........	GEMINI VIRGO SAGITTARIUS PISCES

Every sign has both an element and a quality associated with it. The element indicates the basic makeup of the sign, and the quality describes the kind of activity associated with each.

Signs can be grouped together according to their *element* and *quality*. Signs of the same element share many basic traits in common. They tend to form stable configurations and ultimately harmonious relationships. Signs of the same quality are often less harmonious, but they share many dynamic potentials for growth as well as profound fulfillment.

THE FIRE SIGNS

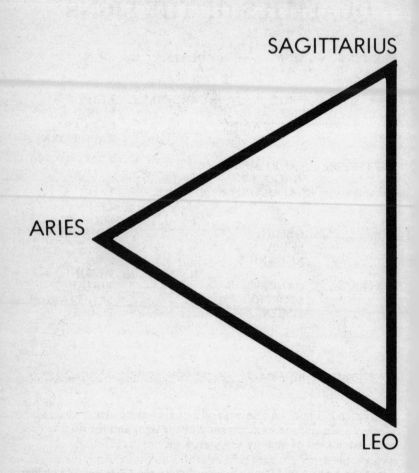

This is the fire group. On the whole these are emotional, volatile types, quick to anger, quick to forgive. They are adventurous, powerful people and .act as a source of inspiration for everyone. They spark into action with immediate exuberant impulses. They are intelligent, self-involved, creative and idealistic. They all share a certain vibrancy and glow that outwardly reflects an inner flame and passion for living.

THE EARTH SIGNS

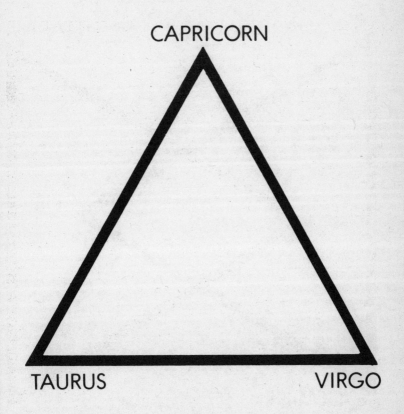

This is the earth group. They are in constant touch with the material world and tend to be conservative. Although they are all capable of spartan self-discipline, they are earthy, sensual people who are stimulated by the tangible, elegant and luxurious. The thread of their lives is always practical, but they do fantasize and are often attracted to dark, mysterious, emotional people. They are like great cliffs overhanging the sea, forever married to the ocean but always resisting erosion from the dark, emotional forces that thunder at their feet.

THE AIR SIGNS

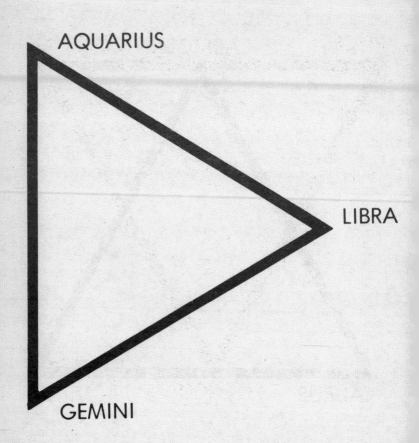

AQUARIUS

LIBRA

GEMINI

This is the air group. They are light, mental creatures desirous of contact, communication and relationship. They are involved with people and the forming of ties on many levels. Original thinkers, they are the bearers of human news. Their language is their sense of word, color, style and beauty. They provide an atmosphere suitable and pleasant for living. They add change and versatility to the scene, and it is through them that we can explore new territory of human intelligence and experience.

THE WATER SIGNS

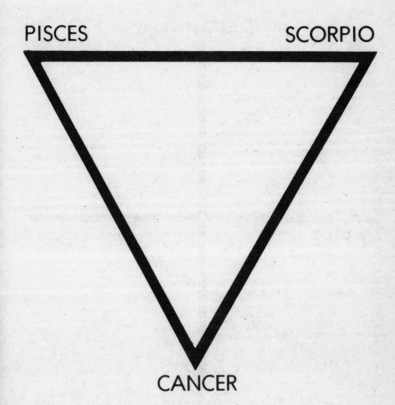

PISCES   SCORPIO

CANCER

This is the water group. Through the water people, we are all joined together on emotional, non-verbal levels. They are silent, mysterious types whose magic hypnotizes even the most determined realist. They have uncanny perceptions about people and are as rich as the oceans when it comes to feeling, emotion or imagination. They are sensitive, mystical creatures with memories that go back beyond time. Through water, life is sustained. These people have the potential for the depths of darkness or the heights of mysticism and art.

THE CARDINAL SIGNS

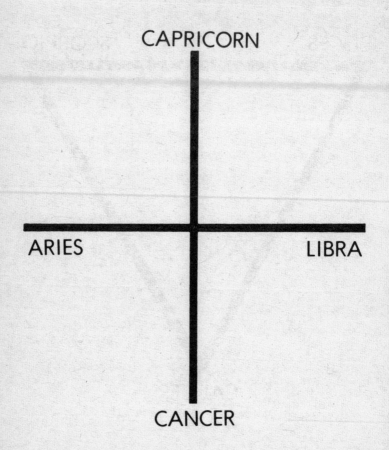

Put together, this is a clear-cut picture of dynamism, activity, tremendous stress and remarkable achievement. These people know the meaning of great change since their lives are often characterized by significant crises and major successes. This combination is like a simultaneous storm of summer, fall, winter and spring. The danger is chaotic diffusion of energy; the potential is irrepressible growth and victory.

THE FIXED SIGNS

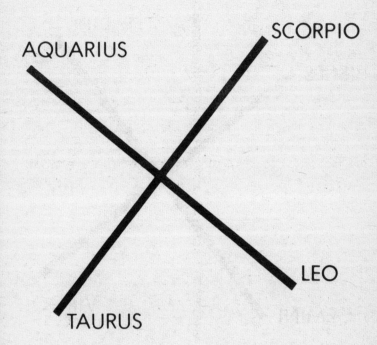

Fixed signs are always establishing themselves in a given place or area of experience. Like explorers who arrive and plant a flag, these people claim a position from which they do not enjoy being deposed. They are staunch, stalwart, upright, trusty, honorable people, although their obstinacy is well-known. Their contribution is fixity, and they are the angels who support our visible world.

THE MUTABLE SIGNS

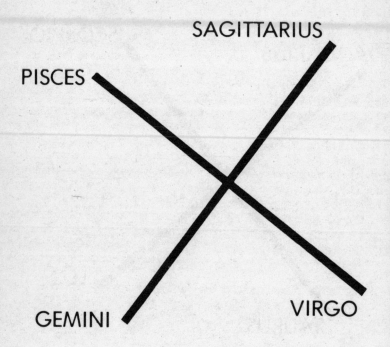

Mutable people are versatile, sensitive, intelligent, nervous and deeply curious about life. They are the translators of all energy. They often carry out or complete tasks initiated by others. Combinations of these signs have highly developed minds; they are imaginative and jumpy and think and talk a lot. At worst their lives are a Tower of Babel. At best they are adaptable and ready creatures who can assimilate one kind of experience and enjoy it while anticipating coming changes.

HOW TO APPROXIMATE YOUR RISING SIGN

Apart from the month and day of birth, the exact *time* of birth is another vital factor in the determination of an accurate horoscope. Not only do the planets move with great speed, but one must know how far the Earth has turned during the day. That way you can determine exactly where the planets are located with respect to the precise birthplace of an individual. This makes *your* horoscope *your* horoscope. In addition to these factors, another grid is laid upon that of the Zodiac and the planets: the houses. After all three have been considered, specific planetary relationships can be measured and analyzed in accordance with certain ordered procedures. It is the skillful translation of all this complex astrological language that a serious astrologer strives for in his attempt at coherent astrological synthesis. Keep this in mind.

The horoscope sets up a kind of framework around which the life of an individual grows like wild ivy, this way and that, weaving its way around the trellis of the natal positions of the planets. The year of birth tells us the positions of the distant, slow-moving planets like Jupiter, Saturn, Uranus and Pluto. The month of birth indicates the Sun sign, or birth sign as it is commonly called, as well as indicating the positions of the rapidly moving planets like Venus, Mercury and Mars. The day of birth locates the position of our Moon, and the moment of birth determines the houses through what is called the Ascendant, or Rising Sign.

As the Earth rotates on its axis once every 24 hours, each one of the twelve signs of the Zodiac appears to be "rising" on the horizon, with a new one appearing about every two hours. Actually it is the turning of the Earth that exposes each sign to view, but you will remember that in much of our astrological work we are discussing "apparent" motion. This *Rising Sign* marks the Ascendant and it colors the whole orientation of a horoscope. It indicates the sign governing the first house of the chart, and will thus determine which signs will govern all the other houses. The idea is a bit complicated at first, and we needn't dwell on complications in this introduction, but if you can imagine two color wheels with twelve divisions superimposed upon each other, one moving slowly and the other remaining still, you will have some idea of how the signs keep shifting the "color" of the houses as the Rising Sign continues to change every two hours.

The important point is that the birth chart, or horoscope, actually does define specific factors of a person's makeup. It contains a picture of being, much the way the nucleus of a tiny cell contains the potential for an entire elephant, or a packet of seeds contains a rosebush. If there were no order or continuity to the world, we could plant roses and get elephants. This same order that gives continuous flow to our lives often annoys people if it threatens to determine too much of their lives. We must grow from what we were planted, and there's no reason why we can't do that magnificently. It's all there in the horoscope. Where there is limitation, there is breakthrough; where there is crisis, there is transformation. Accurate analysis of a horoscope can help you find these points of breakthrough and transformation, and it requires knowledge of subtleties and distinctions that demand skillful judgment in order to solve even the simplest kind of personal question.

It is still quite possible, however, to draw some conclusions based upon the sign occupied by the Sun alone. In fact, if you're just being introduced to this vast subject, you're better off keeping it simple. Otherwise it seems like an impossible jumble, much like trying to read a novel in a foreign language without knowing the basic vocabulary. As with anything else, you can progress in your appreciation and understanding of astrology in direct proportion to your interest. To become really good at it requires study, experience, patience and above all—and maybe simplest of all—a fundamental understanding of what is actually going on right up there in the sky over your head. It is a vital living process you can observe, contemplate and ultimately understand. You can start by observing sunrise, or sunset, or even the full Moon.

In fact you can do a simple experiment after reading this introduction. You can erect a rough chart by following the simple procedure below:

1. Draw a circle with twelve equal segments.

2. Starting at what would be the nine o'clock position on a clock, number the segments, or houses, from 1 to 12 in a *counterclockwise direction*.

3. Label house number 1 in the following way: 4 A.M.-6 A.M.

4. In a counterclockwise direction, label the rest of the houses: 2 A.M.-4 A.M., MIDNIGHT-2 A.M., 10 P.M-MIDNIGHT, 8 P.M.-10 P.M., 6 P.M.-8 P.M., 4 P.M.-6 P.M., 2 P.M.-4 P.M., NOON-2 P.M., 10 A.M.-NOON, 8 A.M.-10 A.M., and 6 A.M.-8 A.M.

5. Now find out what time you were born and place the sun in the appropriate house.

6. Label the edge of that house with your Sun sign. You now have a description of your basic character and your fundamental drives. You can also see in what areas of life on Earth you will be most likely to focus your constant energy and center your activity.

7. If you are really feeling ambitious, label the rest of the houses with the signs, starting with your Sun sign, in order, still in a *counterclockwise direction.* When you get to Pisces, start over with Aries and keep going until you reach the house behind the Sun.

8. Look to house number 1. The sign that you have now labeled and attached to house number 1 is your Rising sign. It will color your self-image, outlook, physical constitution, early life and whole orientation to life. Of course this is a mere approximation, since there are many complicated calculations that must be made with respect to adjustments for birth time, but if you read descriptions of the sign preceding and the sign following the one you have calculated in the above manner, you may be able to identify yourself better. In any case, when you get through labeling all the houses, your drawing should look something like this:

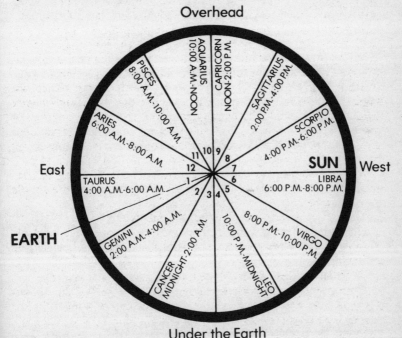

Basic chart illustrating the position of the Sun in Scorpio, with the Ascendant Taurus as the Rising Sign.

This individual was born at 5:15 P.M. on October 31 in New York City. The Sun is in Scorpio and is found in the 7th house. The Rising sign, or the sign governing house number 1, is Taurus, so this person is a blend of Scorpio and Taurus.

Any further calculation would necessitate that you look in an ephemeris, or table of planetary motion, for the positions of the rest of the planets for your particular birth year. But we will take the time to define briefly all the known planets of our Solar System and the Sun to acquaint you with some more of the astrological vocabulary that you will be meeting again and again. (See page 21 for a full explanation of the Moon in all the Signs.)

THE PLANETS AND SIGNS THEY RULE

The signs of the Zodiac are linked to the planets in the following way. Each sign is governed or ruled by one or more planets. No matter where the planets are located in the sky at any given moment, they still rule their respective signs, and when they travel through the signs they rule, they have special dignity and their effects are stronger.

Following is a list of the planets and the signs they rule. After looking at the list, go back over the definitions of the planets and see if you can determine how the planet ruling *your* Sun sign has affected your life.

SIGNS	RULING PLANETS
Aries	Mars, Pluto
Taurus	Venus
Gemini	Mercury
Cancer	Moon
Leo	Sun
Virgo	Mercury
Libra	Venus
Scorpio	Mars, Pluto
Sagittarius	Jupiter
Capricorn	Saturn
Aquarius	Saturn, Uranus
Pisces	Jupiter, Neptune

THE PLANETS
OF THE
SOLAR SYSTEM

Here are the planets of the Solar System. They all travel around the Sun at different speeds and different distances. Taken with the Sun, they all distribute individual intelligence and ability throughout the entire chart.

The planets modify the influence of the Sun in a chart according to their own particular natures, strengths and positions. Their positions must be calculated for each year and day, and their function and expression in a horoscope will change as they move from one area of the Zodiac to another.

Following, you will find brief statements of their pure meanings.

THE SUN

SUN

This is the center of existence. Around this flaming sphere all the planets revolve in endless orbits. Our star is constantly sending out its beams of light and energy without which no life on Earth would be possible. In astrology it symbolizes everything we are trying to become, the center around which all of our activity in life will always revolve. It is the symbol of our basic nature and describes the natural and constant thread that runs through everything that we do from birth to death on this planet.

To early astrologers, the sun seemed to be another planet because it crossed the heavens every day, just like the rest of the bodies in the sky.

It is the only star near enough to be seen well—it is, in fact, a dwarf star. Approximately 860,000 miles in diameter, it is about ten times as wide as the giant planet Jupiter. The next nearest star is nearly 300,000 times as far away, and if the Sun were located as far away as most of the bright stars, it would be too faint to be seen without a telescope.

Everything in the horoscope ultimately revolves around this singular body. Although other forces may be prominent in the charts of some individuals, still the Sun is the total nucleus of being and symbolizes the complete potential of every human being alive. It is vitality and the life force. Your whole essence comes from the position of the Sun.

You are always trying to express the Sun according to its position by house and sign. Possibility for all development is found in the Sun, and it marks the fundamental character of your personal radiations all around you.

It is the symbol of strength, vigor, wisdom, dignity, ardor and generosity, and the ability for a person to function as a mature individual. It is also a creative force in society. It is consciousness of the gift of life.

The underdeveloped solar nature is arrogant, pushy, undependable and proud, and is constantly using force.

MERCURY

Mercury is the planet closest to the Sun. It races around our star, gathering information and translating it to the rest of the system. Mercury represents your capacity to understand the desires of your own will and to translate those desires into action.

In other words it is the planet of Mind and the power of communication. Through Mercury we develop an ability to think, write, speak and observe—to become aware of the world around us. It colors our attitudes and vision of the world, as well as our capacity to communicate our inner responses to the outside world. Some people who have serious disabilities in their power of verbal communication have often wrongly been described as people lacking intelligence.

Although this planet (and its position in the horoscope) indicates your power to communicate your thoughts and perceptions to the world, intelligence is something deeper. Intelligence is distributed throughout all the planets. It is the relationship of the planets to each other that truly describes what we call intelligence. Mercury rules speaking, language, mathematics, draft and design, students, messengers, young people, offices, teachers and any pursuits where the mind of man has wings.

VENUS

Venus is beauty. It symbolizes the harmony and radiance of a rare and elusive quality: beauty itself. It is refinement and delicacy, softness and charm. In astrology it indicates grace, balance and the aesthetic sense. Where Venus is we see beauty, a gentle drawing in of energy and the need for satisfaction and completion. It is a special touch that finishes off rough edges. It is sensitivity, and affection, and it is always the place for that other elusive phenomenon: love. Venus describes our sense of what is beautiful and loving. Poorly developed, it is vulgar, tasteless and self-indulgent. But its ideal is the flame of spiritual love—Aphrodite, goddess of love, and the sweetness and power of personal beauty.

MARS

This is raw, crude energy. The planet next to Earth but outward
from the Sun is a fiery red sphere that charges through the horoscope with force and fury. It represents the way you reach out for
new adventure and new experience. It is energy and drive, initiative,
courage and daring. The power to start something and see it
through. It can be thoughtless, cruel and wild, angry and hostile,
causing cuts, burns, scalds and wounds. It can stab its way through
a chart, or it can be the symbol of healthy spirited adventure, well-
channeled constructive power to begin and keep up the drive. If you
have trouble starting things, if you lack the get-up-and-go to start
the ball rolling, if you lack aggressiveness and self-confidence,
chances are there's another planet influencing your Mars. Mars
rules soldiers, butchers, surgeons, salesmen—any field that requires
daring, bold skill, operational technique or self-promotion.

JUPITER

This is the largest planet of the Solar System. Scientists have recently learned that Jupiter reflects more light than it receives from the Sun. In a sense it is like a star itself. In astrology it rules good luck and good cheer, health, wealth, optimism, happiness, success and joy. It is the symbol of opportunity and always opens the way for new possibilities in your life. It rules exuberance, enthusiasm, wisdom, knowledge, generosity and all forms of expansion in general. It rules actors, statesmen, clerics, professional people, religion, publishing and the distribution of many people over large areas.

Sometimes Jupiter makes you think you deserve everything, and you become sloppy, wasteful, careless and rude, prodigal and lawless, in the illusion that nothing can ever go wrong. Then there is the danger of over-confidence, exaggeration, undependability and over-indulgence.

Jupiter is the minimization of limitation and the emphasis on spirituality and potential. It is the thirst for knowledge and higher learning.

SATURN

Saturn circles our system in dark splendor with its mysterious rings, forcing us to be awakened to whatever we have neglected in the past. It will present real puzzles and problems to be solved, causing delays, obstacles and hindrances. By doing so, Saturn stirs our own sensitivity to those areas where we are laziest.

Here we must patiently develop *method,* and only through painstaking effort can our ends be achieved. It brings order to a horoscope and imposes reason just where we are feeling least reasonable. By creating limitations and boundary, Saturn shows the consequences of being human and demands that we accept the changing cycles inevitable in human life. Saturn rules time, old age and sobriety. It can bring depression, gloom, jealousy and greed, or serious acceptance of responsibilities out of which success will develop. With Saturn there is nothing to do but face facts. It rules laborers, stones, granite, rocks and crystals of all kinds.

The Outer Planets

The following three are the outer planets. They liberate human beings from cultural conditioning, and in that sense are the law breakers. In early times it was thought that Saturn was the last planet of the system—the outer limit beyond which we could never go. The discovery of the next three planets ushered in new phases of human history, revolution and technology.

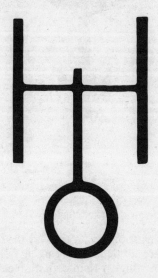

URANUS

Uranus rules unexpected change, upheaval, revolution. It is the symbol of total independence and asserts the freedom of an individual from all restriction and restraint. It is a breakthrough planet and indicates talent, originality and genius in a horoscope. It usually causes last-minute reversals and changes of plan, unwanted separations, accidents, catastrophes and eccentric behavior. It can add irrational rebelliousness and perverse bohemianism to a personality or a streak of unaffected brilliance in science and art. It rules technology, aviation and all forms of electrical and electronic advancement. It governs great leaps forward and topsy-turvy situations, and *always* turns things around at the last minute. Its effects are difficult to ever really predict, since it rules sudden last-minute decisions and events that come like lightning out of the blue.

NEPTUNE

Neptune dissolves existing reality the way the sea erodes the cliffs beside it. Its effects are subtle like the ringing of a buoy's bell in the fog. It suggests a reality higher than definition can usually describe. It awakens a sense of higher responsibility often causing guilt, worry, anxieties or delusions. Neptune is associated with all forms of escape and can make things seem a certain way so convincingly that you are absolutely sure of something that eventually turns out to be quite different.

It is the planet of illusion and therefore governs the invisible realms that lie beyond our ordinary minds, beyond our simple factual ability to prove what is "real." Treachery, deceit, disillusionment and disappointment are linked to Neptune. It describes a vague reality that promises eternity and the divine, yet in a manner so complex that we cannot really fathom it at all. At its worst Neptune is a cheap intoxicant; at its best it is the poetry, music and inspiration of the higher planes of spiritual love. It has dominion over movies, photographs and much of the arts.

PLUTO

Pluto lies at the outpost of our system and therefore rules finality in a horoscope—the final closing of chapters in your life, the passing of major milestones and points of development from which there is no return. It is a final wipeout, a closeout, an evacuation. It is a distant, subtle but powerful catalyst in all transformations that occur. It creates, destroys, then recreates. Sometimes Pluto starts its influence with a minor event or insignificant incident that might even go unnoticed. Slowly but surely, little by little, everything changes, until at last there has been a total transformation in the area of your life where Pluto has been operating. It rules mass thinking and the trends that society first rejects, then adopts and finally outgrows.

Pluto rules the dead and the underworld—all the powerful forces of creation and destruction that go on all the time beneath, around and above us. It can bring a lust for power with strong obsessions.

It is the planet that rules the metamorphoses of the caterpillar into a butterfly, for it symbolizes the capacity to change totally and forever a person's life style, way of thought and behavior.

FAMOUS PERSONALITIES

ARIES: Hans Christian Andersen, Pearl Bailey, Marlon Brando, Wernher Von Braun, Charlie Chaplin, Joan Crawford, Da Vinci, Bette Davis, Doris Day, W. C. Fields, Alec Guinness, Adolf Hitler, Billie Holiday, Thomas Jefferson, Nikita Khrushchev, Elton John, Arturo Toscanini, J. P. Morgan, Paul Robeson, Gloria Steinem, Lowell Thomas, Vincent van Gogh, Tennessee Williams

TAURUS: Fred Astaire, Charlote Brontë, Carol Burnett, Irving Berlin, Bing Crosby, Salvador Dali, Tchaikovsky, Queen Elizabeth II, Duke Ellington, Ella Fitzgerald, Henry Fonda, Sigmund Freud, Orson Welles, Joe Louis, Lenin, Karl Marx, Golda Meir, Eva Peron, Bertrand Russell, Shakespeare, Kate Smith, Benjamin Spock, Barbra Streisand, Shirley Temple, Harry Truman

GEMINI: Mikhail Baryshnikov, Boy George, Igor Stravinsky, Carlos Chavez, Walt Whitman, Bob Dylan, Ralph Waldo Emerson, Judy Garland, Paul Gauguin, Allen Ginsberg, Benny Goodman, Bob Hope, Burl Ives, John F. Kennedy, Peggy Lee, Marilyn Monroe, Joe Namath, Cole Porter, Laurence Olivier, Harriet Beecher Stowe, Queen Victoria, John Wayne, Frank Lloyd Wright

CANCER: "Dear Abby," David Brinkley, Yul Brynner, Pearl Buck, Marc Chagall, Jack Dempsey, Mildred (Babe) Zaharias, Mary Baker Eddy, Henry VIII, John Glenn, Ernest Hemingway, Lena Horne, Oscar Hammerstein, Helen Keller, Ann Landers, George Orwell, Nancy Reagan, Rembrandt, Richard Rodgers, Ginger Rogers, Rubens, Jean-Paul Sartre, O. J. Simpson

LEO: Neil Armstrong, Russell Baker, James Baldwin, Emily Brontë, Wilt Chamberlain, Julia Child, Cecil B. De Mille, Ogden Nash, Amelia Earhart, Edna Ferber, Arthur Goldberg, Dag Hammarskjöld, Alfred Hitchcock, Mick Jagger, George Meany, George Bernard Shaw, Napoleon, Jacqueline Onassis, Henry Ford, Francis Scott Key, Andy Warhol, Mae West, Orville Wright

VIRGO: Ingrid Bergman, Warren Burger, Maurice Chevalier, Agatha Christie, Sean Connery, Lafayette, Peter Falk, Greta Garbo, Althea Gibson, Arthur Godfrey, Goethe, Buddy Hackett, Michael Jackson, Lyndon Johnson, D. H. Lawrence, Sophia Loren, Grandma Moses, Arnold Palmer, Queen Elizabeth I, Walter Reuther, Peter Sellers, Lily Tomlin, George Wallace

LIBRA: Brigitte Bardot, Art Buchwald, Truman Capote, Dwight D. Eisenhower, William Faulkner, F. Scott Fitzgerald, Gandhi, George Gershwin, Micky Mantle, Helen Hayes, Vladimir Horowitz, Doris Lessing, Martina Navratalova, Eugene O'Neill, Luciano Pavarotti, Emily Post, Eleanor Roosevelt, Bruce Springsteen, Margaret Thatcher, Gore Vidal, Barbara Walters, Oscar Wilde

SCORPIO: Vivien Leigh, Richard Burton, Art Carney, Johnny Carson, Billy Graham, Grace Kelly, Walter Cronkite, Marie Curie, Charles de Gaulle, Linda Evans, Indira Gandhi, Theodore Roosevelt, Rock Hudson, Katherine Hepburn, Robert F. Kennedy, Billie Jean King, Martin Luther, Georgia O'Keeffe, Pablo Picasso, Jonas Salk, Alan Shepard, Robert Louis Stevenson

SAGITTARIUS: Jane Austen, Louisa May Alcott, Woody Allen, Beethoven, Willy Brandt, Mary Martin, William F. Buckley, Maria Callas, Winston Churchill, Noel Coward, Emily Dickinson, Walt Disney, Benjamin Disraeli, James Doolittle, Kirk Douglas, Chet Huntley, Jane Fonda, Chris Evert Lloyd, Margaret Mead, Charles Schulz, John Milton, Frank Sinatra, Steven Spielberg

CAPRICORN: Muhammad Ali, Isaac Asimov, Pablo Casals, Dizzy Dean, Marlene Dietrich, James Farmer, Ava Gardner, Barry Goldwater, Cary Grant, J. Edgar Hoover, Howard Hughes, Joan of Arc, Gypsy Rose Lee, Martin Luther King, Jr., Rudyard Kipling, Mao Tse-tung, Richard Nixon, Gamal Nasser, Louis Pasteur, Albert Schweitzer, Stalin, Benjamin Franklin, Elvis Presley

AQUARIUS: Marian Anderson, Susan B. Anthony, Jack Benny, Charles Darwin, Charles Dickens, Thomas Edison, John Barrymore, Clark Gable, Jascha Heifetz, Abraham Lincoln, John McEnroe, Yehudi Menuhin, Mozart, Jack Nicklaus, Ronald Reagan, Jackie Robinson, Norman Rockwell, Franklin D. Roosevelt, Gertrude Stein, Charles Lindbergh, Margaret Truman

PISCES: Edward Albee, Harry Belafonte, Alexander Graham Bell, Frank Borman, Chopin, Adelle Davis, Albert Einstein, Jackie Gleason, Winslow Homer, Edward M. Kennedy, Victor Hugo, Mike Mansfield, Michelangelo, Edna St. Vincent Millay, Liza Minelli, John Steinbeck, Linus Pauling, Ravel, Diana Ross, William Shirer, Elizabeth Taylor, George Washington

ARIES

CHARACTER ANALYSIS

People born under the astrological sign of Aries are often strong-willed and energetic. Ariens are seldom afraid of taking a risk, provided that it is well-calculated. They are people who dare; they are sometimes impulsive but almost never irrational. The Aries man or woman likes to keep busy. They are not a people who like to while away the time in an aimless fashion. Ariens are known for their drive and their boldness. They generally know how to make proper use of their energies; they are positive and productive people who seldom doubt themselves. They know what they want out of life and they go after it. They generally have a pioneering sort of spirit and are always anxious to begin something new. They know how to make use of opportunity when it appears. Many Ariens have no trouble in achieving success.

The strong and positive sort of Arien knows how to channel his energies properly so that he will get the most out of what life has to offer. He is a sensible, practical person, who does not only think about himself but does what he can to help those in less fortunate positions than himself. If a plan goes awry, he does not hesitate to see what he can do to fix it. The Arien is usually quick to initiate a change if it seems necessary to do so. He is an activist, generally, and does not believe in sitting about, waiting for good things to tumble into his lap. If good fortune does not appear, the positive Arien will go out and look for it; his search does not end until he has it. Obstacles do not frighten the Aries man or woman. In fact, contrary situations or people seem to spur him on. The Arien often thrives on adversity. He knows how to turn a disadvantage to an advantage in short order. Not easily discouraged, he will forge ahead on a plan or idea until it is exactly the way he wants it. The

Arien knows how to shift for himself. He won't wait for others to lend a helping hand, but starts himself, without assistance. Some find the Aries person a little too ruthless in his manner for getting what he wants. Patience is a virtue some Ariens lack; they are people who are usually interested in fast results. They want to see the fruits of their investments as quickly as possible.

The average Arien is a person who has many ideas; he is never at a loss for a new approach to an old or familiar situation. He is ever adaptable and knows how to make a profit out of a loss. In emergency situations, the Arien is always quick to act. When an accident occurs, he often knows the proper remedy. Decision-making does not frighten the strong Aries man or woman. They have the ability to think clearly and to direct their interests and energies toward their ultimate goal. Aries people are easily attracted to anything that is new and interesting. They have naturally inquiring minds.

Although Ariens are often alert and quick to act, they are sometimes easily distracted by side issues. Almost everything interests them and this can have its disadvantages, especially when a one-track mind is needed in order to solve a problem. Ariens can sometimes make a mess of things in their eagerness to get things done as soon as possible.

The weak or poorly directed Arien sometimes has a problem trying to put all of his eggs in one basket. He is easily distracted and often argumentative. He sometimes finds it difficult to see the forest for the trees. In trying to get many things accomplished at one time, he achieves nothing. In spite of his short-comings, he is apt to be quite caught up with what he fancies to be his virtues. He will underestimate the intelligence and abilities of others, especially if they seem to threaten his position in one way or another. The confused Arien is always ready for a quarrel. He will often refuse to see the other person's point of view and dismiss their opinions as so much poppy-cock. The Aries man or woman who does not know how to concentrate his or her energies effectively, easily jumps from one mistake to another, leaving things in an incomplete and jumbled state. The weak Arien will seldom admit his faults, although he will eagerly point out those of others . . . or what he imagines to be those of others.

The misdirected Arien more often than not misses his mark. He is too anxious to succeed. He wants success fast and is in too much of a hurry to prepare himself adequately. The weak Aries man or woman can be as stubborn as a mule. When intent on some illusory goal they will seldom take the time to listen to others. Not afraid of taking a risk, the ill-prepared Arien often finds himself leaping from one unsuccessful plan to the other. His optimism often makes a fool of him. He is the type of person who leaps before looking. Although he is easy to anger, his temper quickly cools off. When hurt, he can rant and rave for an hour but once he has defended himself, he will drop the matter altogether and move on to something else. The Arien seldom carries a grudge. In love, too, the Aries man or woman who has not learned how to curb impulsiveness, often finds him- or her- self in a pot of hot water. Love at first sight is not uncommon to this sort of Aries person; he is romantic for as long as the impulse carries him. He is not averse to fly-by-night romances, and is liable to throw caution to the winds when in love.

Because the Aries person has an enterprising nature, he never finds it difficult to keep busy. He is an extremely independent person —sometimes to a fault. Others sometimes find him rather haughty and arrogant. This weak sort of Aries finds it difficult to be objective in anything. He resents criticism even when it is due, yet he will not find it difficult to criticize others. He is the kind of person who takes any dare as an opportunity to prove his worth. Others are often annoyed by the manner in which he presses an issue. He is capable of becoming quite aggressive when the situation calls for tact and understanding. If the weak Arien made an attempt to see or understand both sides of one story, he could improve his own insight into problems. He should do what he can to develop a balanced sense of judgment. It is important for this sort of Aries person to prepare himself adequately before taking on a new project. He should avoid overdoing as that only ends in total exhaustion and very little actual progress is made.

Health

People born under the sign of Aries are generally quite healthy. Their physical condition tends to be good. Still, it is necessary that they take steps not to abuse their health by overdoing. The Arien is sometimes accident-prone because he is careless in his actions, particularly when intent on achieving a particular goal. The head and the face are areas of the body that are often injured. It is important that Ariens learn to relax. The Aries man or woman usually does fairly well in sports. Their bodies are generally well-developed and lithe. The Arien's constitution is almost always good. He is capable of great physical strength for short periods of time. This, or course, has its disadvantages as well as advantages. The Arien can achieve more if he learns how to apply his spurts of strength correctly. Sports where staying power is important are not likely to be ones in which he can excel. The sign of Aries governs the head; nerves, head, and stomach are apt to be the weak points under this sign.

Headaches and fevers are not uncommon complaints. As was mentioned before, it is essential that the person born under this first sign of the Zodiac learn how to relax. It is often the case that they wear out easily because they are impulsive and headstrong; they do not know how to channel their energies in a consistent manner. This can sometimes lead to a breakdown. The Arien is so intent on achieving his goal that he allows himself to overwork. Self-control must also be learned. Sometimes the Arien is too free in expressing himself— this can lead to emotional bankruptcy. He is a person who is quick to anger; he worries. Controlling negative emotions is vitally important as bad moods can often affect his health. People born under this sign should always get their proper rest. Adequate sleep can help an exhausted Arien to regain his strength. A sensible, well-balanced diet is also important. Overeating or immoderate drinking habits can, to some extent, incorrectly influence the general disposition of the Aries man or woman. The Arien does not like to be ill. Sickness makes him restless and impatient. He does not like to spend too much time recuperating from an illness. Because of his drive and enthusiasm, the Arien often recovers more quickly than others. An illness may strike him hard, but he is soon on his feet again. The person born under this sign is almost lively and enterprising. Ariens generally lead long and active lives; to some, they never seem to grow old. The Aries person who learns how to conserve his energies as well as to correctly channel them, can add years to his life-span. Good health habits should be continually observed.

Occupation

The Arien is an active, industrious person. He should find a career in which he can best put his talents to use. Although an Arien is apt to have many interests, he should try to find out which interest is the most suited to his actual means and abilities. He is a person who is sincerely interested in getting on in the world and making a success of himself.

The sign of Aries governs the head and the intellect. The person born during the period, March 21 to April 20, is usually quite ambitious and enterprising. He is not a person who can sit still when there is something to do. Some Ariens have an artistic bent and do well in creative work. Others have some trouble in making up their minds about what kind of work they should do because they are interested in so many things and can handle them all reasonably well. Generally speaking, whatever profession the Arien chooses to enter, he makes a good job of it. The Aries man or woman is never lacking in personality and charm. Quite often they do well in work that requires them to come in direct contact with the public. Quite often they are clever conversationalists. They know how to deal with people—how to amuse them, how to convince them. Others often turn to Aries for advice or counsel when in difficulty. The Aries person can usually handle a position that requires authoratative behavior without any problem at all. They make good leaders and advisors. Ariens are inventive and forward-looking. They have plenty of energy and drive; many have a talent for successfully realizing their plans and dreams.

Aries is a person of action. Quite often he does well in the military or in organized sports. Some Ariens make excellent doctors and nurses. Other do remarkably well as dentists and draftsmen. They are a resourceful people—men and women who often know what they want to achieve in life.

The person born under the sign of Aries is more often than not an individualist. He prefers giving orders to taking them. He is not a "group" sort of person. He enjoys working by himself more than working in a team. A modern person, he usually sees to it that he keeps abreast of the new developments in his field.

One fault often found in the underdeveloped Arien, is that he will undertake a project with much enthusiasm, then as his interest flags he will readily give it up for something new. In such cases, he will often pass the unfinished chore or project on to someone else. Some Ariens make a habit of starting things, then turning them over to others. The sort of Arien who falls into this habit often does it unknowingly. New plans and ideas attract people of this sign quickly. They are always off for new fields to conquer. The strong Arien, however, seldom has difficulties of this sort; he knows how to stick with one job until it is done. He will do his utmost to direct his efforts and energies toward one goal. This sort of Ram makes a success of his life without much effort.

The Aries man or woman is seldom a person who is only interested in work and material gain. He or she knows how to go about having a good time. Some are quite happy when they are able to combine business with pleasure. Ariens usually are not hard materialists, but they know well what money can do. They busy themselves earning money, but they sometimes spend it as soon as it comes into their pockets. The Aries man or woman is generally honest when it comes to money matters. If he or she directs him- or her- self to one goal, there is a good chance that it will be attained without too much effort. The Arien has a driving and courageous personality. In work, this often stands him in good stead.

People born under the sign of Aries generally like to be surrounded by fashionable furnishings and the like. Luxury makes them feel comfortable and successful and often has an important influence in making them positive and enterprising. Shabby or old surroundings are apt to depress the Aries person. He is modern and forward-looking; he must live in an environment that is suited to his general disposition.

Some Ariens tend to be rather careless with their money. Saving is something of a problem for them. They would rather spend what they earn instead of putting something aside for a rainy day. They know how to live for the moment. The weak Arien often invests unwisely or mismanages his joint finances without regard for his partner or mate. The wise Arien avoids impulsive spending and thinks of the future. He sees to it that he learns how to budget his expenses in an effective manner.

Home and Family

The Aries man or woman is a home-loving person by nature. Home means a lot to the Ram. Here he can relax at the end of a hard day and enjoy the comfort of his surroundings. Aries woman are generally excellent home-makers. They have a way with furnishings and color arrangement. They know how to make a home radiate harmony and comfort. Invariably, they have good taste. They can beautify a room or a home without much difficulty. The Aries home usually gives one the feeling of freedom and roominess. A guest is not apt to feel himself confined or uncomfortable.

The Arien enjoys entertaining his friends and family. Nothing pleases him more than people dropping in. He knows how to make the best of a social situation even if it occurs on the spur of the moment. They know how to please visitors and enjoy company. Friends generally respect them and their homes.

In family matters, the Aries man or woman is very emotional—in the good sense of the word. Affection and love between members of his or her immediate family are essential for getting along. The Arien is keenly interested in keeping his home peaceful and harmonious. If possible, the Aries husband or wife tries to exert a strong influence in household matters. The Arien feels that his guidance is important to others.

The person born under this sign of the Zodiac is usually quite fond of children. They understand children and children usually feel close to them. The Arien himself usually has something youthful about his nature. Children have no difficulty in getting along with them and generally enjoy having them join them in some of their activities. Ariens know the value of a good joke and children love them for this. A sense of humor that is rich and well-balanced makes them a favorite with children. Aries people seldom forget the joys of their own youth and enjoy living somewhat vicariously through the adventures and games of their own children.

Although the Aries man or woman is not much of a disciplinarian, they do become rather disappointed if their children do not live up to their expectations in later life. Aries generally thinks he knows what is best for his children and can become rather overbearing if his children are not inclined to agree. The Arien is a person who enjoys being popular and respected and he can be a proud parent.

Social Relationships

The Aries person usually has no trouble in making new friends. He is generally outgoing and generous. He enjoys having many friends. People are easily attracted to the Arien because of his bright and pleasant personality. He knows how to make people feel at ease and encourages them in their self-expression. People often turn to an Arien when they are in trouble. The Aries man or woman knows how to counsel a friend in trouble; he or she is sometimes willing to share the burden or responsibilities of a good friend.

On the other hand, Aries people often make a habit of jumping from one friend to another. As long as a person remains new, interesting, and somewhat mysterious, he remains a friend. As soon as an Arien becomes aware of this friend's limitations, he is apt to try to find someone new to replace him. This is the pattern an uncultivated Arien follows in work. As long as the project is new, it absorbs his interest. As soon as it becomes old hat, he turns it over to someone else and starts something new.

Ariens make friends quickly. If they are really impressed, they will place the new friend on a very high pedestal. Some Ariens become very possessive of their friends and if someone else shows an interest in them, they become rather jealous and resentful. If a friend becomes tiresome or dull, the tactless Arien will not hesitate to handle him in an inconsiderate manner.

Although Ariens generally have a talent for making friends quickly, they also are apt to lose them rather fast if they are not careful. Some Ariens tend to neglect their friends and acquaintances as soon as something new catches their fancies. The weak Arien is sometimes a bit of a gossip and finds it hard not to supply others with the secrets of their friends. This sort of Aries person generally takes people for what they appear to be and not for what they actually are.

LOVE AND MARRIAGE

Romance and the Aries Woman

The Aries woman is more often than not charming. The opposite sex generally find her attractive, even glamorous. She is a woman who is very interested in love and romance. The female Arien has plenty of affection to give to the right man—when she meets him. Women born under this sign are usually very active and vigorous; their intelligence and strong character are also qualities which make them attractive to men. The Aries woman has no trouble in communicating with a man on an intellectual plane; she can easily hold her own in any conversation. She should, however, try to curb her eagerness to talk; quite often she winds up dominating the conversation. The Arien who has cultivated the talent of being a good listener generally does not have any trouble in attracting the sort of man who might propose to her.

The Aries woman is not the sort to sit back and wait for the right man to come along. If she sees someone who interests her, she will more than likely take the lead. She can usually do this in such a charming fashion, that the object of her affection hardly notices that he is being coaxed into a romance.

The Aries woman has no trouble in being true to the man she loves. She is true to herself and believes in remaining faithful to the man she has chosen. She usually makes a thoughtful and considerate companion. When her man is in need of advice she is often able to give him wise counsel. Aries women are generally able to voice an intelligent opinion on just about any subject. Their range of knowledge—just as their range of interests—is quite broad. They are imaginative and know how to keep a relationship alive and interesting.

The woman born under the sign of the Ram makes an excellent wife. It is seldom that she will bother her mate or partner with matters that she can easily handle herself. She has a way of transforming almost any house or apartment into a very comfortable home. With household budgeting, she often turns out to be a mastermind. All in all, the Aries woman is very considerate and dependable; she has all the qualities it takes to make an excellent wife or partner. She knows how to bring up children correctly. She is fond of children and affectionate. She is often the kind of mother who enjoys a large family.

Romance and the Aries Man

The Aires man is often quite romantic and charming when courting the opposite sex. He knows how to win the heart of the woman he loves. The Arien in love is as persuasive and energetic as he is in anything else that interests him. He makes an attentive and considerate lover. A direct and positive person, he has no trouble in attracting women. They are often taken by his charming and dashing manner. The opposite sex feels very safe and confident when with an Aries man—for he knows how to make a woman feel wanted and appreciated. However, the Aries man is sometimes so sure of himself that he frightens the more sensitive woman away.

Although the man born under the sign of the Ram, is usually quite faithful when married, he does not mind "playing the field" as long as he remains single. He can be quite a flirt; sometimes the Aries man goes from one romance to the other until he finds the right girl. Making conquests on the battlefield of love is apt to give his ego quite a boost. The Aries man never has very much trouble with rivals. When he is intent on love he knows how to do away with all opposition—and in short order. The Arien is a man who is very much in need of love and affection; he is quite open about this and goes about attaining it in a very open way.

He may be quite adventurous in love while he is single, but once he settles down, he becomes a very reliable and responsible mate. The Aries man is really a family-type man. He enjoys the company of his immediate family; he appreciates the comforts of home. A well-furnished and inviting home is important to a man born under this sign. Some of the furnishings may be a little on the luxurious side; the Arien feels often inspired to do better if he is surrounded by a show of material comfort. Success-oriented, he likes his home to radiate success.

The Aries man often likes to putter around the house, making minor repairs and installing new household utensils. He is a man who does not mind being tied down as long as he does not really feel it. He will be the head of the house; he does not like the woman to wear the pants in the family. He wants to be the one who keeps things in order. He remains romantic, even after marriage. He is tremendously fond of children and is quite apt to spoil them a bit. He makes an affectionate father. Children make him happy when they make him feel proud of them.

Man—Woman

ARIES MAN
ARIES WOMAN

The Aries man will be contented with the Aries woman so long as she reflects his qualities and interests without trying to outshine him. Although he may be progressive and modern in many things, when it comes to pants-wearing, he's downright conventional: it's strictly male attire. The best position an Aries woman can take in the relationship is a supporting one. He's the boss and that's that. Once that is settled and thoroughly accepted by his Aries spouse, then it's clear sailing.

The Aries man, with his seemingly endless drive and energy, likes to relax in the comfort of his home at the end of an action-packed day, and the Aries wife who is a good homemaker can be sure of his undying affection. He's a lover of slippers and pipe and a comfortable armchair. The Aries wife who sees to it that everything in the house is where her man expects to find it—including herself—will have no difficulty keeping the relationship ship-shape.

When it comes to love, the Aries man is serious and constant, and the object of his affection should be likewise. He is generally not interested in a clinging-vine kind of wife; he justs wants someone who is there when he needs her; someone who listens and understands what he says; someone who can give advice if he should ever have to ask for it—which is not likely to be often. Although he can appreciate a woman who can intelligently discuss things that matter to him, he is not interested in a ranting chatterbox who, through her fondness for earbending, is liable to let the apple pie burn up in the oven.

The Aries man wants a woman who is a good companion and a good sport; someone who will look good on his arm without hanging on it too heavily. He is looking for a woman who has both feet on the ground and yet is mysterious and enticing . . . a kind of domestic Helen of Troy whose face or fine dinner can launch a thousand business deals if need be. The cultivated Aries woman should have no difficulty in filling such a role.

The Aries man and woman have similar tastes when it comes to family style: they both like large ones. The Aries woman is crazy about kids and the more she has, the more she feels like a wife. Children love and admire the affectionate Aries mother. She knows how to play with them and how to understand them. She's very anxious that they do well in life and reflect their good homelife and upbringing. However, both Aries parents should try not to smother their offspring with too much love. They should be urged to make their own decisions—especially as they grow older—and not rely unnecessarily on the advice of their partents.

ARIES MAN
TAURUS WOMAN

The woman born under Taurus may lack the sparkle or dazzle you often like your women to have. In many respects, she's very basic—never flighty—and puts great store in keeping her feet flat on the ground. She may fail to appreciate your willingness to jump here, then there, especially if she's under the impression that there's no profit in it. On the other hand, if you do manage to hit it off with a Taurus woman you won't be disappointed at all in the romance area. The Taurus woman is all woman and proud of it, too. She can be very devoted and loving once she decides that her relationship with you is no fly-by-night romance. She's pretty rugged, too, or can be, when the situation calls for a stiff upper lip. It's almost certain that if the going ever gets too rough she won't go running home to mother. She'll stick by you, talk it out, fight it out, or whatever. When bent on a particular point of view, she can be as hard as nails —without having it adversely affect her femininity. She'll stick by you through thick and thin. She can adjust to hard times just as graciously as she can to good times. You may lose your patience with her, though, if when trying to explain some new project or plan to her, she doesn't seem to want to understand or appreciate your enthusiasm and ambition. With your quick wit and itchy feet, you may find yourself miles ahead of your Taurus woman. At times, you are likely to find this distressing. But if you've developed a talent for patience, you won't mind waiting for her to catch up. Never try grabbing her hand and pulling her along at your normal speed—it is likely not to work. It could lead to flying pots and pans and a fireworks display that would put the Fourth of July to shame. The Taurus woman doesn't anger readily but when prodded often enough, she's capable of letting loose with a cyclone of illwill. If you treat her correctly, you'll have no cause for complaint. The Taurus woman loves doing things for her man. She's a whiz in the kitchen and can whip up feasts fit for a king if she thinks they will be royally appreciated. She may not fully understand you but she'll adore you and be faithful to you if she feels you're worthy of it. She won't see green, either, if you compliment another woman in her presence. When you come home late occasionally and claim that there were a lot of last-minute things to attend to at the office, she won't insinuate that one of those last-minute things was most likely your new, shapely secretary. Her mind doesn't run like that. She's not gullible, but she won't doubt your every word if she feels there is no reason to. The woman born under Taurus will make a wonderful mother for your children. She's a master at keeping children cuddled, well-loved, and warm. You may find, however, that when your offspring reach the adolescent stage you'll have to intervene: Taureans are not very sympathetic to the whims of ever-changing teenagers.

ARIES MAN
GEMINI WOMAN

You may find a romance with a woman born under the sign of the Twins, a many-splendored thing. In her you can find the intellectual companionship you often crave and so seldom find. A Gemini girlfriend can appreciate your aims and desires because she travels pretty much the same route as you do, intellectually . . . that is, at least part of the way. She may share your interests, but she will lack your stick-to-it-iveness. Her feet are much itchier than yours, and as a result, she can be here, there—all over the place, and all at the same time, or so it seems. It may make you dizzy. However, you'll enjoy and appreciate her liveliness and mental agility.

Geminians often have sparkling personalities; you'll be attracted by her warmth and grace. While she's on your arm, you'll probably notice that many male eyes are drawn to her—she may even return a gaze or two, but don't let that worry you. All women born under this sign have nothing against a harmless flirtation; they enjoy this sort of attention and, if they feel they're already spoken for, they'll never let it get out of hand.

Although she may not be as handy in the kitchen as you'd like, you'll never go hungry for a filling and tasty meal. She's in as much a hurry as you and won't feel like she's cheating by breaking out the instant mashed potatoes or the frozen vegetables. She may not be handy at the kitchen range but she can be clever—and with a dash of this and a suggestion of that, she can make an uninteresting TV dinner taste like something out of a Jim Beard cookbook. Then again, maybe you've struck it rich with your Gemini and have one who finds complicated recipes a challenge to her intellect. If so, you'll find every meal a tantalizing and mouth-watering surprise.

When you're exercising your brain over the Sunday crossword puzzle and find yourself bamboozled over 23 Down and 11 Across, just ask your Gemini friend; she'll give you the right answers without batting an eye. Chances are she probably went through the crossword phase herself years ago and gave them up because she found them too easy.

She loves all kinds of people—just like you do. Still, you're apt to find that you're more particular than she. Often, all that a Gemini requires is that her friends be interesting—and stay interesting. One thing she's not able to abide is a dullard.

Leave the party-organizing to your Gemini sweetheart or mate and you'll never know what a dull moment is. She'll bring the swinger out in you if you give her half a chance.

With kids, woman born under Gemini seem to work wonders. Perhaps this is because they are like children themselves in a way:

restless, adventurous, and easily bored. At any rate, the Gemini mother is loving, gentle, and affectionate with her children.

ARIES MAN
CANCER WOMAN

Romancing a girl born under the sign of the Crab may occasionally give you a case of the jitters. It may leave you with one of those "Oh, brother . . . what did I get into now" feelings. In one hour she can unravel a whole gamut of emotions that will leave you in a tizzy. If you do fall in love with a Cancerian, be prepared for anything. She'll keep you guessing, that's for sure. You may find her a little too uncertain and sensitive for your tastes. You'll most likely have to spend a good deal of your time encouraging her, helping her to erase her foolish fears. Tell her she's a living doll a dozen times a day and you'll be well-loved in return. Be careful of the jokes you make when you are with her—and for heaven's sake don't let any of them revolve around her, her personal interests, or her relatives. Chances are if you do, you'll reduce her to tears. She can't stand being made fun of. It will take bushels of roses and tons of chocolates, not to mention the "I'm sorrys", to get you back in her good graces again.

In matters of money-managing, she may not easily come around to your way of thinking. Ariens are often apt to let money burn a hole in their pockets. Cancerians are just the opposite. You may think your Cancerian sweetheart or mate is a direct descendant of Scrooge. If she has it her way, she'll hang onto that first dollar you ever earned. She's not only that way with money, but with everything from bakery string right on to jelly jars. She's a saver and never discards anything no matter how trivial.

Once she returns your "I love you", you'll find that you have a very loving, self-sacrificing and devoted friend on your hands. Her love for you will never alter unless you want it to. She'll put you high up on a pedestal and will do everything—even if it's against your will—to see that you stay up there.

Cancer women make reputedly the best mothers of all the signs of the Zodiac. She'll consider every minor complaint of her child a major catastrophe. She's not the kind of mother who will do anything to get her children off her hands; with her, kids come first. You'll run a close second. You'll perhaps see her as too devoted and you may have a hard time convincing her that the length of her apron-strings is a little too long. When Junior or Sis is ready for that first date, you may have to lock your Cancer wife in the broom closet to keep her from going along. As an Arien you are apt to understand your children more as individuals than your wife. No matter how many times your Cancer wife insists that no man is good enough for your daughter, you'll know it's all nonsense. If you don't help her to curb her super-maternal tendencies, your Cancer wife may have a good chance of turning into a formidable mother-in-law.

ARIES MAN
LEO WOMAN

If you can manage a girl who likes to kick up her heels every once in a while, the Leo woman's your mate. You'll have to learn how to put away your jealous fears—or at least forget about them—when you take up with a woman born under this sign, because she's often the sort that makes heads turn and sometimes tongues wag. You don't necessarily have to believe any of what you hear; it's most likely just jealous gossip or wishful thinking. She's usually got more than a good share of grace and glamor. She knows it, generally, and knows how to put it to good use. Needless to say, other women in her vicinity turn green with envy and will try anything short of shoving her into the nearest lake in order to put her out of commission, especially if she appears to be cramping their style.

If she has captured your heart and fancy, woo her full-force if your intention is to eventually win her. Shower her with expensive gifts, take her regularly to Ciro's, and promise her the moon—if you're in a position to go that far—and you'll find that Miss Leo's resistance will begin to weaken. It's not that she's so difficult—she'll probably make a lot over you once she's decided you're the man for her—but she does enjoy a lot of attention. What's more, she feels she's entitled to it. Her mild arrogance, though, is becoming. The Leo woman knows how to transform the crime of excessive pride into a very charming misdemeanor. It sweeps most men right off their feet . . . in fact, all men. Those that do not succumb to her leonine charm are few and far between.

If you've got an important business deal to clinch and you have doubts as to whether it will go over well or not, bring your Leo wife along to that business luncheon or cocktail party and it will be a cinch that you'll have that contract in your pocket before the meeting is over. She won't have to say or do anything . . . just be there at your side. The grouchiest oil magnate can be transformed into a gushing, dutiful schoolboy if there's a Leo woman in the room.

If you're a rich Arien, you may have to see to it that your Leo wife doesn't become to heavy-handed with the charge accounts and credit cards. When it comes to spending, Leos tend to overdo. If you're a poor Arien, then you have nothing to fear—for Miss Leo, with her love of luxury, will most likely never give you the time of day, let alone exchange vows.

As a mother, she can be strict and easy-going at the same time. She can pal around with her children and still see to it that they know their places.

ARIES MAN
VIRGO WOMAN

The Virgo woman may be a little too difficult for you to understand at first. Her waters run deep. Even when you think that you do know her, don't take any bets on it: she's capable of keeping things hidden in the deep recesses of her womanly soul—things she'll only reveal when she is sure that you're the one she's been looking for. It may take her sometime to come around to this decision. Virgo women are finnicky about almost everything; everything has to be letter-perfect before they're satisfied. Many of them have the idea that the only people who can do things correctly are other Virgos. Nothing offends a Virgo woman more than sloppy dress, character, or careless display of affection. Make sure your tie's not crooked and your shoes sport a bright shine before you go calling on this lady. Keep your off-color jokes for the locker-room; she'll have none of that. Take her arm when crossing the street. Don't rush the romance. Trying to corner her in the back of a cab may be one way of striking out. Never criticize the way she looks—in fact, the best policy would be to agree with her as much as possible. The Arien, however, with his outspoken, direct, and sensible nature, may find a Virgo relationship too trying. All those Do's and Don't's you'll have to observe if you want to get to first base with a Virgo may be just a little too much to ask of you. After a few dates, you may come to the conclusion that she just isn't worth all that trouble. However, the Virgo woman is mysterious enough, generally, to keep her men running back for more. Chances are you'll be intrigued by her airs and graces.

Love means a lot to you and you may be disappointed at first in Virgo's cool ways. However, underneath that glacial facade lies a hot cauldron of seething excitement. If you're patient and artful in your romantic approach, you'll find that all that caution was well worth the trouble. When Virgos love, they don't stint. It's all or nothing as far as they're concerned. Once they're convinced that they love you, they go all the way right off the bat, tossing all cares to the wind. One thing a Virgo can't stand in love is hypocrisy. They don't give a hoot about what the neighbors might say as long as their hearts tell them "go ahead." They're very concerned with human truths. So much so that if their hearts stumble upon another fancy, they're liable to take up with that new heart-throb and leave you standing in the rain. She's that honest—to her own heart, at any rate. But if you are earnest about your interests in her, she'll know, and will respect and reciprocate your love. Do her wrong once, however, and you can be sure she'll come up with a pair of sharp scissors and cut the soiled ribbon of your relationship.

As a housewife, she'll be neat and orderly. With children, she can be tender and strict at the same time. She can be a devoted and loving wife—it all depends on you.

ARIES MAN
LIBRA WOMAN

That girl born under the sign of Libra is worth more than her weight in gold. She's a woman after your own heart. With her, you'll always come first, make no mistake about that. She'll always be behind you, no matter what you do. And when you ask her for advice about almost anything, you'll most likely get a very balanced and realistic opinion. She's good at thinking things out and never lets her emotions run away with her when clear logic is called for. As a homemaker, she's hard to beat. She is very concerned with harmony and balance; your home will be tastefully furnished and decorated. A Libran cannot stand filth or disarray—it gives her goose bumps. Anything that does not radiate harmony, in fact, runs against her orderly grain.

She's chock-full of charm and womanly ways; she can sweep just about any man off his feet with one winning smile. When it comes to using her brains, she can out-think anyone and sometimes with half the effort. She's diplomatic enough, though, never to let this become glaringly apparent. She may even turn the conversation so that you think that you were the one who did all the brain work. She couldn't care less, really, just as long as you wind up doing what is right. She's got you up there on a pretty high pedestal. You're her man and she's happy if you make all the decisions, big and small—with a little help from her if necessary. In spite of her masculine approach to reason, she remains all woman in her approach to love and affection. You'll literally be showered with hugs and kisses during your romance with a Libra woman. She doesn't believe in holding out. You shouldn't, either, if you want to hang on to her. She's the kind of girl who likes to snuggle up to you in front of the fire on chilly autumn nights. She'll bring you breakfast in bed Sundays then cuddle beside you and tuck a napkin under your chin so you won't get any crumbs on the blankets.

She's very thoughtful about anything that concerns you. If anyone dares suggest that you're not the grandest guy in the world, your Libran is bound to defend you. She'll defend you with her dying breath. When she makes those marriage vows she means every word. As an Arien who also has a tendency to place people you like on a pedestal, you won't be let down by a girl born under the sign of Libra. She'll be everything you believe she is . . . even more. As a mother of your children, she'll be very attentive and loving. However, you won't have to take the backseat when Junior comes along. You'll always come first with her—no matter if it's the kids, the dog, or her maiden aunt from Keokuk. Your children will be well-mannered and respectful. She'll do everything in her power to see that you're treated like a prince.

ARIES MAN
SCORPIO WOMAN

The Scorpio woman can be a whirlwind of passion—perhaps too much passion to suit you. When her temper flies, better lock up the family heirlooms and take cover. When she chooses to be sweet, you're apt to think that butter wouldn't melt in her mouth . . . but of course, it would. She can be as hot as a *tamale* or as cool as a cucumber, but whatever mood she is in, it's no pose. She doesn't believe in putting on airs.

Scorpio women are often quite seductive and sultry—their charm can pierce through the hardest of hearts like a laser ray. She doesn't have to look like Mata Hari (quite often Scorpio women resemble the tomboy next door) but once you've looked into those tantalizing eyes, you're a goner. Life with her won't be all smiles and smooth-sailing; when prompted she can unleash a gale of venom. Generally, she will have the good grace to keep family battles within the walls of your home; when company visits she's apt to give the impression that married life with you is one great big joy-ride. It's just one of her ways of expressing her loyalty to you—at least in front of others. She may fight you tooth and nail in the confines of your living room but at a ball or during an evening out, she'll hang on your arm and have stars in her eyes. She doesn't consider this hypocrisy; she just firmly believes that family quarrels should stay a private matter.

She's pretty good at keeping secrets. She may even keep a few hidden from you if she feels like it. This sort of attitude, of course, goes against the Arien's grain; you believe in being open and straight-from-the-shoulder.

Never cross her up, not even in little things; when it comes to revenge, she's an eye-for-an-eye woman. She's not keen on forgiveness if she feels she's been done wrong. You'd be well-advised not to give her cause to be jealous, either. When she sees green, your life will be made far from rosy. Once she's put you in the dog-house, you can be sure that you're going to stay there an awfully long time.

There's a good possibility that you may find your relationship with a Scorpio too draining. Although she may be full of the old paprika and bursting with dynamite, she still is not the girl you'd exactly like to spend the rest of your natural life with. You'd prefer someone gentler and more direct; someone who won't go throwing pots and pans at the mention of your secretary's name; someone who's flexible and understanding; someone who can take the highs along with the lows and not bellyache; someone who can ride with the punches. If you've got your sights set on a shapely Scorpio, you'd better forget that sweet girl of your dreams. True: a woman born under Scorpio can be heavenly, but she can also be the very devil when she chooses.

ARIES MAN
SAGITTARIUS WOMAN

You most likely won't come across a more good-natured girl than the one born under the sign of Sagittarius. Generally, they're full of bounce and good cheer. Their sunny dispositions seem almost permanent and can be relied upon even on the rainiest of days. No matter what she'll ever say or do, you'll know that she always means well. Women born under this sign are almost never malicious. If ever they seem to be, it is only superficial. Sagittarians are quite often a little short on tact and say literally anything that comes into their pretty little heads, no matter what the occasion. Sometimes the words that tumble out of their mouths seem downright cutting and cruel. They're quite capable of losing their friends—and perhaps even yours—through a careless slip of the lip. On the other hand, you're liable to appreciate their honesty and good intentions. To you, qualities of this sort play an important part in life. With a little patience and practice, you can probably help cure your Sagittarian of her loose tongue; in most cases, it will be worth the effort.

Chances are she'll be the outdoors-type of girlfriend; long hikes, fishing trips, and water skiing will most likely appeal to her. She's a busy person; she could never be called a slouch. She sets great store in being able to move about. She's like you in that respect: she has itchy feet. You won't mind taking her along on camping or hunting trips. She is great company most of the time and generally a lot of fun. Even if your buddies drop by for an evening of poker and beer, she'll manage to fit right in. In fact, they'll probably resent it if she doesn't join in the game. On the whole, she is a very kind and sympathetic woman. If she feels she's made a mistake she'll be the first to call your attention to it. She's not afraid of taking the blame for a foolish deed.

You might lose your patience with her once or twice, but after she's seen how upset you get over her short-sightedness, and her tendency to talk too much, chances are she'll do everything in her power not to do it again. She is not the kind of wife who will pry into your business affairs. But she'll always be there, ready to offer advice if you ask for it. If you come home from a night out with the boys and tell your Sagittarius wife that the red stains on your collar came from cranberry sauce, she'll believe you. She'll seldom be suspicious; your word will almost always be good enough for her.

Although she can be a good housewife, her interests are generally too far-reaching and broad to allow her to confine her activities to just taking care of the house. She's interested in what is going on everywhere.

As a mother, she'll be a wonderful and loving friend to her children. She's apt to spoil them if she is not careful.

ARIES MAN
CAPRICORN WOMAN

If you're not a successful businessman or at least on your way to success, it's quite possible that a Capricorn woman will have no interest in entering your life. She's generally a very security-minded female and will see to it that she only invests her time and interests in sure things. Men who whittle away their time and energy on one unsuccessful scheme or another, seldom attract a Capricorn. Men who are interested in getting somewhere in life and keep their noses close to the grindstone quite often have a Capricorn woman behind them, helping them to get ahead. Although she is a climber herself, she is not what one could call cruel or hard-hearted. Beneath that cool, seemingly calculating exterior there's a warm and desirable woman. She just happens to feel that it's just as easy to fall in love with a rich or ambitious man as it is with a poor or lazy one. She's practical. Although she is keenly interested in rising to the top, she's not aggressive about it. She'll seldom step on someone's feet or nudge competitors away with her elbows. She's quiet about her wishes. She sits, waits, and watches. When an opening or an opportunity does appear, she'll latch on to it, lickety-split. For an on-the-go Arien, an ambitious Capricorn wife or girlfriend can be quite an asset. She can probably give you some very good advice about your business affairs and when you invite the boss and his wife to dinner, she'll charm them both right off the ground. She's generally thorough in whatever she undertakes. She'll see to it that she is second to none in good housekeeping.

Capricorn women make excellent hostesses as well as guests. Generally, they are very well-mannered and gracious, no matter what their background is. They seem to have a built-in sense of what is right and proper. Crude behavior or a careless comment can offend them no end.

If you should marry a woman born under Capricorn you need never worry about her going on a wild shopping spree. Capricorns are very careful about every cent that comes into their hands. They understand the value of money better than most women and have no room in their lives for careless spending. If you turn over your paycheck to her at the end of the week, you can be sure that a good hunk of it will wind up in the bank.

Capricorn girls are generally very fond of family—their own, that is. With them, family ties run very deep. Never say a cross or sarcastic word about her mother. She won't stand for that sort of nonsense and will let you know by not speaking to you for days. In fact, you'd better check her family out before you decide to get down on bended knee, because after you've taken that trip down the aisle, you'll undoubtedly be seeing an awful lot of them.

With children, she's loving and correct. They'll be well brought up and polite.

ARIES MAN
AQUARIUS WOMAN

If you find that you've fallen head over heels for the woman born under the sign of the Water Bearer, better fasten your safety belt. It may take a while before you actually discover what she's like and even then you may have nothing to go on but a string of vague hunches. This girl is like the rainbow—full of all bright and shining hues; she's like no other girl you've known. There's something elusive about her, something delightfully mysterious—you'll most likely never be able to put your finger on it. It's nothing calculated, either; Aquarians don't believe in phoney charm. There will never be a dull moment in your romance with the Water Bearing woman. She seems to radiate adventure, magic, and without even half trying. She'll most likely be the most open-minded woman you've ever met. She—like you—has a strong dislike of injustice and prejudice. Narrow-mindedness runs against her grain.

She is very independent by nature and is quite capable of shifting for herself if necessary. She may receive many proposals for marriage and from all sorts of people. Marriage is one heck of a big step for her; she wants to be sure she knows what she's getting into. If she thinks that it will seriously curb her independence and her love of freedom, she's liable to shake her head and give you back your engagement ring—if she's let the romance get that far.

The line between friendship and romance is a pretty fuzzy one for an Aquarian. It's not difficult for her to remain buddy-buddy with someone with whom she's just broken off. She's tolerant, remember? So, if you should ever see her on the arm of an ex-lover, don't jump to any hasty conclusions.

She's not a jealous person, and doesn't expect you to be, either. You'll find her pretty much of a free spirit most of the time. Just when you think you know her inside-out, you'll discover that you don't really know her at all.

Very sympathetic and warm, she can be helpful to people in need of assistance and advice.

She's often like a chameleon and can fit in anywhere without looking like she doesn't belong.

She'll seldom be suspicious even if she has every right to be. If the man she loves slips and allows himself a little fling, chances are she'll just turn her head the other way and pretend not to notice that the gleam in his eyes is not meant for her. That's pretty understanding. Still, a man married to a woman born under Aquarius should never press his luck in hanky-panky. After all, she is a woman—and a very sensitive one at that.

She makes a fine mother, of course, and can easily transmit her positive and big-hearted qualities to her offspring.

ARIES MAN
PISCES WOMAN

Many a man dreams of a Piscean kind of a girl—and an Arien is no exception. She's soft and cuddly, and very domestic. She'll let you be the brains of the family; she's content to just lean on your shoulder and let you be master of the household. She can be very lady-like and proper; your business associates and friends will be dazzled by her warmth and femininity. She's a charmer, though, and there's much more to her, generally, than just her pretty exterior. There's a brain ticking away in that soft, womanly body. You may never become aware of it, that is, until you're married to her. It's no cause for alarm, however; she'll most likely never use it against you. Still, if she feels that you're botching up your marriage through inconsiderate behavior, or if she feels you could be earning more money than you do, she'll tell you about it. But, then, any wife would, really.

She'll never try to usurp your position as breadwinner of the family. She'll admire you for your ambition and drive. No one had better dare say one bad word about you in her presence. It's liable to cause her to break into tears. Pisces women are usually very sensitive beings and their reactions to adverse situations is sometimes nothing more than a plain, good, old-fashioned cry. They can weep buckets when inclined.

She'll have an extra-special dinner waiting for you to celebrate your landing a new and important account. Don't bother to go into the details, though, at the dinner table; she doesn't have much of a head for business matters, usually, and is only too happy to leave all that to you.

She can do wonders with a home. She's very fond of soft and beautiful things. There will always be a vase of fresh flowers on the hall table. She'll see to it that you always have plenty of socks and handkerchiefs in the top drawer of your dresser. You'll never have to shout downstairs, "Don't I have any clean shirts left?" She'll always see to it that you have. Treat her with tenderness and the relationship will be an enjoyable one.

She'll most likely be fond of chocolates. A bunch of beautiful flowers will make her eyes light up. See to it that you never forget her birthday or your anniversary. These things are very important to her. If you ever let them slip your mind, you can be sure of sending her off to the bedroom for an hour-long crying fit. An Arien with patience and tenderness can keep a Pisces woman happy for a lifetime.

She's not without faults herself, however, and after the glow of love-at-first-sight has faded away, you may find yourself standing in a tubful of hot water. You may find her lacking in imagination and zest. Her sensitivity is liable to get on your nerves after a while. You may even feel that she only uses tears in order to get her own way.

Pisces make strong, sacrificing mothers.

Woman—Man

ARIES WOMAN
ARIES MAN

The mating of Aries with Aries could lead to some pretty frantic fireworks, but it does not necessarily have to. As strong in her ways as he is in his, the Aries woman will make her Aries man happiest by supplementing his drives and dreams. An Aries woman can understand and respect a man born under the same sign if she puts her mind to it. He could be that knight in shining armor that Aries women are often in search of. Women born under the sign of the Ram are hard to please and are not interested in just getting a man. They know just what kind of a man he should be and usually do not settle for anything less than their ideal. They are particular. As far as love goes, neither of them shilly-shally with passion. They play for keeps. An Aries-Aries union could be something strong, secure, and romantic. If both of them have their sights fixed in the same direction and have mutual appreciation for each other, there is almost nothing they could not accomplish. It is a block-buster of a combination.

However, if the Aries wife chooses to place her own interests before those of her husband, she can be sure of rocking the boat . . . and perhaps eventually torpedoing it. The career-minded Aries woman, out to do better than her Aries husband, generally winds up doing herself in. He won't stand for it and your relationship won't stand the strain it will bring about. The Aries wife who devotes herself to teas and evenings of bridge will find that she's burned the one bridge she didn't intend to. The homeloving Aries man finds hastily scribbled notes on the dining-room table and TV dinners in the freezer equally indigestible. When you get home from that night out with the girls, he'll take his heartburn out on you instead of reaching for the Alka-Seltzer. If you want to avoid burps and bumps in your marriage, be on hand with his favorite meals, snacks, plus a generous amount of affection. The way to an Arien's stomach is through his heart.

Homemaking, though, should present no problems to the Aries wife. With her, it's second nature. With a pot of paint and some paper, she can transform the dreariest domicile into a place of beauty and snug comfort. The perfect hostess—even when friends just happen by—she knows how to make guests feel at home and this is what makes her Arien man beam with pride. Home is where some people hang their hat; for an Arien, it's where you hang your heart. It's his castle. Marriage can coast along royally for the Aries couple if the little woman keeps the home fires burning and wholeheartedly stands behind her man. This is no problem for the sensitive Aries wife.

ARIES WOMAN
TAURUS MAN

It is the Aries woman who has more than a pinch of patience and reserve who can find her dream-come-true in a man born under the sign of the Bull.

The steady and deliberate Taurean is a little slow on the draw; it may take him quite a while before he gets around to popping that question. For the Arien women who has learned the art of twiddling her thumbs and who doesn't care if her love life seems like a parody of "Waiting for Godot," the waiting and anticipating almost always pays off in the end. Taurus men take their time. Every slow step they take is a sure one—they see to that, especially when they feel that the path they're on could lead them to the altar.

Any Aries woman looking for a whirlwind romance had better cast her net in shallower waters. Moreover, most Taureans prefer to do the angling themselves. They're not keen on women taking the lead—once she does, he's liable to drop her like a dead fish. Once the Aries woman lets herself get caught on his terms, she'll find that her Taurean has fallen for her: hook, line and sinker.

The Taurus man is fond of comfortable homelife. It's as important to him as it is to the Aries woman. The Arien who centers her main activities on keeping those home fires burning will have no worries about keeping that flame in her hubby's heart aglow. The Aries woman, with her talent for homemaking and harmony, is sometimes the perfect match for the strong, steady, and protective bull. He can be the anchor for her dreams and plans, and can help her acquire a more balanced outlook and approach to her life and her goals. Not one for wild schemes, himself, the Taurean can constructively help her to curb her impulsiveness. He's the man who is always there when you need him. Taureans are rather fond of staying put, especially when it's near someone they love and cherish. When tying her knot with a Taurean, the Aries woman can put away all fears about creditors pounding on the front door. Taureans are practical about everything including bill-paying. When he carries you over that threshold, you can be certain that the entire house is paid for.

As a housewife, the Arien married to a Taurus man, need not worry about having to put aside her many interests for the sake of back-breaking house chores. He'll see to it that you have all the latest time-saving appliances and comforts.

The Aries mother can forget about acquiring premature gray hairs due to unruly, ruckus-raising children under her feet. Papa Taurus is a master at keeping offspring in line. He's crazy about his kids, but he also knows what's good for them. And although he may never resort to the rod, he'll never allow himself to spoil his child, either. Children respect Taurean authority and will usually do their best to make papa proud of them.

The Taurus spouse or lover is generous, patient, and easy-going. He's no slouch and it can lead to disaster if the ambitious Aries wife misinterprets his plodding ways for plain laziness. He knows where he's going. Make no bones about that. Stick with him even if sometimes he seems as slow as molasses on a cold day, and your marital life will be all sweetness and light.

The Taurus man is a steady-Eddy—the kind of man the Aries woman often needs. He appreciates her interest in his work, and pays heed to her helpful suggestions because they pay off. Taureans are faithful and never flirt. All his love and attention are riveted to the woman of his choice, as long as she shows that she's deserving.

ARIES WOMAN
GEMINI MAN

The Aries woman and the Gemini man are a twosome that can make beautiful music together. Perhaps that is due to the fact that they are alike in certain respects. Both are intelligent, witty, outgoing, and tend to be rather versatile. An Aries woman can be the Miss Right that Mr. Gemini has been looking for—his prospective better half, as it were. One thing that causes a Twin's mind and affection to wander is a bore, and it's highly unlikely that an Arien would ever be accused of that. He'll admire the Ram for her ideas and intellect—perhaps even more than her good cooking and flawless talent for homemaking. She needn't feel that once she's made that vow that she'll have to store her interests and ambition in the attic somewhere. He'll admire her for her zeal and liveliness. He's the kind of guy who won't pout and scowl if he has to shift for himself in the kitchen once in a while. In fact, he'll enjoy the challenge of wrestling with pots and pans himself for a change. Chances are, too, that he might turn out to be a better cook than his Mrs., that is, if he isn't already.

The man born under the sign of the Twins is like an intellectual mountain goat leaping from crag to crag. There aren't many women who have pep enought to keep up with him. But this doesn't fluster the spry Ram. In fact, she probably knows before he does which crag he's going to spring onto next. In many cases, she's always a couple of jumps ahead of him—and if she's the helpful wife Ariens usually are, she won't mind telling him when and how to jump. They're both dreamers, planners, and idealists. The woman born under the sign of the Ram, though, is more thorough and possesses more stick-to-it-iveness. She can easily fill the role of rudder for her Gemini's ship-without-a-sail. He won't mind it too much, either. If he's an intelligent Twin, he'll be well aware of his shortcomings and won't mind it if somebody gives him a shove in the right direction—when it's needed. The average Gemini does not have serious ego hangups and will even accept a well-deserved chewing out from his mate quite gracefully.

You'll probably always have a houseful of interesting people to entertain. Geminis find it hard to tolerate sluggish minds and dispositions. You'll never be at a loss for finding new faces in your living room. Geminis are great friend-collectors and sometimes go about it the same way kids go about collecting marbles—the more they sparkle and dazzle, the greater their value to him. But then in a day or two, it's not unusual to find that he has traded yesterday's favorites for still brighter and newer ones. The diplomatic Arien can bring her willy-nilly Gemini to reason and point out his folly in friendships in such a way that he'll think twice before considering an exchange of old lamps for new.

As far as children are concerned, it's quite likely that the Aries wife will have to fill the role of house disciplinarian. Geminis are pushovers for children, perhaps because they understand them so well and have that childlike side to their nature which keeps them youthful and optimistic. They have no interest in keeping a child's vigor in check.

Gemini men are always attractive to the opposite sex and vice-versa. The Aries woman with her proud nature will have to bend a little and allow her Gemini man an occassional harmless flirtation—it will seldom amount to more than that if she's a proper mate. It will help to keep his spirits up. An out-of-sorts Twin is capable of brewing up a whirlwind of trouble. Better to let him hanky-pank—within eyeshot, of course—than to lose your cool; it might cause you to lose your man.

ARIES WOMAN
CANCER MAN

It's quite possible that a man born under this sign of the Crab may be a little too crabby for the average Aries woman; but then, Cupid has been known to perform some pretty unlikely feats with his wayward bow and arrow. Again, it's the Arien with her wits about her who can make the most out of a relationship with the sensitive and occassionally moody Cancerian. He may not be altogether her cup of tea, but when it comes to security and faithfulness—qualities Aries women often value highly—she couldn't have made a better choice.

It's the perceptive Arien who will not mistake the Crab's quietness for sullenness, or his thriftiness for pennypinching. In some respects he can be like the wise old owl out on a limb; he may look like he's dozing but actually he hasn't missed a thing. Cancers often possess a storehouse of knowledge about human behavior; they can come across with some pretty helpful advice for those troubled and in need of an understanding shoulder to cry on. The Aries girl about to rush off for new fields to conquer had better turn to her Cancerian first. Chances are he can save her from making unwise investments in time and—especially—money. He may not say much, but he's capable of being on his toes even while his feet are flat on the ground.

The Crab may not be the match or catch for many a Ram; in

fact, he might seem downright dull to the ambitious, on-the-move Arien. True to his sign, he can be fairly cranky and crabby when handled in the wrong way. He's sensitive, perhaps more sensitive than is good for him. The talkative Arien who has a habit of saying what is on her mind had better think twice before letting loose with a personal criticism of any kind, particularly if she's got her heart set on a Cancerian. If she's smart as a whip, she'd better be careful that she never in any way conveys the idea that she considers her Crab a little short on brain power. Browbeating is a sure-fire way of sending the Crab angrily scurrying back to his shell, and it's quite possible that all of that ground lost might never be recovered.

Home is an area where the Aries woman and the Cancer man are in safe territory. Both have serious respect and deep interest in home life, and do their best to keep things running smoothly and harmoniously there. The Crab is most comfortable at home. Once settled in for the night or the weekend, wild horses couldn't drag him any further than the gate post—that is, unless those wild horses were dispatched by his mother. Cancerians are often Momma's boys. If his mate doesn't put her foot down, the Crab will see to it that his mother always comes first whenever possible. No self-respecting Arien would ever allow herself to play second fiddle, even if it is to her old gray-haired mother-in-law. If she's a tactful Ram, she may find that slipping into number-one position can be as easy as pie (that legendary apple pie that his mother used to make). She should agree with her Cancerian when he praises his mother's way with meat loaf, then go on to prove herself a master at making a super-delicious chocolate souffle. All Ariens are pretty much at home in the kitchen; no recipe is too complicated for them to handle to perfection. If she takes enough time to pamper her Cancerian with good-cooking and comfort, she'll find that "mother" turns up less often, both at the front door and in daily conversations.

Crabs make grand daddies. They're protective, patient, and proud of their children. They'll do everything to see that their upbringing is as it should be.

ARIES WOMAN
LEO MAN

For the Arien who doesn't mind being swept off her feet in a royal, head-over-heels, fashion, Leo is the sign of love. When the Lion puts his mind to romancing, he doesn't stint. It's all wining, dining, and dancing till the wee hours of the morning—or all poetry and flowers, if you prefer a more conservative kind of wooing. The Lion is all heart and knows how to make his woman feel like a woman. The Aries lass in constant search of a man whom she can admire, need go no farther: Leo's ten-feet tall—if not in stature, then in spirit. He's a man not only in full control of his faculties but of just about every situation he may find himself in, including of course, affairs of the heart. He may not look like Tarzan, but he knows how to roar and beat his chest if he has to. The Aries woman who has had her fill of weak-kneed men, at last finds in a Leo someone she can lean upon. He can support you not only physically, but also as far as your ideas and plans are concerned. Leos are direct and don't believe in wasting time or effort. They see to it that they seldom make poor investments; something that an Arien is not apt to always do. Many Leos often rise to the top of their profession and through their example, are a great inspiration to others.

Although he's a ladies' man, he's very particular about his ladies, just as the Arien is particular about her men. His standards are high when it comes to love interests. The idealistic Arien should have no trouble keeping her balance on the pedestal the Lion sets her on, so long as he keeps his balance on hers. Romance between these two signs is fair give-and-take. Neither stands for monkey business when involved in a love relationship. It's all or nothing. Aries and Leo are both frank, off-the-shoulder people. They generally say what is on their hearts and minds.

The Aries woman who does decide upon a Leo mate, must be prepared to stand behind her man with all her energies. He expects it, and usually deserves it. He's the head of the house and can handle that position without a hitch. He knows how to go about breadwinning and, if he has his way (and most Leos do have their way), he'll see to it that you'll have all the luxuries you crave and the comforts you need.

It's unlikely that the romance will ever die out of your marriage. Lions need love like flowers need sunshine. They're amorous and generally expect similar amounts of attention and affection from their mates. Fond of going out occasionally, and party-giving, the Lion is a very sociable being and will expect you to share his interest in this direction. Your home will be something to be proud of. The Joneses will have to worry about keeping up with you.

Leos are fond of their children but sometimes are a little too strict in handling them. The tactful Aries spouse, though, can step in and sooth her children's roughed-up feelings if need be.

ARIES WOMAN
VIRGO MAN

Quite often the Virgo man will seem like too much of a fuss-budget to wake up deep romantic interests in an Arien. Generally, he's cool, calm and very collected. Torrid romancing to him is just so much sentimental mush. He can do without it and can make that quite evident in short order. He's keen on chastity and if necessary can lead a sedentary, sexless life without caring too much about the fun others think he's missing. In short, the average Aries woman is quite likely to find him a first-class dud. His lack of imagination and dislike for flights of fancy can grate on an Arien's nerves no end. He's correct and likes to be handled correctly. Most things about him will be orderly. "There's a place for everything and everything in its place," is likely an adage he'll fall on quite regularly.

He does have a heart, however, and the Aries woman who finds herself attracted to his cool, feet-flat-on-the-ground ways, will find that his is a constant heart, not one that cares for flings or sordid affairs. Virgos take an awfully long time before they start trying to rhyme moon with spoon and June, but when and if they get around to it, they know what they're talking about.

The impulsive Arien had better not make the mistake of kissing her Virgo friend on the street—even if it's only a peck on the cheek. He's not at all demonstrative and hates public displays of affection. Love, according to him, should be kept within the confines of one's home, with the curtains drawn. Once he believes that you're on the level with him, as far as your love is concerned, you'll see how fast he can lose his cool. Virgos are considerate, gentle lovers. He'll spend a long time, though, getting to know you. He'll like you before he loves you.

An Aries-Virgo romance can be a life-time thing. If the bottom ever falls out, don't bother to reach for the Scotch tape. Nine times out of ten, he won't care about patching up. He's a once-burnt-twice-shy guy. When he crosses your telephone number out of his address book, he's crossing you out of his life for good.

Neat as a pin, he's thumbs-down on what he considers "sloppy" housekeeping. An ashtray with just one stubbed-out cigarette in it can be annoying to him, even if it's just two-seconds old. Glassware should always sparkle and shine. No smudges please.

If you marry a Virgo, keep your kids spic-and-span, at least by the time he gets home from work. Chocolate-coated kisses from Daddy's little girl go over like a lead balloon. He'll expect his children to observe their "thank yous" and "pleases."

ARIES WOMAN
LIBRA MAN

Although the Libran in your life may be very compatible, you may find this relationship lacking in some of the things you highly value.

You, who look for constancy in romance, may find him a puzzlement as a lover. One moment he comes on hard and strong with

"I love you," the next moment you find that he's left you like yesterday's mashed potatoes. It does no good to wonder "What did I do now?" You most likely haven't done anything. It's just one of Libra's ways.

On the other hand, you'll appreciate his admiration of harmony and beauty. If you're all decked out in your fanciest gown or have a tastefully arranged bouquet on the dining-room table, you'll get a ready compliment—and one that's really deserved. Librans don't pass out compliments indiscriminately and generally they're tactful enough to remain silent if they find something is distasteful or disagreeable.

Where you're a straight-off-the-shoulder, let's-put-our-cards-on-the-table person, Librans generally hate arguing. They'll go to great lengths just to maintain peace and harmony—even lie if necessary. The frank Aries woman is all for getting it off her chest and into the open, even if it does come out all wrong. To the Libran, making a clean breast of everything sometimes seems like sheer folly.

The Aries woman may find it difficult to understand a Libran's frequent indecisiveness—he weighs both sides carefully before committing himself to anything. To you, this may seem like just plain stalling.

Although you, too, greatly respect order and beauty, you would never let it stand in the way of "getting ahead." Not one who dilly-dallies, the Aries may find it difficult to accept a Libran's hestiation to act on what may seem like a very simple matter.

The Libra father is most always gentle and patient. They allow their children to develop naturally, still they see to it that they never become spoiled.

Money burns a hole in many a Libran's pocket; his Aries spouse will have to manage the budgeting and bookkeeping. You don't have to worry about him throwing his money around all over the place; most likely he'll spend it all on you—and lavishly.

Because he's quite interested in getting along harmoniously chances are he won't mind an Aries wife taking over the reins once in a while—so long as she doesn't make a habit of it.

ARIES WOMAN
SCORPIO MAN

Many find the Scorpio's sting a fate worse than death. The Aries woman quite often is no acception. When he comes on like "gangbusters," the average Aries woman had better clear out of the vicinity.

The Scorpio man may strike the Aries woman as being a brute

and a fiend. It's quite likely he'll ignore your respect for colorful arrangements and harmonious order. If you do anything to irritate him—just anything—you'll wish you hadn't. He'll give you a sounding out that would make you pack your bags and go back to mother —if you were that kind of a girl. Your deep interest in your home and the activities that take place there will most likely affect him indifferently. The Scorpio man hates being tied down to a home— no matter how comfortable his Aries wife has made it. He'd rather be out on the battlefield of life, belting away at what he feels is a just and worthy cause. Don't try to keep those homefires burning too brightly too long—you may just run out of firewood.

As passionate as he is in business affairs and politics, he's got plenty of pep and ginger stored away for romance. Most women are easily attracted to him, and the Aries woman is no acception. That is, at least before she knows what she might be getting into. Those who allow a man of this sign to sweep them off their feet, shortly find that they're dealing with a cauldron of seething excitement. He's passion with a capital P, make no bones about that. And he's capable of dishing out as much pain as pleasure. Damsels with fluttering hearts who, when in the embrace of a Scorpio, think "This is it," had better be in a position to realize "This isn't it," some moments later. Scorpio's are blunt. If there's not enough powder on your nose or you have just goofed with a sure-fire recipe for Beef Stroganoff (which is unlikely, you being an old hand with pots and pans) he'll let you know and in no uncertain terms. He might say that your *big* nose is shiny and that he wouldn't serve your Stroganoff to his worst enemy—even your mother. She might be sitting right beside him when he says this, too.

The Scorpio's love of power may cause you to be at his constant beck-and-call.

Scorpios often father large families and generally love their children even though they may not seem to give them the attention they should.

ARIES WOMAN
SAGITTARIUS MAN

The Aries woman who's set her cap for a man born under this sign of Sagittarius, may have to apply an awful amount of strategy before being able to make him say "I do." Although Sagittarians may be marriage-shy, they're not ones to shy away from romance. An Aries woman may find a relationship with a Sagittarian—whether a fling or "the real thing"—a very enjoyable experience. As a rule, Sagittarians are bright, happy, and healthy people and they can be a source of inspiration to the busy, bustling Aries woman. Their deep sense of fair play will please you, too. They're full of ideas and drive. You'll be taken by the Sagittarian's infectious grin and his light-hearted friendly attitude. If you do choose to be the woman in his life, you'll find that he's apt to treat you more like a buddy than like the woman he deeply loves. But it is not intentional; it's just the way he is. You'll admire his broadmindedness in most matters—including that of the heart. If, while you're dating, he claims he still wants to play the field, he'll expect you to do the same. The same holds true when you're both playing for keeps. However, once he's promised to love, honor, and obey, he does just that. Marriage for him, once he's taken that big step, is very serious business. The Aries woman with her keen imagination and love of freedom will not be disappointed if she does tie up with a Sagittarian. They're quick-witted, generally, and they have a genuine interest in equality. If he insists on a night out with the boys once a week, he won't scowl if you decide to let him shift for himself in the kitchen once a week while you go out with the girls.

You'll find he's not much of a homebody. Quite often he's occupied with far away places either in daydreams or reality. He enjoys —just as you do—being on the go or on the move. He's got ants in his pants and refuses to sit still for long stretches at a time. Humdrum routine—especially at home—bores him. At the drop of a hat, he may ask you to whip off your apron and dine out for a change instead. He'll take great pride in showing you off to his friends; he'll always be a considerate mate and never embarrass or disappoint you intentionally. His friendly, sun-shiny nature is capable of attracting many people. Like you, he's very tolerant when it comes to friends and you'll most likely spend a great deal of time entertaining people. He'll expect his friends to be your friends, too, and vice-versa. The Aries woman who often prefers male company to that of her own sex, will not be shunted aside when the fellows are deep in "man talk." Her Sagittarian will see to it that she's made to feel like one of the gang and treated equally.

When it comes to children, you may find that you've been left to handle that area of your marriage single-handedly. Sagittarians are all thumbs when it comes to tots.

ARIES WOMAN
CAPRICORN MAN

Chances are the Aries woman will find a relationship with a Capricorn man a bit of a drag. He can be quite opposite to the things you stand for and value. Where you are generally frank and open, you'll find the man born under the sign of the Goat, closed or difficult to get to know—or not very interesting once you've gotten to know him. He may be quite rusty in the romance department, too, and may take quite a bit of drawing out. You may find his seemingly plodding manner irritating, and his conservative, traditional ways downright maddening. He's not one to take chances on anything. "If it was good enough for my father, it's good enough for me" may be his motto. He follows a way that is tried and true.

Whenever adventure rears its tantalizing head, the Goat will ring up a No Sale sign; he's just not interested. He may be just as ambitious as you are—perhaps even more so—but his ways of accomplishing his aims are more subterranean or at least, seem so. He operates from the background a good deal of the time. At a gathering you may never even notice him, but he's there taking everything in and sizing everyone up, planning his next careful move. Although Capricorns may be intellectual, it is generally not the kind of intelligence an Arien appreciates. You may find they're not quick-witted and are a little slow to understand a simple joke. The Aries woman who finds herself involved with a Capricorn may find that she has to be pretty good in the "cheering up" department, as the man in her love life may act as though he's constantly being followed by a cloud of gloom. If the Arien and the Capricorn do decide to tie the knot, the area of their greatest compatibility will most likely be in the home and decisions centered around the home. You'll find that your spouse is most himself when under the roof of home sweet home. Just being there, comfortable and secure, will make him a happy man. He'll spend as much time there as he can and if he finds he has to work overtime, he'll bring his work home rather than stay in the office.

You'll most likely find yourself frequently confronted by his relatives—family is very important to the Capricorn, *his* family, that is—and they had better take a pretty important place in your life, too, if you want to keep your home a happy one.

Although his caution in most matters may all but drive you up the wall, you'll find his concerned way with money justified most of the time. He is no squanderer. Everything is planned right down to the last red penny. He'll see to it that you never want.

As far as children are concerned, you may find that you have to step in from time to time when he scolds. Although he generally knows what is good for his children, he can overdo somewhat when it comes to taking them to the woodshed.

ARIES WOMAN
AQUARIUS MAN

The Arien is likely to find the man born under Aquarius dazzling. As a rule, Aquarians are extremely friendly and open; of all the signs, they are perhaps the most tolerant. In the thinking department they are often miles ahead of others, and with very little effort, it seems. The Aries woman will most likely not only find her Aquarian friend intriguing and interesting, but will find the relationship challenging as well. Your high respect for intelligence and fair play may be reason enough for you to settle your heart on a Water Bearer. There's an awful lot to be learned from him, if you're quick enough. Aquarians love everybody—even their worst enemies, sometimes. Through your relationship with the Aquarian you'll find yourself running into all sorts of people, ranging from near-genius to downright insane—and they're all freinds of his.

In the holding hands stage of your romance you may find that your Water Bearing friend has cold feet that may take quite a bit of warming up before he gets around to that first goodnight kiss. More than likely he'll just want to be your pal in the beginning. For him, that's an important step in any relationship—even love. The "poetry and flowers" stage will come later, perhaps many years later. The Aquarian is all heart, still when it comes to tying himself down to one person and for keeps, he is liable to hesitate. He may even try to get out of it if you breath too hard down his neck. He's no Valentino and wouldn't want to be. The Aries woman is likely to be more attracted by his broadmindedness and high moral standards than by his abilities to romance. She won't find it difficult to look up to a man born under the sign of the Water Bearer—but she may find the challenge of trying to keep up with him dizzying. He can pierce through the most complicated problem as if it were a matter of 2 + 2. You may find him a little too lofty and high-minded, however. But don't judge him too harshly if that's the case; he's way ahead of his time; your time, too, most likely.

In marriage you need never be afraid that his affection will wander. It stays put once he's hitched. He'll certainly admire you for your intelligence and drive; don't think that once you're in the kitchen you have to stay there. He'll want you to go on and pursue whatever you want in your quest for knowledge. He's understanding on that point. You'll most likely have a minor squabble with him now and again, but never anything serious.

You may find his forgetfulness a little bothersome. His head is so full of ideas and plans that sometimes he seems like the Absent-Minded Professor incarnate. Kids love him and vice-versa. He's tolerant and open-minded with everybody, from the very young to the very old.

ARIES WOMAN
PISCES MAN

The man born under the sign of Pisces, may be a little too sluggish for the average Aries woman. He's often wrapped up in his dreams and difficult to reach at times. He's an idealist like you, but unlike you, he will not jump up on a soapbox and champion a cause he feels is just. Difficult for you to understand at times, he may seem like a weakling to you. He'll entertain all kinds of views and opinions from just about anyone, nodding or smiling vaguely, giving the impression that he's with them one hundred percent. In reality, that may not be the case at all. His attitude may be "why bother" to tell someone he's wrong when he so strongly believes that he's right. This kind of attitude can make an Arien furious. You speak your mind; he'll seldom speak his unless he thinks there'll be no opposition. He's oversensitive at times—rather afraid of getting his feelings hurt. He'll sometimes imagine a personal injury when none is intended. Chances are you'll find this sort of behavior maddening and may feel like giving your Pisces friend a swift kick where it hurts the most. It won't do any good, though. It may just add fire to his persecution complex.

One thing you'll admire about this man is his concern and understanding of people who are sickly or who have serious (often emotional) problems. It's his nature to make his shoulder available to anyone in the mood for a good cry. He can listen to one hard-luck story after another without seeming to tire and if his advice is asked he's capable of coming across with some very well-balanced common sense. He often knows what is bugging a person before that person knows it himself. It's amost intuitive with a Pisces, it seems. Still, at the end of the day, he'll want some peace and quiet and if his Aries friend has some problem or project on her mind that she would like to unload in his lap, she's liable to find him rather short-tempered. He's a good listener but he can only take so much.

Pisces are not aimless, although they may often appear to be when viewed through Arien eyes. The positive sort of Pisces man is quite often successful in his profession and is likely to wind up rich and influential—even though material gain is never a direct goal for a man born under this sign.

The weaker Pisces are usually content to stay put on the level they find themselves. They won't complain too much if the roof leaks and the fence is in need of repair. He's capable of shrugging his shoulders and sighing "that's life."

Because of their seemingly free-and-easy manner, people under this sign, needless to say, are immensely popular with children. For tots they play the double role of confidant and playmate.

ARIES

YEARLY FORECAST: 1988

Forecast for 1988 Concerning Business and
Financial Matters, Job Prospects,
Travel, Health, Romance and Marriage
for Those Born with the Sun
in the Zodiacal Sign of Aries.
March 21–April 20

This would seem to be a year when you have something concrete to show for your efforts. The initiative you derive from your ruling planet Mars can be constructively channeled to bring due reward and recognition. Earnings and personal resources should be increased in this year of practical opportunity. For much of 1988 money and other material necessities should come to you, provided you make good use of your chances and do not waste as you earn. You are never one for hanging on to things too long, so it may be that you can use your newfound backing to further your social ambitions which may reach a high point during the year. For the past year or two you will have been building up toward a peak. At some point during this year you may realize you have made it in more ways than one. There can be career changes and you may be keen to progress far beyond previous expectations. Responsibility will, of course, come with promotion or recognition. This you should accept as a fitting reward for your initiative and endurance. You like to work hard for short, sharp periods and take a necessary rest at intervals. If you carry out this plan of action you will have few health problems. Traveling may weary you, but there should be a more inspiring side to any travel you undertake which can keep you well and alert. Business trips seem most likely, and they can boost your ego which is not a bad thing. Activities and contacts nearer home may give you considerable scope to let you relax and keep you happily involved. Home and family will neither interfere with your progress nor influence you unduly as you seek self-expression and status outside the home. Traveling long distances can make you appreciate the true value of your home and you will make good use of the security it offers, as and when it is needed. There may be changes in home conditions as there are possible changes in career, one being linked with the other. Buying and selling of property is therefore possible. Routine work conditions seem to be stable and will be influenced by any changes you seek as you reach out for success. You are in the mood to function according to your needs, so will do all that is asked of you to increase your productivity and financial reward in line with your changing social responsibilities. Changes can affect your romantic life. Social aspirations of many will be centered on marriage and cooperation with their partner. For many, the desire to make conditions more comfortable may be linked with a wish to establish their position and begin to support a family. Your single-mindedness may keep you from being flirtatious, but you seem to have room for all sorts of relationships which could lead you quite unexpectedly to a decision. With plenty of money in your pocket, you can be an attractive proposition, so may be sought after. If you are on the move over long distances, you may appreciate the life of the traditional sailor and have a relationship in every port, perhaps a passing fancy. You may also be looking for perfection and be difficult to please.

You may feel it in your bones that business will prosper this year. Be adaptable and prepared to take on the heaviest load at short notice. Be one step ahead of your competitors and prepare your ground well so that you can react without fear of falling down on the job. Lay down long-term plans in the first six weeks of the year. You will have many well under way, so can finalize preparations in this time. Always have an eye to the future, yet also be conservative enough to choose wisely if there is a choice of project. You should gain recognition, but you do not want this at any price. From the beginning of June until the end of November you may have another chance to review your prospects and tidy up any loose ends. These would have appeared between February and May when you should have been putting your strategy to the practical test. This second spell may allow you to appreciate where changes can be made before the main onslaught gets under way in the last seven or so weeks of the year. You have the ball at your feet throughout December and the end of the year may mark a culminating point for you. Be honest in your business affairs. You could be tempted, or may encounter unscrupulous people who will take advantage of your strength and position. Do not risk reputation. You may find there is some genuine need to be charitable or to use the velvet glove in the boardroom. Throughout the year you may have to travel on business quite a lot. The period between January 8 and February 21 may see you developing overseas or distant markets. From then until about April 6 you may find your-self most active in pushing business. The periods around May 22 and July 12 could be a bit precarious. You should keep an eye on opposition for unfair practices and should see that your inside in-formation and backup are reliable. Private arrangements may help you make progress or outwit competitors.

Money should pose no problem for you. Personal efforts will be rewarding up to March 7, during which period you could be more involved in the pursuit of individual success. It could be a most ac-tive time prior to the period from March to late July when the re-sults will materialize. Assets can increase without apparent effort during the period up to July 21. The fact that you are on the receiving end does not rule out the possibility that you can also distribute funds quite easily. Make sure you direct your resources wisely, for you must maintain your social position and could have heavy overhead. It is essential that you take the opportunity to build up your assets, for the opportunity you have this year will not be repeated for some years to come. Between July 22 and the end of November, you may have more freedom of movement to dis-tribute your material goods or make arrangements for investment. It may be advisable to take professional advice during the year. What better than that of an expert who can guide you on invest-ments so that your funds may increase even more? The whole of December seems to afford you further opportunity to stock up, so you should end the year still going strong. There may be a need to share your resources, or maintain a partnership interest in money. This could be a long-term project and could be particularly impor-tant during April or May. Between June 10 and November 11, academic pursuits or apprenticeship training may restrict your earning power. The end result will be favorable.

The fact that you may have no monetary worries to speak of can be good for your constitution. As you could be getting around quite a lot, you may suffer from exhaustion or travel weariness. Studies can also take the stuffing out of you. From January 10 to February 22 can be a very busy time which may be good for you as your hopes build up. Keep your spirits up and there is nothing you cannot achieve. You do not like to be tied down at the best of times, so should welcome change. But you also appreciate the op-portunity to live it up on an expense account and restore your flagging energies when the occasion arises. Hasty or immoderate actions can bring about unexpected accidents. Take care in the weeks at the beginning of the year just mentioned and from May 23 to near the end of October when you could press yourself really hard. Between August 22 and September 21 you may have some time to review your health conditions, if necessary, so make this a time to have your annual checkup.

Travel can play a considerable part in the year's activities. Between January 1 and February 14, and again between May 27 and December 1, you may be under continual pressure to move around the world or be many miles from your home. Keep a case packed for takeoff at a moment's notice. Business interests or the accumulation of wealth may be one reason for this spreading of wings. Development of resources may coincide with travel between March 8 and July 21 and between November 30 and the end of the year. Concentration on business interests may cancel out some of your holiday travel. You are going places in more ways than one, however, so will find time to enjoy yourself when it is convenient during the year. An extra-busy time may be between January 10 and February 22 may give you little time to see much of your native soil. You may not like this pressure at times, but on the whole will accept the challenge and put your best foot forward. Between July 22 and November 30, you may find more pleasure in local trips, keeping in touch with relatives, and neighborhood interests. Even so, there may be demands on time or money during this break.

Work may be stimulating or boring. If you have success in mind you will welcome the challenge and put up with routine in order to progress. Examinations may be taken before the year is out, prior to your taking on more responsible work. Conditions may be unsettled in the first six weeks of the year and again between May 27 and December 1. You must be prepared for changes if you are to fit in with the changing pattern. You are not lost for initiative so will survive. December can bring due reward and recognition for your efforts as you leave the stress of preparation behind.

A rolling stone gathers no moss. If you are on the move a lot, you may have little time for romance or serious courtship. Taking time to consider the pros and cons was never your strong point. So if you have marriage on your mind you will do something about it. You may be flirtatious between July 21 and November 30 and much more serious or constructive during March to July and in December. There is always the possibility that you may meet someone on your travels who will turn your love life upside down. Between February 9 and March 5 you could be attractive and attracted to the opposite sex. Between September 7 and 30 you may be moved by thoughts of romance, marriage or a family of your own. Love affairs may culminate between October 29 and November 22 when caring and sharing may be put into practice in marriage. It depends on whether you decide to share your lot. Married or single you will succeed.

DAILY FORECAST

January–December 1988

JANUARY

1. FRIDAY. Good. Today should be an exciting kickoff to the New Year. You should be feeling full of energy and raring to go. Loved ones will be helpful to you and will do what they can to start you off keeping to your resolutions. Casual encounters could lead to new romantic connections. Someone you meet through a friend at work could end up playing a very important role in your life. The day should be favorable for visiting relatives you were not able to see over the recent holiday season. Aries people may experience a stroke or two of unexpected good luck. Being in the right place at the right time may bring you some happy experiences.

2. SATURDAY. Disconcerting. People may be very difficult to pin down today. Making special journeys to see associates may not necessarily be the answer. Public transportation systems could be subject to disruptions leading eventually to strikes. Your travel arrangements could be thrown into disarray. You would be far better off dealing with business matters nearer to home. Wait till next week before going afield. You will find this a frustrating period from almost every angle. It looks as though you will have to mark time with some special project you had been hoping to get off the launching pad. Some information you learn during the course of a casual conversation could arouse misgivings in you.

3. SUNDAY. Demanding. This will be one of those days when you should take nothing and no one for granted. Loved ones will be unable to make up their minds, thus changing them radically just when plans appear to have been set. It will be next to impossible to get a decision out of your nearest and dearest about anything at all. You should take some time out to check over your present financial situation. The chances are you have spent more than you had realized on your recent partying and general celebrating. Do not forget to set some time aside for the task of writing thank-you letters to those who remembered you at Christmas with a present.

4. MONDAY. Worrisome. You could be feeling somewhat frustrated today at work. It looks as though you are not being given all the chances that you would have hoped for to show off your natural talents at your office or work place. You must be very careful, however, not to blow your top when talking to your boss. Employers may need you to deal with dull, routine work, even though you feel ready, willing and able to make exciting new starts. This is not the time to try to change your job, though. Do not throw away your security by taking a chance to find something better when unemployment is high. Aries may have to pay a stiff penalty for breaking their word and letting loved ones down.

5. TUESDAY. Inactive. There is not likely to be a lot of action taking place this day. It would be a good time and opportunity for recharging your batteries and for taking stock of your present situation. You might well decide that a new initiative and approach is required when dealing with influential people. The best way to go about this is to make appointments later in the week. Anything to do with your career must be handled in an extremely businesslike way. Work loads will be easier to deal with. You will not be feeling quite so disgruntled with your lot. This should be a good time for showing a greater interest in the affairs of children.

6. WEDNESDAY. Disquieting. You still seem to be running things. You simply cannot bulldoze superiors into acting in a way that will please just you. You must understand that they have lots of other matters to take into consideration. Excessive spending must be guarded against. You simply cannot afford to continue throwing your money around as you appear to have been doing over the Christmas period. The time has come when you are going to have to work out a new budget that all of the family can stick to. Remember all of the heavy winter fuel bills you will soon have to allow for. Romance is likely to be disappointing and frustrating.

7. THURSDAY. Variable. Today should be quite good for consolidating gains made from recent speculations. You should look around for wise investments. This would be as good a time as any to deal with professional people like stockbrokers and accountants. They can and will give you the benefit of their greater experience. New ventures can be given a more solid and a safer foundation. You should find that it is easier to deal with your boss. Employers will take a more sympathetic view of what you have been trying to achieve. It will be favorable for making vacation plans, provided joint finances are up to it.

8. FRIDAY. Good.   It looks as if you have been pushing yourself quite hard during the first few days of this new year. Perhaps you should slow down a little. Certainly you need to take a lot more care of your health. If you have put on a few pounds, due to Christmas overindulgence, you should start to think about a diet. You should aim for one that would get you back to what you consider to be your best weight. It would not be a bad idea to cut down on your alcohol intake, either, if you have been overdoing it a little bit too hard. Research can yield interesting results. If you undertake this on your own, work out a system for recording your findings first. Organization of facts is a key to getting good results.

9. SATURDAY. Fortunate.   All the indications are that this will be an excellent weekend. This pertains not only for pleasure seekers but also for those who would like you to do something meaningful to advance their career prospects. Good work done in the past can win the notice and the recognition of people in positions of authority. Promotions that you thought had passed you by could well be in the pipeline. Superiors will be more sympathetic to granting sickness leave for operations or prolonged medical treatment. This period will be helpful for contacting the authorities in connection with matters of hygiene and sanitation. You may have a good idea for improving general conditions.

10. SUNDAY. Special.   This will be a particularly happy day for you and yours. There are not likely to be any problems when it comes to including your loved ones in your plans for today. Social activities are likely to appeal to young and old alike. You will be pleased that you have the opportunity to get away from the domestic environment at some point in the day. You would find this Sunday rather frustrating if you had no alternative other than to spend all of your time within your own four walls. Close friends or acquaintances can offer valuable legal tips or advice. This will be in an area in which they have had experience.

11. MONDAY. Changeable.   Teamwork is your best bet today. Two heads will definitely be better than one. See what you can do to produce a more cooperative atmosphere at your place of employment. People will be looking to you to give them some sort of a lead. This is not a time for sitting back and expecting the money to come rolling in. You will have to work harder to convince your superiors that your original ideas would be worth backing. But even so, it is important not to demand major results too quickly. Aries can afford to be more daring and experimental in their thinking. Otherwise, they may find themselves behind in the running.

12. TUESDAY. Good. This is probably the best day of the year so far for solving legal disputes. These have been dragging on for all too long. Agreements can be reached with factions with whom you have been warring. But you must be prepared to give a little ground yourself. It would be best to meet others half-way rather than having to go to the expense of appearing before the court. As far as your career is concerned, the search for new and exciting horizons can reveal unlimited possibilities. Aries may jump a difficult hurdle in self-improvement endeavors. The day should be favorable for romance. Involvements with much older or younger people than yourself can be particularly happy.

13. WEDNESDAY. Sensitive. New facts or information may come to light or be brought to your notice that will give you some cause for suspicion or concern. Perhaps you have been a little too trusting with a person who you do not know very well. Don't be too quick to go investing in the get-rich-quick schemes of others. You should rely on yourself and your own opinions. Glib-talking people may be trying to lure you into gambling with your hard-earned cash. But investors born under your sign who have long experience could strike it rich if they rely on their own judgment. Just don't bank on repeating your luck twice over! Lightning can and does strike in the same place twice.

14. THURSDAY. Good. Start by reviewing the first fourteen days of the year. You should feel quite pleased at how you have faired. Even if you did not quite make the progress that you thought you would all along the line you have no call for regret. Influential people will be impressed by your energy and your desire to get to the top. Research or investigative work that you are able to carry out should go off especially well for you. Your attention to detail will win you much praise and you will be highly rated among your colleagues. Romance may contain some exciting new developments. Loved ones can outstrip Aries in their daring.

15. FRIDAY. Sensitive. Differences of opinion can lead to arguments with people at or from distances. It would be best to keep your opinions to yourself. This is not a time when business and

pleasure will mix very successfully. In-laws may try to interfere in
your marital or partnership plans. It will require a good deal of
discipline and self-control on your part to stop your telling people
not to stick their noses in where you do not think they belong. If
you can work on your own, you will benefit. This is a good day for
study and all mental endeavors. The minds of Aries people can be
razor-sharp. But it would be best to confine that quality to the
mind and not to your tongue. Words can cut as razors.

16. SATURDAY. Variable. Attempt to broaden your horizons, and not just for a day. Take on a part-time job if it will sup-
plement your income. Readers who are finding it a bit difficult to
make ends meet should push themselves a little bit harder. It
might even be possible to turn something that you have always
thought of as a pleasant hobby into a well-paid, second-string job.
Loved ones will be helpful and will be sympathetic to what you are
trying to achieve. People at a distance are likely to be lucky for
you. But later in the day they can also cause some anxiety. This
may be caused by sudden illness or an accident.

17. SUNDAY. Difficult. If you are making any journeys today,
you should be sure to allow more time than usual. Road conditions
are likely to be hazardous. Readers who are making trips on buses
or on the railroad are also likely to be subject to holdups. These
could be due to cancellations or to emergency work on the road or
railroad. This would be a pleasant day for visiting flea markets
where you are likely to find that there are quite a few bargains to
be picked up. But the advice of friends could lead to disappoint-
ments and wasted money. It should be favorable for secret and
clandestine romantic affairs. But it is best not to mix with shady or
dubious characters as deception is always a distinct possibility.

18. MONDAY. Variable. Carelessness can lead to lost business
transactions. You may be feeling a little hung over after your
weekend frivolities. It would be smart to get your wits about you
early on as you are likely to have some important work to attend to
first thing. Aries will only have themselves to blame if they go back
on their word. Influential people will not be impressed and will be
far too shrewd to be taken in by empty promises. They will require
something more tangible than mere verbal assurances. Later in the
day will be good for getting new ventures going. They should not
be attempted, however, without serious, advance preparations.

19. TUESDAY. Changeable. Friends can offer valuable encouragement as well as moral support. You will find it very reas-

suring to have people whose opinions you have always respected backing you all the way. This is an important factor for the creative side of your nature. Spare time should be largely devoted toward artistic endeavors if you have any leanings in that direction. It's a good day for concentrating on mental interests through joining groups devoted to philosophical or religious interests. Distant business affairs can help you to swell profits. Currency exchange rates may favor you more than your foreign connection. Make all the use of this advantage while you can.

20. WEDNESDAY. Good. Friends are likely to be lucky for the Ram. Aries-born people who are involved in show business may hear of some interesting new jobs. They may feel that these would be just right for them. It would be best to get your agent to handle the matter for you, rather than your going directly to the producers, though. Generous actions toward others may well repay some past debt you owe. New business opportunities that are proposed to you today are more likely to be worthy of further investigation. Long-treasured dreams and wishes can be realized. These may concern you and your family, or they might be strictly your own. But their impact is sure to affect everyone.

21. THURSDAY. Mixed. Secrecy will be helpful in romantic affairs. You should be very careful who you allow to know what is going on in your personal life. When you are prepared to make an announcement yourself, the secret can be revealed. No matter how much people will vow to keep your best interests at heart, they will still be inclined to gossip. Married readers may be finding themselves increasingly attracted to a member of the opposite sex. They should think very carefully, however, before they get involved in something that could prove too hot to handle. Matters of the heart should be kept private and confidential.

22. FRIDAY. Variable. Compassionate urges are likely to be aroused. Aries may be able to do some particularly good work in obtaining publicity for deserving causes. This is an important day for those of you who are involved with the media in any way. It will be easier to get your own point of view across in any articles that you write. Tact and diplomacy are useful ways for furthering your business and your career affairs. Your more direct methods may not be quite so successful. The evening can give rise to fears about the future. Your imagination may start you thinking along gloomy lines. You worry about making enough money.

23. SATURDAY. Variable. Group and society projects can receive the official go-ahead from the authorities. You should have good reason to feel pleased about some news. It may be contained in the mail or received through a telephone call that you get early on in the day. The breaks are likely to go very much your way in areas where you have simply been feeling your way up till now. Friends can be instrumental in introducing Aries to influential people. Social activities will be happy occasions. You will be able to make the most of your natural charm and your forceful personality. Don't hold back; you will not get a second chance.

24. SUNDAY. Enjoyable. After your most recent achievements, you will be in a much more buoyant mood. You have good reason to be feeling cheerful. Perhaps you will wish to do something out of the ordinary. Certainly you will want to get out and about more and enjoy yourself. Although it is still a little bit premature, you might just decide to have a celebration. You will enjoy the company of friends and family alike. There is not likely to be any friction between the two. It will be good for attending social functions, whether for pleasure or serious motives. New ideas come effortlessly, and self-expression will be easier.

25. MONDAY. Variable. You will have mixed feelings about getting back to work today. On the one hand, you will be quite keen to come to grips with new projects. They could earn you quite a lot of cash if they work out successfully. On the other hand, you will be strongly drawn to giving more attention to domestic issues. It would probably be in your best interests to give more time to outside issues early on in the day. Get finished with them while you have the opportunity to do so. Influential people may not be quite as cooperative with your financial schemes as you might have hoped. Romantic partners can emerge from their crises much wiser for their ordeal.

26. TUESDAY. Useful. Payment of taxes or insurance policies must not be allowed to fall behind. Do not use cash that has been earmarked to pay regular bills to go on spending sprees. You might suppose that you could make up the amounts in savings accounts by the time you need large sums of money. But this would scarcely be possible. Joint financial arrangements may seem to be unfairly biased against Aries people. Some new agreements will certainly have to be reached. Charm and flattery will be useful for infiltrating behind the scenes. Secrecy is helpful to financial affairs involving new developments. Otherwise, the amount of your investment could be a key to the scope of your involvement.

27. WEDNESDAY. Disquieting. Thinking may be faulty, particularly where money is concerned. You must budget more carefully. It might be a good idea to talk to older and more experienced relatives about your cash-flow problems. If you have been overspending, you are going to have to find areas where cutbacks can be made. These will be essential even if you and those who rely on you feel the pinch. You cannot afford to go on living above your means. Short trips or journeys are likely to fail to produce the results that you may have been expecting. It is a wise policy not to leave important financial documents lying around.

28. THURSDAY. Variable. Correspondence, telephone calls, and visits made in person are helpful for contacting people in positions of authority. This would be a good day for signing important business agreements. If you have been offered quite obviously favorable terms, it would certainly be in your best interests to sign on the dotted line. Do not go on haggling about the small print. If you hold out for all of your demands to be met, you may find that the key people will leave you out in the cold and look elsewhere. Difficulty in communicating with people at a distance can cause impatience and lost tempers. It would probably be wisest to travel wherever is necessary to meet face-to-face for discussions.

29. FRIDAY. Mixed. Today will be fortunate for writers, teachers and all of you who earn your living by communicating ideas. You will become rather excited by the ideas of someone who you are attempting to teach. Your own ideas which are similar, strike a chord with persons who obviously have a great deal of natural talent. You will find it easier to concentrate for long spells at a time today. Aries salespeople may be able to attract more customers and thus boost their earnings. This is especially true for those of you who are working on a commission basis. Close relatives may try to impose unwanted burdens and responsibilities.

30. SATURDAY. Deceptive. Potential buyers or sellers of property are best not given much credence. When it comes to the crunch, Aries people may well be let down. This is a difficult day all-around for real estate affairs. You will be disappointed. Attempts to be straightforward with family or household members may fail. Facts can easily become distorted. It will be difficult for the Ram to know who to believe. Your best bet would be to withhold judgment and not make any definite decisions. Evening entertainment is not likely to live up to your expectations. Perhaps you did not give it enough thought in advance.

31. SUNDAY. Variable. The week commences and the month ends with you feeling quite pleased with your start to this new year. You may feel sure that you have failed in one or two areas. The gains that you have made, however, should well offset areas where you feel disappointment. This is a favorable day for spending more of your time alone with loved ones. This is also a valuable period for sorting out all kinds of personal matters. It will be especially good for terminating failed romances on pleasant terms. But sentimentality can interfere with your judgment later in the day. Attempts to finish off work already under way may be given up.

FEBRUARY

1. MONDAY. Disquieting. You will feel somewhat pressured today. The people to whom you have to answer may not give you as much time to deal with important jobs as you require. It might even be necessary for you to work longer hours. That is, of course, if you are going to complete your chores on time and to your own satisfaction. Friends may try to land the Ram in trouble with the law. Do not go along with any questionable propositions that are proposed to you for making extra cash. These might put you on the wrong side of the fence with the authorities. More time spent at home will enable you to straighten out domestic problems in peace and quiet.

2. TUESDAY. Upsetting. There is little doubt about the fact that this is likely to be one of the most difficult days of the year you will have experienced so far. People will simply not be willing to take your point of view into consideration. This will be true no matter how reasonable you may feel you are being. The more that you can work on your own and not rely on others, the better it will be. Influential people should not be asked to grant special favors. Your boss is likely to hit the roof if you put in special requests for time off to attend to personal or family issues. Vacation plans may have to be postponed or even canceled.

3. WEDNESDAY. Fair. Perhaps this month has not gotten off to quite the start that you were hoping for. This will be a slightly better day than the first or second, however. You should be able to catch up with chores that you had to put to one side due to pressure put on you by influential people. This is the right time to sort out any matters that you should have finished off before last month came to a close. Pay your bills and try to get your financial affairs into better order. Speculative enterprises continue to be risky though. Do not allow yourself to be carried away by glib-talking people. This should be a good day for making down payments on holidays.

4. THURSDAY. Important. This will be a helpful kind of a day for getting yourself locked into routine jobs. You may have been conveniently shoving these to one side for too long. Occupational affairs can be dealt with in a successful manner. It would not be too smart for you to bring up points about the future and your prospects with the firm that employs you. It would be best to lay your cards on the table and to give some idea of what your expectations are to your superiors. Chances are, they should feel that they can give you hope for the future. If not, however, then it is best for you to make your plans accordingly.

5. FRIDAY. Difficult. Once again the pendulum swings the other way. For reasons that you find difficult to fathom, there will be arguments erupting at your place of employment between yourself, co-workers and superiors. This is an extremely difficult time for getting on with the people you have to work alongside. The best thing for you to do would be to keep your ideas for change to yourself for the time being. If you propose them seriously for adoption now, they are likely to be shot down in flames. This would most certainly cause a lot of bad feeling among everyone, yourself included. Impatience must be guarded against.

6. SATURDAY. Disturbing. Problems will continue to arise for readers who have to work today. Commitments to your job and your career could easily interfere with romantic plans. You are likely to be in an emotional mood. Perhaps you are unsure of the true feelings of a person who means a lot to you. It might be best not to put him or her on the spot and try to wring any promises from the person about the future. People who you would like to see today may not be available. This is possibly due to ill health. Aries need to take more care of their own physical well-being, especially when it comes to catching colds and chills. They can readily become the forerunners of flu or bronchitis.

7. SUNDAY. Deceptive. The job you face will not be an easy one for you. You have to formulate a concrete plan to deal with many of the issues that have gone wrong for you during the first week of this month. You may be able to work out solutions today while there is peace and quiet. Aries must be careful in their dealings with the police. You could easily find yourself on the wrong side of the law without intending to. Watch your step when driving. Do not speed or make any silly mistakes when behind the wheel, due to lack of concentration. Partnership affairs may not be all that they seem. Loved ones may be hiding something.

8. MONDAY. Mixed. Put more effort into teamwork. If you are working on a special project, try to enlist help from a person who has bags of energy and is someone you have always gotten on well with. Things should then work out satisfactorily for you both and lead to the kind of profits that you have been aiming for. Results of joining forces with others will tend to be more favorable. The advice of friends will be helpful. Discussing personal problems with them may lead to the solutions that you have been looking for. It is important that you do not neglect your responsibilities to people you profess to genuinely care for. You may find it difficult to set enough time aside for this.

9. TUESDAY. Disquieting. There is a risk of misplacing loyalty or love. You certainly must be extremely careful that you do not jeopardize your long-term happiness because of an infatuation. Someone who you have recently met may cast a bit of a spell over you. Perhaps you are not thinking straightforwardly at the moment. Listen to what older friends and relatives have to say. Do so even if some of their advice is hard for you to swallow because of the way you are feeling at the moment. Aries may suddenly see the light, though, and realize that they have made a serious error in trusting unreliable people. Romantic estrangements or separations can seem inevitable.

10. WEDNESDAY. Sensitive. Government authorities may impose higher rates of taxation. Appeals for reductions are unlikely to be granted. Your plans for making extra cash are likely to be dashed by public authorities who could make demands on you. This is not an easy period for balancing the books. This will be especially true if you have a lot of installment-purchase commitments to meet. Misunderstandings with clients over the handling of money on their behalf can involve loss for all concerned. The more you can concentrate on straightening out your own financial problems, the better it will be. Positive thinking will be particularly helpful when it comes to drawing up plans for the future.

11. THURSDAY. Pleasant. The chances are that this is going to be a much more palatable day from both the personal and the business standpoint. For starters you will be in a no-nonsense mood. Aries will not be prepared to sit on the fence. It is important that you straighten out your personal and private problems. That will enable you to concentrate on your work much more easily. It will be favorable for contacting friends or loved ones who live at a distance. People will be more agreeable to suggestions that you make for the coming weekend. Today should be good for sharing academic and self-improvement interests with like-minded people. It is reassuring to know they exist!

12. FRIDAY. Variable. Trouble has long been brewing in connection with people at or from distant places. This may at last come to a head. You are most likely to find yourself in some sort of confrontation type of situation. It would be best to lay your cards on the table at this juncture and give voice to your feelings. Stand up and be counted. It is no good beating about the bush any more. Quarrels may be helpful for clearing the air. Aries may make a sudden and long-awaited breakthrough in their study or self-improvement endeavors. This could result in your being able to open up whole new areas of employment opportunities.

13. SATURDAY. Mixed. This will only be a so-so day. You must not allow yourself to get too far down in the dumps. It is true that you have suffered some serious setbacks during the first two weeks of this month. You must admit, however, that things could be a lot worse. Be the optimistic Ram. Do not mix with associates who take a jaundiced view of life. Show more grit and determination. In that way, superiors will believe that you really do want to get to the top. Accept the fact that there are certain goals in your life that you cannot achieve just yet. Then it will be much easier to get your priorities straight and move forcefully ahead.

14. SUNDAY. Special. This will be a excellent day for dealing with jobs that you can handle on your own and at your own pace. Aries natives who are involved in any sort of research work will find it easier to concentrate. Comparatively speaking, there will not be too many interruptions. Attending to jobs of the detailed and analytical kind is recommended. Even though it is a Sunday, reputations can be improved. Public opinion will be easier to sway than usual. You will be able to win people around with your charm and your no-nonsense approach. Aries cannot afford to sit on the fence any longer. Decide on a goal, and the time you mean to achieve it first. Then charge ahead and keep going till you do; there's no reason to hold back.

15. MONDAY. Variable. Friends can provide Aries with introductions to influential people. It should be a good day for making the best of any well-placed contacts that you may have. Business and pleasure will mix together rather well. Just be careful that you do not overindulge if you attend any public functions. They could have a bearing on your career, especially so if the alcoholic beverages were flowing freely. You may think that you are capable of keeping firm control of yourself. But you just might become rowdy and go way over the top. People in positions of authority tend to be more courteous than usual.

16. TUESDAY. Productive. Don't be extravagant and don't be irresponsible. You must keep the impulsive side of your nature in check. Then all will be well. This applies particularly strongly where money is concerned. Today should be favorable for signing business financial agreements and contracts. But group and club activities must not be allowed to lure you into additional expense. Aries will find this is a lucky day for dealing with people at a distance. It will be very good for shopping expeditions and for buying in bulk in order to cut down on household spending. Friends may turn into lovers. This can happen suddenly and unexpectedly.

17. WEDNESDAY. Fair. See if you can do more for others. You will enjoy involving yourself in charitable work, especially if the cause is very dear to your heart. Humanitarian or philanthropical ventures should make excellent progress. You will find that certain friends are extremely generous. You will undoubtedly be collecting on behalf of people who are less well off than those in your own circle. Behind-the-scenes maneuvering can lead to unexpected developments at your place of employment. It will be a good day for dealing with secret enemies. Some information may come into your hands that gives you the edge over someone who has been gunning for you.

18. THURSDAY. Rewarding. This will probably be the best day of the week so far, and quite possibly of this month. You will be in a fighting mood. You will also have boundless energy. Perhaps, you will feel inspired to make a start on an artistic project that means a lot to you. You should be able to present your original ideas to influential people in such a way that they will feel as excited as you do. They might even wish to give you some sort of financial backing. It would be a good time for discussing confidential matters with bankers. The results of agreements made with professional people should be kept strictly secret.

19. FRIDAY. Mixed. A mixed sort of trends is indicated for today. Don't let people force you to resort to panic measures to meet schedules first thing. You must do all that you can to ensure that the work you are turning out is of the highest possible standard. As the day matures, so the pace will slow down somewhat. It will be good for contacting influential people who operate away from the public eye. The kind of information that you are able to obtain would not normally be readily available to you. Informal conversations with such people will bring interesting facts to light. You never know when you might find these of great importance.

20. SATURDAY. Good. Go all-out to obtain the goodwill and the cooperation of others. Try to heal wounds that are souring relationships with associates. It would benefit you financially to cooperate with them. This is a day when Aries people will find it much easier to mix in with all sorts of different circles. It should be good for discovering ways of using your artistic abilities to make more money. New romantic attractions may be formed. They could possibly evolve through the introductions of friends or through parties and social gatherings. Personal charm can be irresistible. You have probably made that discovery by now.

21. SUNDAY. Enjoyable. You should take into consideration all of the good things that took place yesterday. Couple those with today's activities and you should then be able to look back on this weekend as a fairly memorable one. You will have fine opportunities to mix business with pleasure. Do not fail to respond positively to any invitations that are extended to you to attend social gatherings. There you would have the chance to meet people from different walks of life that yours and of different age groups. A cheerful and optimistic approach can bring the desired results. People will be more willing to place their confidence in you.

22. MONDAY. Variable. Hunches may pay off; one never knows. This is a good day for going with your intuition, as it is not likely to play you false. Tips that are passed on to you to speculate should be investigated further. It could be that, with some sort of streamlining, they have a good chance of bringing you in dividends. All artistic and creative ventures, in particular, can be made more lucrative. But higher earnings may result in higher taxation and overheads. The advice of friends who live by their wits will tend to be unreliable. Erratic actions must not be allowed to endanger reputations. These are easily ruined, and extremely difficult to redeem, so it's best to proceed carefully.

23. TUESDAY. Disturbing. Some news that comes through to you early on in the day is likely to throw you into something of a panic. People may be making financial demands upon you that you consider to be most unreasonable. Perhaps you will be asked to settle up a debt in a shorter period than was originally arranged. This is an especially sensitive period for all career and business matters. The way things look, it would be best not to put in any special requests to superiors for the time being. Extra tact and diplomacy will be required if you are going to avoid getting people's backs up. If you feel unable to talk with others in a calm, reasonable manner, it would be best not to talk at all. Get away from whatever subject it is and turn your mind to other matters.

24. WEDNESDAY. Mixed. Publicity drives and advertising campaigns may lead to Aries-born people getting into trouble with the authorities. If you are involved in show business you must be careful that you do not do anything that could offend public morals or taste. Remember it is not always the case that all publicity is good publicity. Attempts to obtain information before it is officially released are unlikely to be successful. Correspondence to government officials or other people in authority may be lost or mislaid. The evening should be favorable for making new friends. You will probably join in some group activity.

25. THURSDAY. Happy. This will be a much happier day for you and yours. Despite some recent setbacks, it would appear that there is a lot of grit and determination about you today. You will not be willing to take things lying down. It would be extremely unwise for your competitors to write you off when you are in your present frame of mind. Letters written with charm, and perhaps some flattery, can succeed in obtaining the desired results. Today should be good for composing love letters, or for contacting loved ones by telephone. New romantic attractions can be formed while you are traveling around. This is a favorable time for making arrangements to look into real estate markets.

26. FRIDAY. Variable. Domestic and family affairs will be more than usually sensitive. Perhaps you should try to do a little more for your nearest and dearest. Your mate or partner may feel neglected because of all the time that you have spent away from home recently. It might be a good idea to arrange for a special treat for this evening. You could rely on the cooperation of mutual friends to make this go with a swing. Routine business transactions may be brought to a standstill by unexpected events. Later in the day, influential people can be helpful in unusual ways. It may be that they can advance a loan for a project you are planning.

27. SATURDAY. Important. This should be an especially jolly day. The atmosphere at your place of employment will be very much improved. It seems that your boss is determined to make it easier for the staff to cooperate with one and other. There will be good bonus incentive payments made to those of you who can finish chores ahead of schedule. You will be keen to make a good impression where it counts. Those of you who have been seriously contemplating making important changes in your career are likely to have second thoughts now. Property values can be increased. Articles made or prepared at home can command good prices. Parents may offer financial assistance.

28. SUNDAY. Disquieting. Aries' enthusiasm for getting new projects off the ground may be excessive. You must not be too forceful with people who obviously do not want to fall in with all of your ideas as they relate to creative work. More time should also be spent with family members. Do not be so insensitive as to neglect the emotional needs of your nearest and dearest. There is no point in making new starts before operations that are already under way have been brought to a satisfactory conclusion. Overly casual behavior can be found offensive by parents or other household members. Remember that as long as you are a family member living at home you must abide by whatever rules apply.

29. MONDAY. Productive. This leap-year day is especially favorable for wheeling and dealing behind the scenes. You should be able to come to some very lucrative agreement with the people whom you are meeting behind closed doors. Explore all possible avenues that might be open to you that could lead to an increase in profits. Anything that requires secrecy should be easier to straighten out. Subtlety and diplomacy are the best ways of obtaining the support of influential people. Such people may be willing to stretch the rules, provided they can be assured that no one will find out. Be sure you do not inadvertently leak the information. Your helpers would be most unhappy.

MARCH

1. TUESDAY. Good. You appear to be in a very determined mood today. You seem to be determined to get your own way and determined to make more progress in your career. Influential people are likely to admire your style. You should not have too much difficulty in getting the support of those in authority. This is also a starred day for readers who make a living through their artistic and creative talents. You will come up with some excellent original ideas that ought to win you general support. The evening is especially favorable for romance. New attractions may be formed. You might even meet the man or woman who you will marry.

2. WEDNESDAY. Rewarding. Carry on with the good work. This is a follow-up day when you ought to have the opportunity to consolidate the gains that you have recently made. Occupational and career affairs will make smooth progress. You should not have any difficulty in getting along with people in authority. More exertion put into routine activities can meet with recognition and financial remuneration. Personal connections will be helpful for obtaining the assistance of professional people. Romance continues to look most promising for the footloose and fancy-free amongst you. Take advantage of invitations you receive. Any one might open the door to a whole new beginning.

3. THURSDAY. Disquieting. Employment affairs offer opportunities for improving future prospects as well as economic security. Your first priority now should be to make sure that provisions are made to maintain your living standards and those of your nearest and dearest. This may entail some cutting back on extravagancies. Loved ones may be resentful if you take them to task for throwing money around in a careless fashion. But you must do what you know will be right for the long term. It seems more than likely that you will be bogged down with routine jobs at your place of employment. There won't be quite as many opportunities to make exciting new starts.

4. FRIDAY. Disconcerting. Aries may be offered work under more favorable conditions. Superiors will make it plain, however, that rewards will only be matched by future performance.

Perhaps your health will be somewhat below par. You might even have to take some time off during office or factory hours to see your doctor during office hours. You are only likely to make progress by fits and starts on jobs that you do attend to. The outcome of legal proceedings cannot be anticipated. Unexpected decisions may make alimony settlements less favorable to Aries people. Business transactions must be kept aboveboard and well documented.

5. SATURDAY. Deceptive. The month started out on what appears to have been a bright and optimistic note. But it is likely to end on a somewhat sour one. Arguments with colleagues may be based on misunderstandings. Don't lose your temper before you have armed yourself with all of the facts available relating to your associates' recent actions. Business reputations can be endangered by mixing with disreputable people or organizations. This is not a time when you should try to make money the easy way. This will be especially true if speculation is involved. It will be a lucky day for romance. Loved ones can bring great happiness. They may spring a big surprise on you this weekend.

6. SUNDAY. Pleasant. It should be a happy and somewhat carefree day. You seem to have been giving a lot of attention to your work recently. Why not let your hair down and enjoy yourself with the people with whom you like to be the most. It will be favorable for contacting close associates and friends whom you have not seen for a long time. You will find that there is a good deal to discuss which is of great mutual interest. It's a happy day for romance. Readers who are contemplating making a relationship more permanent are not likely to have any regrets if they become engaged or even name the day for marriage. It should be good for giving parents a surprise treat.

7. MONDAY. Mixed-up. You will be in two minds today as to what action you ought to take. This will be in regard to quite an important business deal. It might be best to err on the side of conservatism. This would certainly be so if you have to invest quite a lot of capital without any written guarantee of a fairly reasonable return on it. The risk is great and the results are problematical. Failure to agree with others may result in lost opportunities. This is not a day when team effort will be particularly easy to promote. New starts that you were hoping to make may have to be postponed or canceled altogether. Romantic affairs should be favorable for people in different age groups.

8. TUESDAY. Fair. Investments may yield surprising results. Some money that you plowed into a speculative venture some time ago may return to you, and with surprising dividends. This would seem to be a much more promising day from the financial point of view. It will be easier to get along with business associates. Teamwork is definitely favored. Two heads should be better than one. Legacies or inheritances may be cleared or received. Those who handle cases or possessions on behalf of others may be given more work than they can cope with. The day should be good for contacting influential people who operate away from the public eye.

9. WEDNESDAY. Easygoing. Readers who have been burning the candle at both ends should find it easier to slow down a little today. This does not mean that there will not be a great deal to keep you meaningfully occupied. The facts, in reality, are quite the contrary. But you should not have to rush quite as much as you have been doing. This is a fine period for dealing with desk jobs and paying the bills that were due at the end of last month. Do not keep small shopkeepers waiting for their accounts to be settled. You do not want to get a reputation for being lax in straightening out your debts. This is a helpful day for doing research work. Try to find some place to do it where there will not be interruptions.

10. THURSDAY. Routine. Those Aries-born readers who are left at home to cope with domestic duties and to look after very small children might get a little frustrated. This is one of those dreary days when you are going to have to make your own entertainment. Friends with whom you would like to team up may not be available. Today is favored for doing good turns. This will be true especially if you are involved in any sort of charitable work. It is a good day for drawing up plans for distant travel, but not for making any journeys just yet. Aries should try to use the day to rise above petty, emotional and practical problems and see things in a broader perspective.

11. FRIDAY. Productive. Some forward movement can be made today. You seem to have quite a lot of work to contend with, however. There are many jobs that you should want to get out of the way today. You do not want to know that they are hanging over your head when it comes to taking a weekend break. The day is favorable for signing business financial agreements. Delays that have been obstructing your making progress can now be resolved. There will be a better atmosphere at your place of employment. It would appear that you can be assured of higher profits in the future. This should be a favorable time for getting in touch with large business firms and corporations and start negotiating.

12. SATURDAY. Deceptive. Don't go rushing headlong into making new agreements. This especially applies if you would be required to use your own money in a way that could only be described as speculative. You need to be much more circumspect in your career and your public dealings. People and situations may not be what they seem. The evening is favorable for deepening and strengthening existing romantic involvements. Your love life should be taking on an added glow. You will enjoy any sort of entertainment that is artistically stimulating. If your favorite type of music is involved, you will be up on cloud nine.

13. SUNDAY. Important. This is a tip-top start to the week. You seem to be a lot happier about how things have gone for you during the first part of the month. Compared with almost all of February, this half of March is super. You should have the opportunity to spend more time at home with your nearest and dearest today. But this does not mean to say that you will not have the opportunity to attend to one or two important business matters. It is better to contact influential people on a purely informal and casual basis. Making friends of such people could turn out to be helpful to future career affairs. You never know when a chance conversation can turn into a windfall of good fortune.

14. MONDAY. Disquieting. You might not be prepared for what takes place first thing. Events move so fast that you are in danger of being overtaken. Be very cautious about making any promises that you might not be able to live up to. This is one of those days when you are likely to be held to your word some time hence, causing you no little embarrassment. Friends may abuse their privileged position to obtain cash from Aries people. Neither so-called friends nor money may ever be seen again. Spouses and loved ones can be unreasonably extravagant where money is concerned. It will be a day that warns against all speculation. Wait until market conditions improve before you take any flings.

15. TUESDAY. Rewarding. You have the knack of bouncing back again despite the most tremendous odds. Just when people have written you off, you are likely to pull yourself together and make spectacular gains. You are never more dangerous than when you are underrated. The day will be favorable for attending social functions and activities. You will be much in demand today. People will warm to you because of your lively personality and outward-looking attitude. The day will be an important one for readers who are involved in organizations to make the world a better place for the underprivileged to live in. Just knowing you are doing all you can to help such a worthy cause should spur you on.

16. WEDNESDAY. Good. This will be another favorable day for attempts to further charitable projects and schemes. Aries are likely to be the ideal people for obtaining publicity for deserving organizations or ventures. But the Ram should try to be more flexible and accommodating in financial and career affairs. In this way, they can assure their own advantage, as well. Charm and tact can bring you in more money. It is important that you do all that you can to show superiors how keen you are to get ahead in your career. You can count on successful shopping expeditions. Work will be enjoyable for readers who are in direct contact with the public. There will be mutual feelings of faith and goodwill.

17. THURSDAY. Fair. Today will be good for completing minor matters. Clearing the decks for new activities will also be favored. You have been wishing you could embark upon these fairly soon. Get caught up on your correspondence as well as your accounts. Try to get a clearer picture of your financial situation in its entirety. It will be favorable for visiting sick friends or relatives who are confined to their homes or are in hospital. Your face peeking around the door is likely to cheer them up considerably. Secret financial agreements could turn out to be especially lucrative. But romance can be stressful or even quite unhappy.

18. FRIDAY. Deceptive. Aries can be overly naive and gullible. People who appeal to their idealism or compassionate instincts may be merely out to exploit them. Shady business transactions would only damage your reputation in the long run. You may be feeling bored and this could cause you to take risks. Normally, you would not ever dream of taking chances this way. But new propositions received from tried and trusted associates may turn out to be very worthwhile. People may repay favors done for them in the past. Your company will be much in demand tonight. You could find yourself all set for a busy social weekend.

19. SATURDAY. Easygoing. On the whole, you should be fairly well pleased with the progress that you have made during the past week. Before this Saturday comes to a close, you should take some time for reflection and for planning ahead. It is important that the Ram does not leave too much to chance. This is especially true in all financial programming. Lack of external pressures and obligations should give Aries the opportunity to further their personal plans and interests. This is a happy day for readers who are able to spend more time as a family. It might be wise to start thinking about vacation plans if the whole family is involved.

20. SUNDAY. Fair. Take it easy on this day of rest. Make it a typical family day. There are not likely to be any new pressures placed upon you. Don't give time over to career matters. They would probably be best handled during regular office hours, anyway. The morning period is quite good for going over accounts, paying bills and catching up with correspondence on a personal level. It should be good for going on missions of a secret nature. It will also be favorable for fund-raising and for assisting with worthwhile charities. But partnership finances may give rise to disputes. Just being with friends may turn out to be a great deal duller than you would have imagined.

21. MONDAY. Productive. Use more initiative in business affairs. It is up to you to exploit your powers of leadership to the full. Colleagues will be happy to fall in with your plans if you show yourself capable of updating old methods and techniques. You should find that you have just the right touch when it comes to dealing with difficult people or circumstances. Readers who are involved in delicate union negotiations should win praise from all parties involved. Ambitious urges will be particularly strong as will be your sense of fair play. But influential people cannot be relied upon to keep their word. This can be a disconcerting discovery and could make it difficult for you to know how to act.

22. TUESDAY. Variable. This will not be quite such a difficult day for discussions with influential people. They may have been rather difficult to pin down, to date. Don't stand for any affectations of importance. If people start to beat around the bush, just lay your cards on the table. Tell them exactly what your minimum requirements would be in order to come to a settlement. This is a propitious day for signing contracts. Sign official documents while you can still carry the majority of your supporters with you. Get in touch with superiors who can pull a few strings on your behalf either by phone, letter or in person. But messages may go astray later in the day. You might have to trace them.

23. WEDNESDAY. Good. This will be a useful day for catching up with any tasks that you have fallen behind with. And it will also be an especially important period for giving more attention to your correspondence. Write letters to friends and relatives who have been resident overseas for quite awhile. News and views from home will give great pleasure to people you care for. They undoubtedly feel quite a bit out of touch. You will not have to rush, either in your personal or in your career affairs. Aries readers will enjoy shopping expeditions and should be able to pick up some bargains. Any time of the year is good for charity work.

24. THURSDAY. Variable. Not much of any great importance is likely to take place at any time today. You may have to mark time with a new project. You had been hoping to launch it sometime this week. The reason for this delay is that the influential people whose backing you require may not be available for meetings. You were hoping these could take place soon in order to finalize details of their support. Family or domestic emergencies may even require Aries to take time off from their regular jobs. This could seriously affect overtime and bonus payments. But property transactions can be made more lucrative. You may be trying to sell a lot in a prime real estate area.

25. FRIDAY. Upsetting. It would be in the best interests of all Aries-born people to take no one and nothing for granted today. Move ahead with caution. On the whole, it would be best to stick to the jobs that you know and understand. If you attempt to make any new starts now you could leave yourself open for criticism. It is vital that you prove yourself to be steady and reliable to your boss. Do not give competitors a chance to steal a march on you. Major errors or miscalculations may require Aries business people to retrace steps that they took earlier in the week. But it will be a favorable day for all investments, especially those in property.

26. SATURDAY. Variable. The more money that you can invest in beautifying your home and property, the better it will be for you. Do all that you can to improve the look of your home. Not only will it be more attractive to the eye but it will also have a higher value on the market. There are many little fix-up jobs that you can handle yourself if you take the time to figure out how and then concentrate on doing. It will be an important day for gardeners. You will enjoy any physical work that takes you out into the fresh air. This should be all the more true if you have spent a good deal of your time in an office or factory this week.

27. SUNDAY. Variable. Influential people try to encourage Aries to take risks with money. But no matter how much you respect people in positions superior to your own, and however much you want to please them, you must act very cautiously. Look over all speculative propositions very carefully before you risk any of your own money. Returns are not likely to live up to what you had been led to expect. It would be best to decline politely any offers that you get to have a piece of the action. Stick to what you know and understand. Current romantic involvements can become exciting and dynamic. Passionate feelings will help to blow away the cobwebs of familiarity and habit.

28. MONDAY. Easygoing. This will be a slow and a steady start to the working week. You should be able to work yourself easily into the groove at your place of regular employment. People with whom you come into contact will be pleasant, if perhaps a little withdrawn. This will suit you as you won't be in the mood for a lot of chatter. This should be a good period for attending to any jobs that you can handle on your own. This is also the right time for boning up for any examinations that you may be taking soon. Devoting spare time to hobbies and creative activities at this point is also recommended. These serve to take your mind off worries.

29. TUESDAY. Exciting. This looks as if it is going to be one of the happiest and most exciting days that you have had this month. Plans that you have been plugging away patiently with have a much better chance of coming to fruition. They will also stand a good chance of bringing you in a profit. Your relationship with influential people should be very good indeed. You should find yourself on just the same wavelength as those who have some sort of authority over you. Aries business people will come to discover it easier to obtain the acceptance of others for their original ideas and suggestions for procedures.

30. WEDNESDAY. Variable. Bosses and other influential people are misleading guides. In fact, they may even fail to follow up the advice that they are dishing out to you. You will have to be very careful that you do not allow yourself to get carried away on the wave of another's enthusiasm. You must look at all investment plans with a cool head and an eagle eye. Hunches and intuitions are not likely to turn out to be very reliable. People in positions of authority tend to be suspicious of compassionate and charitable urges. But it should be a day favorable for all artistic and imaginative work. You can excel and gain satisfaction from your talents.

31. THURSDAY. Mixed. Daydreaming can impair efficiency to a great degree. You must keep your mind on the work in hand. Readers who earn their livings dealing with large sums of money must be alive to the dangers of error. Be firm with friends or relatives who try to bother you at your place of employment. Your business and your personal lives must be kept in strictly separate compartments. Trying to mix them can cause you big trouble. This can be a valuable day as long as your get your priorities right. Work out a plan of campaign well in advance. But leave yourself more time for getting to and from the office or factory.

APRIL

1. FRIDAY. Disturbing.   You might not be able to fulfill all of your plans. This is an extremely difficult day for readers who had high hopes of making new starts in this second quarter of the year. The main problem is likely to be that you will have to take time off to deal with difficult situations within the home. The ill health of partners, in particular, will require your attention. Failure to abide by legal technicalities can involve expense which should have been avoided. Later in the day, loved ones and spouses may tend to be evasive, or even downright dishonest. Try to get to the bottom of why they are acting in such an unusual way.

2. SATURDAY. Frustrating.   Aries certainly have influential and important people on their side. But nothing can really be accomplished without gaining the cooperation and support of spouses or colleagues. You will feel very frustrated today as you will be able to see the way ahead all right. So it will be very hard for you to understand why people are acting the way they are. In reality, they should have your best interests at heart. It will be difficult for you to decide just how far you should go along with the plans of others. Compromise, in this instance, will probably not work to anyone's advantage.

3. SUNDAY. Sensitive.   Matters that have been bubbling under the surface are likely to be brought out into the open. There could be arguments erupting within the home. Although this may be painful at the time, it is important that you and your mate or partner speak your minds. This will be the best way to clear the air and make teamwork a possibility in the future. Perhaps you may be accused of giving too much time to outside interests. It might certainly make life a lot easier if you were to divide your time more evenly. Your home should rightfully take precedence over your place of employment. Try to give your nearest and dearest a fair deal. They will understand if work seems to preoccupy you.

4. MONDAY. Variable. Investments may possibly increase in value. Review all your holdings very carefully. Make sure that you have placed savings where they can earn you the most interest. This should be a good day for dealing with professional people like bank managers, accountants and stock brokers. But you must beware of channeling too great a portion of your assets into single investments. The risk of doing so is too great. Homelife should be happier and more contented than has been true of late. This will make it easier for you to devote more attention to getting on in your career. Valuable contracts and agreements may be forthcoming. If they are due, but late, be sure to follow up on them.

5. TUESDAY. Variable. Aries people must be careful that they do not tread on any toes today. They could easily say or do something that others would find offensive. They must be sure to think before they blurt out an ill-chosen remark. Someone who you work alongside may be going through a bit of an emotional upset. What you meant to be a lighthearted remark could easily be taken the wrong way. Do not do anything that could damage your reputation in the eyes of your superiors. People can consider your original ideas eccentric or downright freakish. But the day is good for doing back-up research on current business ventures.

6. WEDNESDAY. Tedious. Get your affairs in order. This is the right time for Aries who have been worried about income tax and insurance matters to pay more attention to paperwork. Be sure that you keep all your receipts for purchases for which you may be able to deduct on your income tax. If you are unable to back up your deductions, they could be disallowed. This should be a good time for checking up on distant business contacts. You would be wise to ensure that people who you are not able to go and see personally aren't up to any mischief. The advice of professional experts and consultants can be particularly valuable.

7. THURSDAY. Easygoing. This will be a fairly easygoing day. You will have the opportunity to deal with many matters that have been left to one side. It will be a good day for Aries people to do a bit of spring-cleaning. Get rid of articles that are shoved away in cupboards. You really do not have any use for them if they are just sitting out of sight. You may be able to help charitable organizations with clothing and accessories that you no longer want to wear or keep. Some part of the day should also be given over to study and reading. Catch up on pet subjects that you would like to know a good deal more about. This could be an auspicious day for approaching publishers with manuscripts.

8. FRIDAY. Deceptive.   Be very wary about putting too much trust in people who come to you with get-rich-quick schemes. This is not the right day to risk your money in speculative gambits. The people you are trying to convince to back your creative projects are likely to be very suspicious and cautious. Aries may feel frustrated that they are unable to take advantage of current opportunities. But new ventures that can be successfully launched could turn out to be especially lucrative. You must be on the alert at all times, however, against being taken in by glamorous people or situations that seem too good to be true.

9. SATURDAY. Disturbing.   You may become somewhat worried because you do not seem able to maintain concentration for any appreciable length of time. It may be that your mind keeps wandering to whatever pleasure plans you are going to have for the weekend. You must try harder to impress your superiors. Any lapses on your part now are very likely to be noticed immediately. That could well count against you when promotions and salary bonus payments are being considered. The advice that you get from older and more experienced people could well be both unrealistic and unreasonable. You do not have to say so, but do not follow it.

10. SUNDAY. Changeable.   Arguments are likely to flare up between you and your friends. It will not be easy to get close associates to go along with your plans for having a good time. People may think that you are being far too extravagant. They dislike the way you seem to want to throw your money around. It seems that you are taking a bit of a live-for-the-moment attitude toward your financial situation at the moment. This might be a good time for expounding your views and ideas to groups of people. Audiences can be particularly sympathetic, as well as being impressed. Friendships can take on a romantic overtone. But Aries can misunderstand the motives or actions of others.

11. MONDAY. Good.   You will be glad to go back to work after a rather indifferent weekend. You should be well pleased to come to grips with jobs and new ventures. You were not able to round these off successfully last week. Your relationship with superiors at your place of employment is likely to be very good indeed. Those of you with specialist skills and abilities are likely to find that their services are very much in demand. It will be favorable for giving more time and attention to business financial affairs. Ways can be found for reducing overheads and increasing profits. Influential people will be impressed by the organizational abilities of the Ram. This should be a boon to your career.

12. TUESDAY. Exciting. Carry on as you have been doing. You seem to have improved your future prospects tremendously. You should be feeling very much more secure in your present job. Your confidence will be growing all the time. You may hear a whisper that you are in line for promotion or a salary increase fairly soon. You will get a lot of pleasure from any work that allows you to show off your creative talents in a favorable light. Some time spent working away from the public can lead to greater fame and recognition. Secret money-making ventures can bring you in a handsome profit. Friends may try to find out how you are suddenly comparatively well off. Keep it a secret.

13. WEDNESDAY. Quiet. This midweek day is a fine time to pause for reflection. Whatever you do today, you must not rush. Go over recent events carefully in your mind. See where silly mistakes could have been avoided if you had not been so impulsive. Try to find ways so that you do not repeat costly errors. You will enjoy yourself if you have the opportunity to spend more time at home. This should be a good day for the self-employed. Those of you who can please themselves as to what hours they can work will also find today will be useful. It will be possible to get caught up on small chores. Try not to leave washing piling up for the weekend.

14. THURSDAY. Sensitive. Your attempts to further personal plans and interests could meet with the concerted opposition of others. It would probably be advisable to keep your original ideas to yourself for the time being. You had hoped to alter working schedules. Allow others to take the lead. You will not lose either face or favor by keeping your opinions to yourself. All impulsive moves should be avoided. People in the business world can be hypocritical in appealing to double standards or morality and fair play. Later in the day, friends can offer valuable support and encouragement. You will welcome sympathy and understanding.

15. FRIDAY. Good. Make hay while the sun shines. With the weekend coming up, you appear very likely to make important financial gains before you take a break. Home life will be happy and contented. You are not apt to meet with any stiff opposition from loved ones. They will be understanding even if you feel that you have to give more time to outside interests. It would be necessary in order to improve your career prospects. You will also have a chance to put some of your more exciting personal plans into action in your spare time. You will find it easier to put your ideas across to other people in a way that makes them understandable.

16. SATURDAY. Important. You should round off the working week in fine form. People will be very impressed by the way you can stick to a task doggedly. You never quit until you have seen it through to a satisfactory conclusion. Influential people will be greatly impressed at the high standards you always set for yourself. The morning is favorable for turning over a new leaf. Break with old habits once and for all. You will find it easier to exert willpower over such practices as smoking and drinking. Total withdrawal and abstinence are more likely to be successful than gradual methods. But everyone is different and has his or her own way of handling such personal matters.

17. SUNDAY. Disquieting. No matter how hard you try, this will be a day when you are going to find it extremely difficult to relax. You will perhaps be rather full of nervous tensions. It may well be that the action-packed week has left you drained, but unable to slow down. You must try to take more care of your health. It is vital that you eat well and maintain a diet that is both satisfying and nutritious. Financial problems may require some attention before they start getting out of hand. While going over accounts, you may be shocked to discover how much money you and your family have been spending. Declare an emergency meeting and discuss ways to cut back.

18. MONDAY. Routine. This slow-moving day is just the start to the working week that you want. You are unlikely to have to exert yourself too much. It would be best to bring outstanding affairs to a conclusion rather than making any attempts at new starts. There will be opportunities to go over the books and to straighten out your financial problems. Accountants will be sympathetic and will come up with some constructive advice. They can show you how you can make greater savings in the immediate future. Try to anticipate a modest level of spending for the next few months. Budgeting can not only come in useful but will, in all certainty, be absolutely essential.

19. TUESDAY. Rewarding. Pull out all the stops! Go all-out to show superiors exactly what you can achieve when given the opportunity. Your dynamic personality can only impress upon your boss that you should be given a position of greater responsibility. This is also a good time for requesting favors. You will be able to increase profits to a considerable degree. This is a fine period for readers who earn their livings through buying and selling. Commission will give your earnings an even greater boost. Friends may make their feelings known to you by acting in a deliberately beguiling manner. Casual encounters can lead to new attractions.

20. WEDNESDAY. Excellent. This should be still another day when you will make a fine impression on your boss. Favors that you apply for are likely to be granted. Love life should be extremely happy. Aries-born people, who have not had a steady partner for some time, should feel quite excited. The reason for this is the way a new love affair is progressing. You will be feeling a lot more secure within yourself now. Financial support is likely to be forthcoming for your original ideas. You are not likely to find yourself short of supporters for your creative projects. Reputations can be enhanced. Money-making schemes can be clever and astute. All in all, this should be a day you will long remember.

21. THURSDAY. Variable. Are you an Aries-born person who is involved in the business of buying and selling property for a living? If so, you should be able to increase your profits to a considerable extent. Real estate that you have had on your books for some time is likely to become more fashionable. If that is true in your area, it should move fairly quickly. But you do have to be wary of the people with whom you are dealing. You must be on the look-out for shady customers. Do not place too much reliance on promises that are only made to you verbally. Even names and addresses that are given to you may be false. Personal spending should be whittled down and kept within reasonable bounds.

22. FRIDAY. Important. Today will be favorable for channeling charitable and compassionate urges into practical action. Aries people could find that their minds dwell constantly on third world emergencies. These, as well as poverty conditions on the home front, could result in their attempting to transform their feelings into acts of assistance. You frequently do what you can to alleviate the sufferings of people who are less well off than you are. You might be able to round up quite a lot of support for your worthy causes. Discuss your goals and plan of action with friends and family. This evening would be a good time for working on hobbies that give free rein to your creativity.

23. SATURDAY. Tricky. Quick money-making schemes that are proposed to you may seem very lucrative at first glance. On deeper analysis, however, you might discover that they simply do not hold water. Get-rich-quick projects could also turn out to be illegal. Do not get involved in anything that would put you on the wrong side of the law. Keep all of your business dealings strictly on the up-and-up. Extra expense may be incurred through the need to pay for damage done by youngsters. This will be a trying day for the Aries parent. You will have some difficulty in controlling your temper. Your best bet would be to avoid normal routine.

24. SUNDAY. Variable. Try a little bit harder to relax. Do something unusual. This will not be a difficult day as long as you decide to make it easy for you. Do not allow yourself to act in a gloomy and despondent manner. Dwelling on mistakes made in the past is foolish. You cannot do anything about them now. You should be planning how to make the future more secure for you and yours. Be more of a realist. Gambling urges need to be restrained. Do not try to make up for financial losses by speculation. Don't listen to tips that are passed on to you by friends to have a fling. This evening should be good for taking loved ones out for a special treat.

25. MONDAY. Fair. Friends may be able to assist you in straightening out your financial problems. Of course, they may not wish to offer you direct assistance. But they may be able to put you in touch with a very bright accountant or some other professional expert in financial matters. This person could well specialize in the sort of problems you are encountering at the moment. It will be favorable for formalizing new business arrangements by signing on the dotted line. This will be an exciting day for Aries who are starting a new job. You should not find it too difficult to settle down in your new surroundings. But deliberate action might have to be taken to minimize expenditure on taxation and insurance.

26. TUESDAY. Mixed. Friends, or so-called friends, may be trying to pressure you into becoming involved in their money-making schemes. Be strong-willed. Do not back projects that you do not believe in one hundred per cent. The time may have come when you must speak your mind, even if you make yourself rather unpopular by doing so. This is an important day for your career. By putting more effort into your job, you can make an excellent impression on people in authority. They are in a key position to help you to advance. Superiors are likely to lean over backward to be of assistance. This fact alone should convince you to make all-out efforts to prove your worth and get exposure.

27. WEDNESDAY. Variable. Alertness and quick thinking can help to make routine jobs more lucrative. Bright ideas that come to you may help you to up your take-home pay quite considerably. Bonus payments might be earned. Do all that you can to promote team effort. You should find that you and your associates are very much on the same wavelength. This helps when it comes to rounding off jobs that have been dragging on for all too long. Those of you who earn their living through buying and selling may devise some gimmick to attract more customers. This, of course, would result in increased earnings. But you might encounter some difficulty in concentrating as the day progresses.

28. THURSDAY. Disquieting. Partners and colleagues can act erratically. You may be rather puzzled by the antics of your opposite number. Agreements that you made with regard to cutbacks in expenditure may be ignored by other members of your family. You will find some difficulty in controlling your temper with people who you feel are taking advantage of you. When dealing with your work today, you may find yourself under considerable strain. The reason for this is the result of the many different types of people that you have to cater to. This is a sensitive period for readers who are in the travel and holiday business. The outcome of legal proceedings cannot be relied upon, even though you are right.

29. FRIDAY. Deceptive. Misunderstandings can easily arise between Aries people and their loved ones. You may be accused of taking a somewhat selfish attitude and not pulling your weight at home. You should try to see things from the point of view of your mate or partner a little more often. Perhaps you have been guilty of neglecting domestic issues far too frequently of late. Partners may be hypersensitive. You must therefore do all that you can to help them to gain better control of their emotions. Teamwork can result in chaos if fundamental matters are neglected. Placing all the emphasis on minor issues will only add to the confusion and create disharmony.

30. SATURDAY. Happy. The week and the month come to an end with you back in the driver's seat. All in all, you should be feeling fairly well pleased with your progress of late. This holds even though you have had to deal with one or two minor setbacks. Home life should be very much more settled. You and your opposite number should have been able to iron out quite a lot of your differences. Past disagreements can be forgotten and forgiven. Later in the day, partners may have original ideas for swelling mutual funds. Spouses should be given greater financial freedom and independence. Otherwise, a certain amount of resentment will gradually build up as your mate suspects your mistrust.

MAY

1. SUNDAY. Disturbing. This is the sort of a day when your long-term plans could go down the drain. You will be lacking in discipline. Any keep-fit or dietary plans that you have recently embarked upon will be extremely difficult to keep up with. Research work can become compellingly interesting. Fascinating discoveries may be just around the corner. You will undoubtedly have lots of bright ideas about the best way to handle business affairs. Your only problem will be to decide when you can try to put them into practice and win the support of influential people. Restrictions on joint spending will be required. Not only will this be fairer but it will also be more practical.

2. MONDAY. Manageable. It is important for you to rely on your own opinions. Well-meaning friends simply cannot help you when it comes to making important decisions connected with your career. It looks as if you may have reached some sort of a crossroads. Perhaps a radical change is due. This would not appear to be the right day to give in your notice, however. Make sure that you have another job definitely lined up before you start thinking about resigning from your present place of employment. Interviews or discussions with influential people will put you in an optimistic frame of mind, though. If you feel sure of yourself and your capabilities, others will have confidence in you.

3. TUESDAY. Quiet. Take a hard look around your home and another look around your place of employment. You will undoubtedly find there are lots of jobs for you to deal with. They may have been left over from April. This rather easygoing sort of a day will give you the opportunity you need to straighten things out a bit. Those Aries people who feel that their home is in a mess will be able to get busy with many of the domestic chores. Important agreements can also be reached with people at or from distances. You will be able to conduct quite a lot of your business today by letter or over the telephone. The latter is faster, of course.

4. WEDNESDAY. Good. It should be an exciting and an important day. The Ram will be feeling much more optimistic. With your newly found confidence, you will be better placed to challenge people at your place of employment. You do not agree with their decisions and you intend to make it known. Just be sure that your opposition is based on facts and what is best for the company. Any personal animosity has no place in such circumstances. Attempts to improve efficiency will have an immediate effect on business profits. Becoming a member of a club or society may be the best and quickest way of gaining know-how in specialist fields of endeavor. Perhaps you have a friend who might want to join.

5. THURSDAY. Disquieting. Perhaps you are expecting too much from this day. You must be a little more realistic about your future career prospects. Those people who are involved in show business may be attending some sort of audition today. It may well be that they are offered a supporting role, not the one they were hoping for. It would certainly be of value to you to bring your present place in the theatrical world into perspective. Don't turn down work out of hand. Career and public affairs may be subject to sudden ups and downs. Even for Aries, the effects can be disconcerting. People can be unduly suspicious, or try to infect Aries with their pessimism. Pay no attention.

6. FRIDAY. Good. This is an important day. It would be of assistance to your plans to get an early start. You may feel sure that you have plenty of time to deal with both work and outside business. But it is likely that a lot of pressure will be placed on you this afternoon. You certainly will not want to be bogged down with routine affairs then. Write letters and pay outstanding bills first thing. Those readers doing the weekend shopping are well advised to get into the stores as early as possible in order to avoid the rush. Put your speculative schemes up to influential people. They may be willing to take a chance and go along with Aries' ideas.

7. SATURDAY. Good. This is an important ending to the week. You should be able to catch up with your social life. It is an excellent period for get-togethers with friends whom you have not had the opportunity to see all week. This was not your fault, but just due to pressures caused by your career. Group and club activities will give you the opportunity to promote worthwhile causes.

There is little likelihood of any sign of the recent friction between you and your mate or partner. It is a happy day for parents born under the first sign of the Zodiac. Your relationship with youngsters will be greatly improved. Valuable information can be gathered and new friends can be made.

8. SUNDAY. Difficult. Aries people may be responsible for the funds and finances of groups or clubs. If so, they would be well advised to bring in an independent auditor. People who are critical of the way you have managed accounts must not be allowed to get your back up. The best way for you to avoid serious arguments is to bring in a third party. He or she must be impartial and their final say cannot possibly be argued with. You may feel rather hurt by some treatment that is meted out to you. Its instigators are those who you always thought you could rely on and trust. This is a better day for family affairs than for social activities.

9. MONDAY. Good. It appears to have been a rather topsy-turvy weekend. You will therefore probably be quite pleased to get back to your routine. This should be a pleasant day, whether you are spending it in traveling around or are sticking to familiar surroundings. Friendship associations may take on a new face. Close acquaintances may turn into lovers. This would be a pleasant, but most unexpected development. Attempts to publicize personal views and ideas are likely to meet with a favorable response. People will be more willing to give you a fair hearing. It will be good for creative endeavors such as writing fantasy and poetry.

10. TUESDAY. Sensitive. You want to get hold of some confidential information that you do not have access to through normal channels of communication. No matter how hard you may try, you are unlikely to be very successful in this endeavor. The people you know who might be able to help you, in a roundabout way, may not feel that this is the right time to divulge what appear to be secret details of new projects. It would be wise to wait for a better day before making such approaches. You will not get what you want by being too pushy. This should be a good time for making legal settlements out of court. Unnecessary expenses and unwanted publicity can thus be avoided.

11. WEDNESDAY. Disturbing. Loved ones may be remote and uncommunicative. This is one of those days when you are going to feel very much alone. You must not get too depressed over today's events. Any setbacks that you suffer in your relationships with people are likely only to be temporary. They are friends who mean a great deal to you. Don't go in for emotional outbursts. These would only tend to alienate people even further. Don't gossip. Seemingly friendly people may be entertaining unfriendly thoughts. Smiles may conceal treachery. You may find it difficult to stand up against competition in the business world.

12. THURSDAY. Tricky. Don't allow the impulsive side of your nature to get the upper hand. This would be a better day for dealing with jobs you know and understand than it is for making any new starts. Speculative propositions that are put to you are likely to be doomed to failure. Do not follow the advice of so-called friends who live off their wits. They might well be looking to you as a meal ticket. You must be very careful that you do not take any action that could tarnish your public image. This would be a favorable time for visiting relatives and other people whom you have not seen for a long time.

13. FRIDAY. Good. Any superstitions that you may feel about this day are likely to be unfounded. This looks as though it could be a very important time in your life. All the pointers are that the Ram is on the verge of making a very important breakthrough. You should now be able to win the confidence and support of people who you always felt were holding something back. Investments that you make now are more likely to reap healthy dividends. Friends can be unexpectedly energetic and helpful in their support of the personal schemes of Aries people. Casual flirtations can lead to new romantic involvements.

14. SATURDAY. Fair. The day will be good for shopping expeditions. You may discover that the initial outlay is rather costly. But you will find that you can save yourself a lot of time and money in the long run. To do so, you purchase in bulk. The Aries woman may at last have the money necessary to buy a new dress, or coat, or some other article that has caught her eye. This is a good period for giving yourself a treat. But partners will continue to place a heavy strain on joint financial affairs. Perhaps by having a serious talk, you will be able to get your opposite number to mend his or her ways.

15. SUNDAY. Variable. It will be up to you to make your own entertainment today. The people whom you had perhaps hoped you would see may be out of town. They might be unavailable for other pressing reasons, even though at home. More time should be given to correspondence and mental endeavors. Younger readers, who will soon be taking important examinations, should not neglect their studies. It should be a good day for turning over a new leaf. Any attempts to get yourself into better shape physically are likely to have a successful outcome. However, later on in the day you may have problems in sticking to your own resolutions.

16. MONDAY. Easygoing. Don't be in too much of a rush if you have any important and detailed paperwork to straighten out. You must not hurry desk jobs. This applies especially if you are handling money on behalf of others. This is not likely to be a very important day if you were hoping to get new projects launched. Influential people may be away on trips. They might even be too busy to give you very much of their time for other reasons. You won't really need to make any long journeys yourself. You can probably achieve as much or possibly more, over the telephone and by correspondence. Telephoning can cut delay by days.

17. TUESDAY. Variable. Good timing may enable the Aries-born to find themselves in just the right place at the right time. You are likely to discover this a lucky day if you have any important social engagements to keep. You may find yourself in the position of hobnobbing with the very people you have long been trying to meet. You can do yourself a lot of good in your career by the contacts and friendships that you forge now. Loved ones will be understanding if you have to spend more time away from home than usual. But at your place of employment, influential people are not likely to take kindly to any changes in financial procedures that you try to initiate. Don't make waves.

18. WEDNESDAY. Variable. There is a distinct possibility of new romantic attractions being formed. Aries people who are traveling today may meet a member of the opposite sex. Each person is drawn to the other immediately. You will find it easier to strike up conversations with strangers in a relaxed and easygoing manner. Those of you who have been keeping steady company for some time will find this is an auspicious period for becoming engaged. Some may even combine it with a proposal of marriage. But home life will be a little depressing. Family and household members may tend to get upset over nothing at all.

19. THURSDAY. Good. Energy will be climbing to its peak now. You should not have any trouble in finishing up the fairly heavy schedule you seem to have set for yourself today. You will definitely be in an aggressive mood. Influential people will be visibly impressed by your determination to get to the top of the heap. The day is favorable for putting more money into home improvements. You should do what you can to increase the value of your property. Do not neglect minor repairs; otherwise, they will rapidly become serious ones calling for urgent attention. Making your home more beautiful can be an ongoing project.

20. FRIDAY. Important. Make the most of this beneficial period while you have it. This is not a day to waste your time or your energies on matters of minor importance. Discussions with influential people can succeed in winning their support for speculative schemes. Propose your original ideas with enthusiasm and confidence. This approach will almost certainly gain acceptance for them. Your loved ones will back you up and give you the support that will boost your morale. This is a good period for the Aries parent to discuss with teachers the progress, or lack of it, of offspring. It is also the right time of year for buying and selling antiques. But you must be prepared to negotiate.

21. SATURDAY. Disquieting. Recreation and sporting activities will involve more cost than anticipated. You may be asked to attend some entertainment today. You should first ascertain just how deeply you are going to have to dig into your pocket. You might decide that your time would be better employed in and around the home. In any case, it is important that you do not neglect loved ones. Your mate or partner would appear to have been very reasonable about the amount of time that you have spent away from home recently. You owe it to them to make up for it. Gamblers should avoid pushing their luck too far.

22. SUNDAY. Good. This should make an excellent start to the week. You will be able to straighten out lots of minor problems. That will clear the decks for any important starts that you may wish to make on Monday. Special outings will go off very well. This will pertain especially if you have decided to take your mate or partner on a trip. You should not need to spend a great deal of money to get the best that this day had to offer. Romantic partners can help to restore self-confidence in Aries people. Even brave Aries need encouragement at times. It will be a good time for putting more exertion into furthering developments.

23. MONDAY. Variable. Teamwork will most certainly net you the best results today. Persuade your mate or partner to assist you with any chores. These can be done more speedily if two pairs of hands are used. Although this can be a pleasant enough day, you should not try to achieve too much. Aim for rendering good, solid work and service rather than for attempting to produce spectacular results. Do whatever you can to make your good name even better. Be wary about overexerting yourself because this could affect your health to its detriment. Doctors do not always have all the answers; they are human and can make mistakes, too.

24. TUESDAY. Good. You will be in a good but determined mood today, one that would be difficult to oppose. You will have plenty of grit and determination for achieving your aims. You will also find today an excellent one for proving other people wrong. But when you do so, use tact and diplomacy. Do not be too bombastic and scathing or you will make enemies. But you will have the opportunity to make a point that happens to be important to you in a very special way. Aries-born people who are contemplating making a job switch could receive an excellent offer. Routine occupational affairs can be made more lucrative. But in order to do so, you must be prepared to put in some overtime.

25. WEDNESDAY. Disturbing. This could be a rather worrisome day. You are likely to be confronted with some difficult situations. And you may be at a loss as to know how to straighten them out for the best. Some of you may have to make an important decision about the future. One way or another, this is likely to be a day fraught with emotion. Members of your family will be very sensitive to criticism. Continued distractions can impair the efficiency of the Ram. Daydreaming can interfere with concentration. Business partners and colleagues may be more trouble than they are worth, at least today.

26. THURSDAY. Difficult. Rely on yourself as much as possible. Don't become involved in any projects for which you would have to put up most of the financial backing. There are friends of yours who live off their wits. They may be attempting to get you to speculate in some way or another. Legal documents should not be signed without first going over the small print very carefully. Misleading phrases may make it hardly worthwhile for Aries to agree to the terms of the new contract. Business associates may try to conceal their mistakes from Aries partners. This sort of deception can make matters even worse for the future.

27. FRIDAY. Variable. Don't sit around moping. It will be up to you to generate whatever action is to be taken. Influential people will be helpful, but only if they feel that you are really determined to make progress in your career. There are not likely to be any special problems to cope with at home. But even though romantic affairs may appear to be going smoothly, basic incompatibilities may begin to reveal themselves. You may not be on quite the wavelength with a member of the opposite sex as you had supposed you were. Differences of opinion will cause friction. It would be best to bring it all out into the open right away. Letting it fester will not accomplish anything positive. Discuss your options.

28. SATURDAY. Exciting. The time is favorable for research work, particularly of the confidential kind. Aries who are involved in jobs that require them to experiment should be very excited about discoveries they make today. The more creative you can be, the more satisfaction you are likely to get from your work. It will be possible to make progress in finding out who secret enemies are. You learned that there has been gossiping and spreading of rumors about you. Today should be good for putting more exertion into furthering charitable causes. Do all you can to obtain publicity from worthwhile ventures.

29. SUNDAY. Demanding. This will be a difficult period for you. There seem to be a lot of jobs that you have to attend to today. You find these extremely boring and run-of-the-mill, with no shred of challenge. However, if you do not sort them out now, they are likely to spill over into next month. That would serve only to increase your backlog. There will not be much opportunity for you to find pleasure and entertainment today. Partners and spouses may be unwilling to go along with Aries' joint financial plans. The results of these discussions could be a deadlock. An extra effort should be made to moderate personal spending. This appears easy in theory. But in practice, it's a different game.

30. MONDAY. Disquieting. Today should be helpful for drawing up plans for the future. You must try to concentrate on what is in the best interests of the overall happiness and security of you and yours. Be more disciplined about your spending habits. You must try harder to cut back in areas where you have been becoming extravagant. Later in the day, you may have reason to doubt the wisdom of an investment that you made. But it will undoubtedly be too late to withdraw now. Driving needs more care as the weather improves. This is especially true if you are traveling in unfamiliar areas. No time gained can be worth the risk of an accident and probable injury.

31. TUESDAY. Disturbing. Your confidence seems to have taken a bit of a beating over the past couple of days. But there does not seem to be much hope of your restoring it today. It would be best to stick to routine as much as possible. If you become involved in wild, speculative moves you will almost certainly become unglued. Don't listen to the advice of so-called friends who live off their wits. Sponsorship for study programs and academic pursuits may be withdrawn. Professional people may refuse to give Aries the benefit of their accumulated wisdom and knowledge. Importing and exporting businesses can run into trouble with the authorities. Customs officials may hold up goods.

JUNE

1. WEDNESDAY. Disturbing. You seem to be smack in the middle of a very tricky, unpleasant period at the moment. Whatever you do, you must not resort to panic measures. Attempt to solve your present difficulties with a well-planned strategy. Sudden breakthroughs may occur in connection with affairs at a distance. But you may not be able to obtain full information on the spot. Local travel and journeys may be interrupted, due to industrial action on the trains. There is also the possibility of electrical faults. Romantic arrangements may have to be canceled at the last moment. This will cause a great deal of unhappiness and frustration. You could be in a tough spot, trying to explain why.

2. THURSDAY. Tricky. Don't believe all that you are told. Promises of support made to you verbally may not be reliable. Fair-weather friends may not be willing to support your new schemes, even if they say they would. This would be especially true if the going gets a bit rough. You can only pull through by relying on yourself more, together with your qualities of grit and determination. Reputations should not be allowed to hang on the words of others. Loyalties could easily be misplaced. It is best not to mix with unreliable people or organizations. But this is a promising day for transactions with large corporations. Be sure you have all your facts straight.

3. FRIDAY. Inactive. It is not likely that there will be very much taking place today. You should be very pleased that you have an opportunity to take things a little easier. Slow down a bit. Look over the past few days and try to discover where you have gone wrong. What is even more important is how to ensure that you will not make the same mistakes all over again. Do what you can to improve your relationship with members of your family. Take a more serious look at the present trends of career and business affairs. Aries people do not seem to be making the progress that they are capable of at the moment. It may be that you are gathering strength for a time and working on a new plan of action.

4. SATURDAY. Fair. Aries will not see a lot of improvement today. It looks as if you will be catching up with odd jobs that you should have gotten rid of some time ago. There will be quite a lot of chores to attend to, in and around the home. Aries readers may find themselves rushed off their feet, trying to clean up. Other members of the family may be somewhat slovenly and not prepared to pull their weight. Friends can let Aries people down when their help and their support are most needed. Group and club activities could easily involve some unforeseen expense. But influential people will be more sympathetic and willing to help.

5. SUNDAY. Good. Today will be like a breath of fresh air to the Ram. You do seem to have taken a bit of battering recently. This is an excellent time for in-depth discussions on personal matters with friends and acquaintances. You should be able to straighten out your differences by speaking your mind. You will be drawn closer to people whom you care about. This has not been the case for some time past. Social functions and gatherings may provide the setting for new romantic attractions. Friends who live at a distance may suddenly put in an unexpected appearance. As long as the visit is temporary, you will be able to spend more time updating news. But you may have made prior engagements.

6. MONDAY. Satisfactory. This may not be the sensational start to the working week that you were hoping for. Any improvement in your current financial situation is welcome. But it is only likely to be brought about by steady and hard work. Aiming for spectacular gains through gambling is like building castles in the air. Pay more attention to your regular job. You can win the loyalty and support of influential people. But you must show that you are not afraid to put in a bit of overtime in order to get a job finished. Ill-feeling between you and your colleagues can be forgotten if all make the effort. Enemies can be turned into friends if there is a willingness to resolve differences.

7. TUESDAY. Variable. Some behind-the-scenes maneuvering could be helpful to furthering major financial ventures. This is an excellent time for doing what you can to set up future moves. You will probably want to make these sometime toward the end of the week. You should try to win the support of influential people in subtle ways. You will not do well by employing hard-sell tactics. Do not allow friends to sponge on you generosity. You should not loan any money to back someone's schemes if the person cannot give you a definite date as to when he or she may be able to pay you back. Why take such a risk? If the project collapses, there would be little chance of your being repaid.

8. WEDNESDAY. Deceptive. Intuitions cannot be relied upon. This is a day for acting on facts and facts alone. Do not make any moves on impulse. Influential people who pass on any tips to you may be well-meaning, but they are also likely to be misinformed. Emotional considerations can distort your opinion on practical and business issues. Self-deception always is a possibility. This is not a day for mixing with dubious people or disreputable organizations. You must not do anything that could cause your reputation to suffer. Getting a bad reputation can be comparatively easy. But trying to shed it could be extremely hard.

9. THURSDAY. Fortunate. This is a much better day than the others this week. Taken as a whole, you do not seem to have been able to make a very promising start to the month of June. But you should be feeling more optimistic now. You will have far more energy than previously at your disposal. This should mean that you can get through jobs that you have been putting off. There are not likely to be any new difficulties on the domestic front that would slow you down. Influential people will be more than willing to talk over your problems with you. They are in a position to give you the benefit of their long and valuable experience. This is a favorable time for casual flirtations and romance.

10. FRIDAY. Variable. Bright ideas should be used to make more money. Older readers should listen to the young up-and-coming generation at their place of employment. With some possible adapt the schemes of junior members of staff should be well worthy of further consideration. The more that you can employ teamwork, the faster you will be able to get rid of boring, routine tasks. It should be a good day for raising meaningful funds for charity. You will be able to use your spare time to assist people who are less fortunate than you are. But bankers may oppose money-making schemes that would involve any sort of speculation. So it is unlikely you could borrow any funds.

11. SATURDAY. Lucky. Overall, it appears to have been a fairly disastrous start to the month of June for you. But it

looks as if you are in for a very good weekend. There are not likely
to be any special pressures placed upon you today. You may
receive some sort of cash benefit without even having to work
for it. This could come in the form of a gift from an older friend
or relative. But, on the other hand, it may be the repayment of a
debt that was incurred some time ago. Anyway, the financial
pressure that has been exerted on you recently should be eased
for the time being. This will bring you tremendous relief and a
sense of freedom from worry. You will enjoy the weekend
much more than usual.

12. SUNDAY. Good. In conjunction with yesterday's happenings, this would appear to be one of your most pleasant and enjoyable weekends. You have not had the good fortune to experience
such for some time. Friends or loved ones may be instrumental in
introducing Aries to influential people. They could be very important in helping them to get ahead in their career. Contacts that you
make today are likely to prove very fortunate for you in the future.
Today should be good for getting out and about more. Make an
effort to meet people from various walks of life different to your
own. Only in this way can you really understand how others live.

13. MONDAY. Disturbing. Words spoken thoughtlessly could
give offense without your having intended to. You must be careful
not to put your foot in your mouth, so to speak. Do not spread
rumors or gossip. People with whom you come into contact will be
on edge. You must be more aware of the danger of arguments
leading to walkouts. You might become very frustrated today.
Putting new plans into operation will be extremely difficult.
Influential people are not likely to be around just when you need
them most. Relatives may try to make Aries feel guilty for past
actions. Driving needs more care than usual. Other drivers as well
as pedestrians, can be particularly thoughtless.

14. TUESDAY. Changeable. Writing and mental endeavors
will contain setbacks. It will not be easy for you to get your original
ideas agreed to. Writers who are trying to have their works accepted by publishers will not be too happy as a result of today's
experience. Dates for submitting your artistic work for approval
may have to be postponed. Ill-health can interfere with your daily
routine. It may not be your own physical well-being that is giving
you cause for concern. It could easily be that of a dear friend or
relative. Publicity drives may fail to provoke a favorable response.
Some thought should be directed toward finding a new approach,
with sparkle.

15. WEDNESDAY. Deceptive. No sooner have you begun to make progress on your job than you are likely to be pulled off. Whatever it was, you will probably be switched to some new task. This will be a frustrating day in many ways. You may feel that people who have some authority over you are really not aware of your abilities. They do not understand what you are attempting to achieve. It is important for you to convince them of your worth. Reference to past experience can be an unreliable guide, though, when it comes to making important decisions now. The present should not be judged by the past.

16. THURSDAY. Encouraging. This will be a good day for trying to catch up with those chores you have put aside lately, for one reason or another. Aries who remain at home during the day will find it easier to deal with domestic chores. There will be little to upset routine or to distract you. Workloads that are finished off ahead of deadlines may bring you in an unexpected bonus. Your relationship with your boss is likely to be very much improved. See what you can do to increase the value of your real estate by carrying out work in and around your home and property. Parents can be especially generous when making loans. Of course, they are eager to help you get ahead and will encourage your ambitions.

17. FRIDAY. Disquieting. Perhaps you will not have your usual amount of energy today. The tasks that you have set for yourself are unlikely to be putting any great strain upon you. But nevertheless you will easily become exhausted and disheartened. It might be best for you to turn to matters that would not take a great deal out of you physically. The earlier part of the day would be quite good for roughing out holiday plans or making vacation arrangements. Attempts to capitalize on your artistic talents may prove to be more successful than before. But you are advised not to get involved in any heavy speculation. The health or circumstances of children are likely to put you to extra expense.

18. SATURDAY. Happy. This is likely to be a complete reversal of yesterday's trend. You should be able to catch up with many of the jobs that you were not able to complete on time. You will be pleased that you have so much more energy at your disposal today. Otherwise, it might have meant that you would have had to spend some time tomorrow dealing with desk jobs and the like. Loved ones will be easier to get along with. No additional, new demands are likely to be made upon you. Romantic urges will tend to be stronger for single Aries. This can be a good day for playing the field and making new conquests. Whatever else you do, take your mind off work and its related problems, for once.

19. SUNDAY. Happy. You get off on the right foot at the start of the week. You should be able to pretty well please yourself as to how you spend this day. What would please you the most is to mix business with pleasure. Sporting activities are likely to be high on the agenda of the more energetic among you. It would be a good day, too, for the Aries parent to spend more time with youngsters. You could discuss school problems with offspring of tender years. Any contact with influential people will help you to arrange important meetings for later in the week. These could be of great help to you in furthering your career. Do everything you can to ensure that such a meeting does take place.

20. MONDAY. Variable. Get down to some serious hard work. Try to push up your output. Perhaps you have not been firing on all your cylinders. This is a good day to show your boss that you still mean business. Prove that you are the one who should be considered when any changes are being made in jobs at the top. You must put all ideas for pleasure-seeking and entertainment out of your mind at work. Wait until you have completed your duties to your own satisfaction and to the satisfaction of your superiors. Official permission is unlikely to be granted for business expansion just now, however. This may delay your plans, but you will just have to be patient.

21. TUESDAY. Mixed. This will not be a particularly important day as far as home and family affairs are concerned. In fact, Aries women readers may become a little bored with routine, run-of-the-mill jobs. If you find yourself bored with your own company, get out of the house. There are plenty of ways in which you can entertain yourself, from visiting museums to calling on a friend. You might be able to persuade someone to accompany you to a show or recital. All career and occupational affairs, routine work, and transactions that you are able to undertake today will be unusually lucrative. But attempts to discuss matters frankly may be a waste of time for all.

22. WEDNESDAY. Deceptive. The earlier in the day that you can get going, the better it will be for you. The morning period will be the best time to discuss important partnership affairs with your opposite number. Loved ones will be unusually helpful and enthusiastic. It should be possible to cut back on the amount of time you spend dealing with routine tasks. Try employing more team effort with greater effect. At your place of employment, however, misunderstandings are likely to arise. You will not get on very well with your associates. You may have to refer a dispute to your boss in order to get it settled impartially. This, in turn, could stir even deeper resentment. You will just have to use all your diplomacy.

23. THURSDAY. Important. Make the most of today and to-morrow! You are more than likely to have some pretty fortunate breaks. Influential people will be more approachable now than they have been lately. Propose your ideas for streamlining certain routine procedures at your place of employment. Your boss will undoubtedly give you a fair hearing. Make the most of the additional energy that you seem to have today. But be sure that you channel it in productive ways. This will be a much smoother day for teamwork and all cooperative efforts. Aries should have a fair idea of just what joint enterprises can achieve if approached in the right way. Close cooperation with all involved is essential.

24. FRIDAY. Good. This should be an excellent follow-up day. Continue to build on the excellent foundations that you have laid for promoting teamwork. A pooling of original ideas with your associates could lead to the streamlining of work patterns. You might even be able to get started on creative jobs. Choose those that really have appeal to your imagination, later in the day. It should be favorable, too, for obtaining legal advice and assistance from professional experts. Today will also be good for contacting partners and loved ones who are living at a distance. And it should be even more favorable for contacting influential people about property investments too.

25. SATURDAY. Disquieting. As you know, things seem to have been going fairly well for you over the past couple of days. But today you are likely to be feeling strangely at odds with your surroundings. Team effort will not go very well. Surprisingly, you will be bankrupt of original ideas. Perhaps you have been pushing yourself a little too hard? It might be a good idea to pay more attention to routine matters. Certainly you should steer clear of get-rich-quick-schemes. Potential joint financial problems may come to a head. This can be a day of reckoning for Aries people who have chosen to ignore the warning signals. You may be faced with some difficult choices.

26. SUNDAY. Sensitive. A sudden increase in business could well have brought in a huge workload. You will doubtless feel that you have to devote quite a lot of your spare time to career matters. This state of affairs is likely to upset your opposite number. Loved ones will feel that you are more interested in your job than in them. There will be some conflict for you today. Perhaps you can avoid confrontations by promising an outing later in the day. But you will feel that you must get rid of your work first. People at or from distances can impose extra responsibilities upon you. You will have an extra burden.

27. MONDAY. Worrisome. Professional people can not only be deliberately not helpful in your view but they can be downright obstructive. You may feel that an accountant or lawyer who should be acting on your behalf is giving more protection to the other party. You might decide that this is a propitious time to discuss the matter with your colleagues. See if they can come up with any name of someone who would represent you and serve your purpose better. Higher education and study courses may take up far more of your time than you had bargained for. They could, in fact, become something of a burden. Spouses may disagree on the best methods to employ when dealing with in-laws.

28. TUESDAY. Disturbing. Aries may be asked to do what goes against the grain. What will annoy you today is that influential people may pass down changes in work programs. They will do this to you without having given you the courtesy of first discussing their changes of plan personally. It is no good having a sensitive skin today, though. You will have to jump when the people who wield power over you call the tune. Lack of self-confidence may have an inhibiting effect on the Ram. You may hesitate that split-second too long before taking the initiative on important activities. Publishers can impose deadlines that are unreasonable. You will just have to fight for your rights.

29. WEDNESDAY. Disturbing. You are likely to want to oppose the voice of authority. It will annoy you to have people, in positions superior to your own, stick their noses in your business. They will try to interfere with work schedules. Hard as you may try to reason with such people they will continue to insist that they know best. You must be very careful about losing your temper. It would be best not to speak your mind, however certain you are that you are in the right. Do not allow yourself to become a spokesman for the grievances of others, either. Don't allow trivial matters to affect your good judgment. That is one of your most valuable assets. Use it to your own best advantage.

30. THURSDAY. Sensitive. You will still have good reason to feel irritated by superiors. Influential people may base their judgments on insufficient data or inaccurate information. Clarifying matters can prove to be difficult. Readers who have the opportunity to work from their home base will find this an altogether better day. They do not have to jump when the voice of authority calls, for one thing. It should be a good day for putting more exertion into furthering matters that allow you to operate from behind the scenes. Secret transactions can prove especially lucrative. Take great precautions against leaking of vital information.

JULY

1. FRIDAY. Sensitive. Friends are quite likely to make unreasonable demands upon you. You will have to be very firm with people who attempt to drag you away from your work. They are only for seeking pleasure and entertainment. This is especially true for Aries people who operate out of their home bases. Money is likely to be the root cause of problems that flair up between you and your close family. Arguments may also arise with business partners over the allocation of net profits. Taxation problems should not be put off to another day. Postponement will only make them worse. You could also run the risk of being late. That would entail a fine which would add to your troubles.

2. SATURDAY. Variable. Get in touch with friends in high positions. They might be able to supply you with important information that you would not be able to get hold of yourself. This is a good period for all business financial negotiations. You might be able to clinch a deal that will bring you in a handsome profit. Contracts that have been hanging fire should be signed now without further delay. It should be a good evening for attending group functions and club activities. Anything you do in the way of entertainment and creation will be good for you. Take your mind off your work and problems.

3. SUNDAY. Encouraging. This will be an important day. You should try to spend at least some of your time this Sunday working in solitude. It would appear that there are a number of jobs to which you should turn your attention. These will require a calm atmosphere. Loved ones will show more understanding if you set aside one or two hours to straighten out desk jobs. Take time to have a careful review, thinking about your future career prospects and how to improve them. The evening can provide you with the opportunity to mingle with influential people in casual and informal surroundings. Useful introductions can be made. These could have long-term implications for you.

4. MONDAY. Disturbing. The chances are you will not be in the mood for work. This is not a day when you can walk away from your responsibilities. If you try to get time off from the office or headquarters, your boss is likely to see through your excuses. You do not want to take any silly risks that could put the future well-being of you and your loves ones in jeopardy. Your powers of resistance are going to be sorely tested. Words spoken in haste, behind other people's backs, may get around. Aries' credibility can be impaired by vagueness and confusion. It is important to stick to the facts or you will run the risk of spreading misinformation.

5. TUESDAY. Deceptive. You must pay more attention to detail. Do not be sloppy when attending to desk jobs. Influential people may well check over your work after you have completed it. You may have to do it all over again without receiving any more money. You could be in trouble if you don't get it right the first time. This will be rather a slow day for attending to personal affairs and activities. Friends may come up with ideas for pleasure-seeking that you will find one big drag. There will tend to be far too much quiet and dullness for the liking of Aries people. Forget whatever that was and find your own entertainment. You are never at a loss for good ideas and novel ways to have fun.

6. WEDNESDAY. Changeable. Government officials and others in authority can interfere with the smooth running of home and family affairs. This is one of those days when you may have to fill out various forms and deal with lots of red tape. Aries who were hoping to make alterations in the garden or build extensions on their homes may find this is easier said than done. You are likely to have to request planning and/or building permits from the proper civil authorities first. Traders in antiques or other valuable objects may be found to be in possession of stolen goods. Be sure that you keep your books straight and up to date if you are in that line of business. Personal plans will be given a boost this evening.

7. THURSDAY. Exciting. The morning is especially favorable for breaking with the past and changing old habits. You may have been feeling that there are many areas of your present life-style in which you have been getting into too much of a rut. Now is the time to set out in new directions. People whom you have only recently met may be a source of inspiration. Their ideas could cause you to think along different lines entirely. You will find that the company of younger people is especially stimulating. Aries should make an extra effort to rise above petty emotional considerations. They should strive to view their lives in a much broader and more adventurous perspective. Strike out on unknown paths.

8. FRIDAY. Useful. There will be plenty of driving force running through you today. Break with the past. There may be one or two people who you continue to see fairly regularly. But since they bore the life out of you, why continue? You will be doing yourself, as well as them, a favor if you allow these relationships to slip silently into the past. This is a time for getting your personal life in better order. It is about time that you do what pleases you and not what you think will satisfy everyone else. This is not a question of being selfish. It is, plain and simple, just being realistic. It will be favorable for entertaining influential people at home. Don't stand for any nonsense from difficult people.

9. SATURDAY. Useful. You will end this week feeling that you have certainly achieved something. This is more likely, though, to be in the personal area of your life. This is a useful day for looking at your present financial situation in its totality. It might be a good idea to channel some of your money from your current account into a Certificate of Deposit. There it would earn you more interest and you would not be tempted by its accessibility. This would also help you as you will have to cut back on needless expenditures. Get in touch with friends and make arrangements for socializing this evening. The poor health of people at or from distances could be a cause for concern.

10. SUNDAY. Sensitive. This will certainly not be a particularly exciting day. But you will be more in tune than usual with your surroundings and with those people who are close to you. Relax and unwind; take your mind right off your problems. It is an important day for Aries who have been working away from home all week. Do all you can to rebuild the relationship that exists between you and your mate or partner. People will be more understanding than usual, and you will find them more easily understood. Since thinking about your career prospects can be confused, postpone any important advance planning you have been mulling over. Concentrate today on anything but work. Rest up.

11. MONDAY. Disturbing.   All forms of speculation should be ruled out. This will be an extremely difficult day for anyone who attempts to earn their living that way. Relying on tips and information that comes from insiders will prove useless. Conditions will make it very hazardous for operating from behind the scenes. Be very careful about who you place your confidence in. Do not pass on secrets that you promised you would not divulge to anyone. People may be trying to force the hand of the Aries-born. They could be trying to get them to take on additional responsibilities before they are ready to do so. You may be thinking a lot about some nice event you enjoyed over the weekend.

12. TUESDAY. Deceptive.   Aries people can be led astray by will-o'-the-wisps. Thinking must be kept practical and down-to-earth. The more that you can rely on regular ways to earn a living, the better it will suit you. Too much sentimentality and nostalgia may make you fail to appreciate just what is happening at the present. You need to look at new acquaintances with fresh eyes. Perhaps you have been reading more into situations than you should have. This is a good day for buying furniture and other articles for the home. There may be some good summer sales going on. Be sure to check out more than one store so you can get comparative prices. Why pay more than necessary?

13. WEDNESDAY. Good.   This midweek day should find you in a much better position to take important action. The recent in-depth thinking that you have been doing might not have come up with all the answers to your present problems. But at least you should be more aware of what your priorities are. What is even more important is to decide how to go about achieving them. More time can also be spent at home. You will be drawn closer to your family, especially your mate or partner. Efforts to close outstanding affairs will be more successful. It will enable you to leave the decks clear for a new bout of activity. That would help ensure its success because you can devote full time to the new project.

14. THURSDAY. Successful.   This is likely to be the first day for a long time that that Aries people will feel really confident of themselves. They will be eager and prepared to take the initiative in affairs of major importance. People will be interested in your ideas for streamlining the way current routine jobs are dealt with. You will be talking with the confidence of a person who is sure of the facts. They can tell that you are also sure of which direction they wish you to aim in. It will be good for concentrating efforts to turn hobbies into major sources of income. It will also be favorable for sports, especially of the more energetic kind. But take it easy if you are out of practice.

15. FRIDAY. Important. This will be still another excellent day. You really must do all you can to take full advantage of the opportunities that exist for you at this time. It will also be a favorable day for combining business with pleasure. Get in touch with influential people with whom you would like to have meetings as early in the day as possible. It might be a good idea to suggest a short lunch break, or a special kind of dinner. This could well be the incentive needed to get someone to talk over important issues with you. People will tend to respond to friendliness in the same spirit. It's an auspicious day for serious romance. A casual affair can deepen into something more serious and meaningful.

16. SATURDAY. Mixed. Today will be favored for setting off on a vacation. If you have the opportunity, try to be away for the weekend, at least. It would do you a lot of good to have a complete change of environment. You seem to have done fairly well over the past two or three days. You should now give your mind and your body the rest and relaxation that they require. You must not overexert yourself. It may be that you cannot get away just now. But you could enjoy putting the finishing touches to holiday plans that you wish to fulfill this summer. It will also be a good day for study and academic endeavors. Leave lots of time for including recreational pursuits. Don't become a stick-in-the-mud.

17. SUNDAY. Variable. Come up with some bright new ideas for ways to improve your general health. Perhaps you could embark on a diet that will help you to get into better shape. Or it may be that you will decide that you require more exercise to tone up your body. Whatever it is that you decide to do, you must be careful that you do not overstrain yourself. There will be a good opportunity for discussing important domestic issues with other members of the family. This will be especially important if it is your hope to make some cuts in expenditures this week. But your thoughts about romance may be rather confused. Continuing in a confused state won't solve anything.

18. MONDAY. Mixed. Monday morning blues can usually make this a painful day. Those of you who were hoping to get some exciting new project launched may be in for a great letdown.

You may not feel quite so confident about your plans in the cold light of day. Gossiping with co-workers may be the only way that you can think of to relieve your boredom. Aries should try to get something special done which they can show to superiors at the end of the day! Any kind of work that you can attend to in your spare time is recommended. Gather information on new insurance or investment schemes. If you take the time and trouble you could probably find some worthwhile investments.

19. TUESDAY. Mixed. You should be feeling especially cheerful and healthy. The results of any recent vigorous exercise course or diet that you have recently embarked upon should be paying dividends now. Keep up the good work. As long as you exercise self-discipline, you should be fairly well pleased with your progress today. You will probably find that you have to give more time to routine matters than to spectacular ways of increasing your income. But you are not likely to be defeated by feelings of frustration. Just be alive to the possibility of accidents and take all necessary precautions. Obey all safety instructions. One silly shortcut could wreak havoc with your life.

20. WEDNESDAY. Variable. Efforts to promote teamwork can be spoiled by basic misunderstandings. An absence of a common goal can lead to wasted time and money. Some readers may have been thinking of joining forces with a friend to write a play or compose a song. Then they may discover that all their enthusiasm for such a project was unjustified. A clash of personalities could reveal graphically that you are better working alone. This is not a day for signing legal documents or binding contracts. But later on in the day will be good for marital and romantic affairs. So that would be a good area to which you should devote time. Otherwise, you will be running in place.

21. THURSDAY. Sensitive. Older people will be more willing to share the wealth of their experience and of their greater understanding. Younger Aries readers will be well advised to seek the advice of older relatives and friends. They will discover that there is plenty of common sense in what they have to say. Partnership affairs and problems will not be such a headache for you. The gentle approach is invariably the best one. You will probably have to discuss some fairly sensitive subjects with other members of the family. Colleagues may make some solid progress in furthering distant business affairs. Influential people can be stubborn and unhelpful but it may be just a passing fit of pique.

22. FRIDAY. Fair. Joint financial affairs can become critical unless some dramatic action is taken. You must make sure that you do all in your power to keep enough cash on hand. There are large, regular bills, like insurance and income tax to meet. If you find that you have been living above your means, you are going to have to make some pretty big cuts. Some of them are bound to hurt and could lead to arguments. But you must stick to what you know to be right in the long run. Hunches may prove to be correct. Superiors will be helpful and may pay long-overdue bonuses or even raises. But be sure that your classification keeps up with your increases.

23. SATURDAY. Good. There seem to have been some strange happenings going on this week. This is a better day for Aries readers who are able to work on their own. It is not so great for those of you who have to promote team effort in order to earn your way. Research work will prove to be fascinating. Those Aries-born who can work from their home base should get all the peace and privacy that they require. They will need both in order to carry out their experiments. It will be a good time for signing property or investment contracts. It will also be good for visiting family members, especially parents, or even for receiving visits from them.

24. SUNDAY. Variable. Minor misunderstandings or distractions can prevent the Aries-born from his or her preferred activities. He or she would like to devote as much time as possible to the more important aspects of their life. You may feel that you are too bogged down in dealing with matters of minor importance. Loved ones will be rather demanding. You might not have the opportunity to spend your spare time as you would really like to do. Study, or reading for pleasure may have to be given up due to your inability to concentrate. It might be a good idea to take off for the beach or the countryside. Only in that way will you be able to get away from it all! That, in itself, would be a good move.

25. MONDAY. Quiet. This will be a pleasant and an easygoing sort of a day. Those Aries readers who had a lot to cope with over the weekend should now be able to get ahead with neglected chores. This is definitely a better time for dealing with hobbies that you can handle on your own. You can also do so in your own time. This should be a good period for drawing up plans for future business activities. But conditions in general will be too slow for making any new moves now. Distant travel may provide a welcome change for Aries. They may feel they have not been getting out and about enough. Whether you travel for business or pleasure, you should allow time for sightseeing and leisure.

26. TUESDAY. Disturbing. Health is likely to be something of a problem for you. It may not necessarily be your own well-being that is giving you cause for concern. If not, it will be that of a dear friend or relative. You may have to alter your plans in order to allow for a visit to your local doctor or the hospital. Academic pursuits can lead to a sudden breakthrough. You should feel more confident than before if you are going to be taking an important examination fairly soon. Aries business people must take steps to ensure that their emotions do not get the better of them. You must concern yourself only with your best interests.

27. WEDNESDAY. Sensitive. It is just as well that you do not have too much on the agenda today. You simply will not be able to cope with any mammoth tasks. Aries must be particularly careful that they do not overdo physically. This is a helpful period for keeping on top of your routine. It will also be good for catching up with neglected odd jobs. It will be easier than usual to concentrate on intricate details. But the day is not forceful enough to warrant making any new starts. Take a more relaxed view to your work. It does not necessarily follow that the more effort put in, the better or more lasting the results. Somehow, the formula does not pan out quite that easily.

28. THURSDAY. Mixed. Aries may have to perform errands for family and household members. You may become a little peeved because you will feel that your loved ones are taking you for granted. Don't be too quick to voice your opinions on this matter, though. A special surprise treat may be planned for you for later in the day. You may even have to take time off from work. You will probably not be too worried about this, however. The progress of your current business negotiations do not seem to be bringing you the results you had been hoping for. This could be the result of a general business slump. If so, time will no doubt be the factor that will change conditions.

29. FRIDAY. Variable. Friends can provide you with just the sort of energetic help and support that you require. In fact, you may be inspired by the efforts of your close associates. It would be a good idea to check over the starts you have recently made, but gave up. They were all related to creative projects. It may well be that you threw the towel in too soon. On reexamination, you might discover that you could make a few little adaptations. Your projects could then be turned into the money-makers you had first believed they were. But influential people should not be approached with such untried proposals just yet. If they prove unsuccessful, such people will be angry.

30. SATURDAY. Sensitive. Group and club activities will be stimulating. You should find that discussions with friends are not only interesting but also informative. They will enable you to improve your knowledge of subjects that you did not know very much at all about. This should be an excellent time for making progress with hobbies and similar pastimes. Aries will be thinking more seriously about profound, philosophical matters. But just be wary about being too frank and honest with casual acquaintances. Some people will take offense at what they consider to be rudeness and lack of tact. Withhold your comments and observations until you are sure you can trust your listeners.

31. SUNDAY. Uneventful. The month comes to an end and the week begins on a quiet note. This will be a pleasant, if rather lackluster day. Make this a typical family-type day. There seems to be little point in taking your search for pleasure to far-flung places. The best bet for you is to stay in your immediate vicinity. That will allow for more time to be meaningfully spent in privacy and seclusion. You must try to balance your natural outgoing tendencies with some introspection and self-evaluation. The results of this can help to make future activities more effective and enduring. All times are good for learning from the lessons of the past so that at least some of your errors can be avoided in the future.

AUGUST

1. MONDAY. Variable. You may awaken in something of a panic. The explanation may be that you had a restless night. Perhaps you found that a dream was rather disturbing? It might have rekindled memories that have been dead and buried long ago. It will not be easy to get into your stride first thing. You must not allow your thinking to become morbid. Try to look on the bright side of things. The future is not likely to be as bleak as some Aries frequently believe. The day should be good for the Aries-born who are in public relations. You should be able to get your advertising campaigns off the ground. New contacts can supply information that will be helpful to personal affairs. Take note.

2. TUESDAY. Sensitive. Make a concentrated effort to get official approval for a speculative enterprise. You have been eager to get this launched for some considerable time. You should find that influential people are much more sympathetic than usual to your aims and your ambitions. This is a good day for trying harder to bring some of your long-term aims and objectives to fruition. This is also the right day to contact teachers to discuss your children's progress at school. Loved ones will be rather inhibited and may not be able to communicate their feelings very freely to you. Put them at their ease and then let them tell you in their own way what is bothering them.

3. WEDNESDAY. Deceptive. The more you can work on your own, the better you will do today. There will be very little action taking place. Do not place too much reliance on the promises of your close associates. Team effort is likely to come to a full stop because others are not pulling their weight. Study and self-improvement programs can give Aries valuable new experience and know-how. Those of you who can operate from their home base will not have too many interruptions to cope with. Be careful that you do not put your foot in it when discussing the future with influential people. Show greater tact and diplomacy. Romance continues to be unsettled.

4. THURSDAY. Disturbing. Problems that arise today will not be easy to solve. You will not be able to take any shortcuts with work that requires great attention to detail. This would be a good day for starting new savings plans, though. You really must try to put more money to one side to meet bills that will be coming due toward the latter end of the month. Bankers and accountants must be watched carefully. They may be inefficient and uninterested when dealing with the personal financial affairs of the so-called little man. They do not intend to be this way. It is simply that they are used to dealing on a grand scale.

5. FRIDAY. Quiet. It is very unlikely that there will be any particularly difficult problems for you to cope with today. This is an easygoing period. If you are planning to take your summer vacation soon you will have the opportunity to make the final arrangements. If you are going abroad, make sure that hotel reservations have been confirmed. You may have to rent a car or get a rail pass, so you should make such arrangements ahead of time.

Check, too, that your passport and visas are up to date and valid. Loved ones will be easier to get along with. There will be a more relaxed atmosphere within the home than there has been recently. This should be a good time for investing in antiques or other valuable objects.

6. SATURDAY. Important.   The week will end on a buoyant note. This would appear to be a day on which you can make an important breakthrough in your career. You will soon find that your relationship with your boss will have improved greatly. Influential people will show greater appreciation not only for what you have been trying to achieve but also for what you have. It will be fine for getting out and about more. Other people can be helpful to the furtherance of your personal plans. Your vitality should be at a high level. The Aries-born person must do everything possible to channel energy into the most constructive activities.

7. SUNDAY. Changeable.   Writing and other creative endeavors can be taken up anew with refreshed perspective. You enjoy these hobbies and other diversions, and they take your mind off dull, workaday problems. Put them out of your mind and relax. Loved ones will be fun and easy to get along with. You are likely to find that recent pressures have been eased somewhat. These had been weighing heavily on you. This will be a good day for getting to know younger children better. Take offspring and their friends on a trip or some kind of outing. This will also be a good day for visiting other relatives like parents, especially if you have not seen them for some time. Neighbors can be something of a nuisance. They want to borrow everything from sugar to tools.

8. MONDAY. Deceptive.   Move forward today with a good deal of caution. Make sure that your associates have a clear understanding of what you are attempting to achieve at your work place. Demonstrate how team work can benefit all concerned. False assumptions can only lead to misunderstandings. You will have more success, when dealing with the members of your family, if you appeal to their emotions. You are trying to persuade them to go along with you in trying to make extra savings. Watch out for deception on the part of your business competitors. They will be prepared to use undercover and subtle methods in order to get the upper hand. Their motto is probably no-holds-barred.

9. TUESDAY. Rewarding.   This should be a happy day for seeing friends or relatives. You have not had an opportunity to talk to any of these people for ages. But if it's impossible to see them, you could surely get in touch with them by telephone or by writing. Don't let it slide or you will find yourself out of touch permanently. You may come across a long-lost address you had been searching for. So it does pay to clean out your desk or sort through old correspondence. This could be a happy day for cementing relationships with children. Trips or outings will bring you closer together. You may discover a hobby you can share with a child.

10. WEDNESDAY. Quiet. Slow down a bit today. You seem to have been pushing yourself fairly hard lately. You may not be feeling the strain yet, but it is probably mounting. You have been living off your nerves in a state of constant tension for some time. Start by checking out your health. If you're overweight, find a good diet and stick with it. If you do not get enough exercise on your own, enroll in a course of keep-fit exercise on a regular basis. You will feel and look a lot better. You can probably finish up your business affairs somewhat earlier this month. Then you can make a point of getting extra rest and some form of relaxation that you enjoy. Take up your favorite hobby again.

11. THURSDAY. Satisfactory. There will be some extra, unexpected expenses you will find you have to shell out for. Children's affairs are a likely cause, requiring the Aries parent to dig deeper into his pocket. It may be that there are school fees to be paid for in advance, or you may have to buy clothes for the coming school year. All of this will prevent your being as successful as you had hoped with your new savings plan. It's possible that you will reap good profits from speculative ventures, but those would probably qualify for heavy taxation. For those of you who are involved in the world of entertainment, such as the theater, today should be a favorable one.

12. FRIDAY. Fortunate. If you are still involved in making plans for a vacation, now is the time to wrap them up. Summer tends to come to a close after Labor Day, at least where school children are concerned. Also, if you are thinking of some kind of Christmas vacation, it's not too early to start planning. Reservations for air travel will be tight and you might find that affordable hotels are already heavily booked. If you postpone acting now, you could be in for a great disappointment later on. You may have decided to take on some academic courses this Fall in an attempt to improve your chances for promotion. Be sure to check these out during the month because the good ones fill up quickly.

13. SATURDAY. Variable. Restlessness will be quite a problem for you today. Aries-born people will find it extremely difficult to remain calm and settled for more than a brief time. You should try to live more for the moment. The ideas that friends dream up for pleasure and entertainment may seem pretty tame to you. But it will be hard for you to come up with anything better. Unless, of course, you are planning to be very reckless with your money. Too much pointless running around will not lead to anything, however, and will only leave you physically exhausted. Commitments and responsibilities to loved ones should not be neglected. You may get so involved with your own personal worries that you tend to overlook these.

14. SUNDAY. Routine. There are not likely to be any special or favorable developments today. This could just become a typical family-type day. There won't seem to be a great deal going on socially to entice you to travel very far afield. But it could be a good day for catching up with routine chores and activities. Tidying up around the home and garden could do a lot for your morale and sense of accomplishment. Pay up on bills that have been outstanding for some time. Try not to keep small shopkeepers and businesses waiting for payment. You could easily get the reputation for being a bad debt. And if you live in a small community, the word would get around quickly.

15. MONDAY. Difficult. This will not be an easy start to the working week. People at your place of employment may seem cold and unfriendly. The atmosphere at the office or store will not be very conducive to making new starts. This, of course, will come as something of a disappointment to you. You will have to work alone if you want to achieve anything of value. Sudden enforced changes of routine may make Aries workers short-tempered, as well. Overtime can leave you exhausted and irritable. Work done under pressure is not likely to be of an especially good quality. Loved ones can be touchy and difficult to please. You will have to grin and bear it, and hope for a better day.

16. TUESDAY. Tricky. Legal matters may not be quite as straightforward as they seem. When dealing with the authorities, you may find yourself answering endless questions. You may then have to answer more, put to you by another person. There will be endless red tape, and then, perhaps, an unsatisfactory outcome. You may find yourself unable to get as much done at your regular job as you would like. But that will be due to circumstances beyond your control. Documents and contracts may contain hidden loopholes. Make sure that you have them checked over by a professional expert in the appropriate field before you sign on the dotted line. Otherwise, you could lose a lot of money.

17. WEDNESDAY. Excellent. This will surely be one of the most successful days you have experienced for ages. And if tomorrow fulfills its promise, you should concentrate on career matters. You can do a great deal to make a good impression on your boss, and should lose no time in doing so. This might mean the difference between remaining in whatever is your current position or winning a much longed-for promotion. The earlier part of the day should be used for lending a helping hand to your partner or spouse. By showing greater interest in their activities, as well as in them, you will earn their gratitude. And they will undoubtedly respond in kind when an opportunity arises. Later, join with your associates in business for some kind of sport.

18. THURSDAY. Important. Discuss your creative enterprises with the people who are in a position to help you get them launched. Any financial help you get is likely to come from fairly unlikely sources. You may learn that some influential person is a great admirer of yours. This will certainly be something you had never before realized. Official support can be won for speculative or risky ventures, much to your surprise. You had not expected this to come through quite so soon. Government and Customs officials will be more helpful than usual with your distant business affairs. Later on, during discussions with a group of friends, the thinking can reach great intellectual depths.

19. FRIDAY. Variable. This will be a day favorable for furthering transactions with large business corporations. You should be able to move another step closer to clinching a very important deal. You will find that you tend to get on extremely well with people who are very much older than yourself. This applies, also, to those very much younger. While it is true that existing ventures can be kept moving forward, the impetus for getting new projects started is likely to be missing. It may be that your immediate boss is the one responsible for this setback. Loved ones will tend to be quarrelsome. You will probably find yourself wanting to keep on the move this evening. You seem restless and somewhat ill at ease.

20. SATURDAY. Disturbing. The week ending will come to a close on something of a sour note. By midweek, it had reached a truly promising peak. So you will be doubly disappointed that you were not able to improve your career prospects even further. Superiors and other influential heads may not agree with results of the investigations that have been conducted recently by Aries people. It does not seem to matter that the results appeared to be conclusive. But Aries-born have a tendency to pretend they know more about some subjects, like philosophy or religion, than they really do. This pretense can be a real drawback at times, and may even have a negative effect on a promotion.

21. SUNDAY. Variable. Try to put your free time to good use on this so-called day of rest. If your desk has become cluttered with miscellaneous bills, ads and letters, you could straighten them out. And if you have unanswered letters, there would probably be enough time to write a few. If you don't keep up with friends in faraway places, both their interest and yours will gradually diminish. And in time, you would undoubtedly lose touch altogether. It's a day when you could also turn to academic pursuits and study. Reading stimulates the mind and might even result in your taking some practical action. Either the morning or afternoon would be favorable for local travel. You might want to go to a beach or take children to a playground.

22. MONDAY. Changeable. Aries should understand that anxiety about the future is pointless. Negative thinking is not only non-productive but it is also harmful. Worrying about situations that you are powerless to alter is ridiculous. Nor should you try to exert influence over someone who lives far from you, perhaps abroad. Even if he or she is a relative, save yourself trouble. There is enough for you to straighten out close to home that has a direct effect on you and your loved ones. If you can do something worthwhile to change some petty rule, concentrate your efforts on that. You may have a sudden idea on how to solve a problem that has baffled you.

23. TUESDAY. Deceptive. Do not place any reliance on promises made to you during social affairs. You may later find out that the person who made the promises is given to talking through his hat. Certainly do not give up a good job on the basis that a new and more exciting one will be available to you very soon. You must be extremely cautious about all such matters connected with your career. Otherwise, you could lose out badly. The Aries-born are sometimes great dreamers. Their wishful thinking is apt to lead them astray, away from the reality of their actual circumstances. Don't fall into the trap of locking yourself away in an ivory tower. It could prove disastrous. Romance can also be confusing today.

24. WEDNESDAY. Challenging. Get-up-and-at-'em early to-day. There will be lots of good opportunities out there today. But you will have to push yourself hard if you hope to make the most of them. Your eagerness to get ahead will not go unnoticed by your boss. Influential superiors will be inclined to help you as much as they can. They do believe in rewarding determination and a positive attitude toward your job. The Aries-born can earn a good reputation for efficiency and adaptability in the face of ever-changing situations. This will be a plus on your record. Now is the time to collect information on various diets and keep-fit exercise courses. You may find exactly the one you want.

25. THURSDAY. Productive. Friends can be lucky for the Ram today. This is an important time for socializing with influential friends. These are people with whom you have always found yourself to be on a very similar wavelength in the past. Creative work looks especially promising. You should be able to make more of your natural talents than you have in the past. Perhaps you will be able to convert what has always been thought of as a hobby into an ongoing, paying proposition. This should be a fortunate day for signing business financial agreements and entering into a new stage of negotiations. More effort and perseverance can lead to the realization that secret hopes and dreams can come true.

26. FRIDAY. Important. This is an important day. You should make a dedicated attempt to place business financial affairs on a more secure and solid foundation. Try to get your finances straightened out. It will be good for meetings with accountants to go over all your income tax problems. This is a good time for becoming a member of societies whose main interest is philosophy, religion, astrology or related subjects. This should be a propitious time for contacting friends who live at a distance. You might be able to arrange a meeting with them in the not-too-distant future. This should make you especially happy as it seems that you have not heard of them for a long while.

27. SATURDAY. Disappointing. Today will see the end of a rather disappointing week. The Aries-born may have had high hopes of getting the opportunity to clinch a lucrative business deal. The possibilities of such are now likely to be ruled out after you hear from an influential person. Someone whom you had thought you could always trust may go back on his or her word. Too much preoccupation with the past may lead to missed opportunities here and now. You may find that you are not able to get through with all the jobs you had planned to do, due to reasons of health. If you wish to win the confidence of others, tact and diplomacy will be key factors. Acting aggressive is often self-defeating.

28. SUNDAY. Unsettling. Health will require special care and protection today. You may have started out feeling under the weather. It is important for you to do all in your power to get yourself back into shape. You certainly do not want to be laid off at work. As usual, there is likely to be a particularly heavy workload in the coming week, due to the fact the month is coming to an end. You want to be sure you can pull your weight when the going gets tough. It may be that you are especially susceptible to summer colds or allergies. Keeping in constant touch with relatives or close friends may be difficult at this time. Somehow, you may have offended someone and are finding it difficult to restore rapport.

29. MONDAY. Mixed. The good news that you have been eagerly expecting may come today via the mail. It may just be tickets for a pop concert or a sporting event, but they're hard to come by. But better still, it may be from a loved one who has been out of sight, but not out of mind, for some time. Casual acquaintances will be more willing than usual to go along with your plans. You should make good headway today with routine desk jobs. It would be a smart move, too, to get your correspondence up to date. Advertising campaigns may well bring in especially favorable results. But do not overdo it. The results could backfire if you try too hard and consequently get people's ire up by promising too much.

30. TUESDAY. Sensitive. Aries and their loved ones may find themselves at cross-purposes today. What might start out as mere discussions over money could become serious arguments. You and your mate or partner may not be able to agree on where spending cuts should be made. In connection with your career, this will be an auspicious time for making long-term plans. Travel can be helpful to business affairs. By so doing, you could clinch a good business deal you might otherwise not have won. Face-to-face meetings far outweigh what can be done by telephone or letter. Your superiors at work can be especially understanding today. They are more likely than usual to recognize your abilities and potential.

31. WEDNESDAY. Satisfactory. Your bright ideas can turn out to be financially viable. You may win the support of someone who has the money and is willing to back you. You need this before you can get your projects going. It is important for you to do a bit of hustling today, though. You are not likely to make any real gains by sitting back and playing a waiting game. Fortune does not simply knock upon doors. This will be an excellent time for fund-raising activities. Not only will you help those less fortunate than yourself but you will gain a great deal of satisfaction from doing so. Tax and insurance matters should be brought up to date. Accountants may fail in following instructions.

SEPTEMBER

1. THURSDAY. Challenging. Start this month off as you mean to finish it! Set your goals and priorities and don't lose sight of either. It is important that you make a special effort to increase your earnings. That is because it is likely that there will be additional bills coming in for heavier household spending. There may be school-related bills as well as fuel and higher food bills. This is a good time to undertake redecorating programs. You can save money by becoming a do-it-yourselfer insofar as possible. If you can improve and brighten up your home, you will add value to your biggest asset. Young adults may want to bring their romantic companion home to meet the family. Love life looks promising.

2. FRIDAY. Changeable. This will be an important day for those who want to set up in business with close acquaintances. Partnership agreements can be negotiated with considerable success. You will undoubtedly feel very excited at the prospect of making a lot of money within a short time. But you must be careful that you do not overlook any important details of management or cash flow in your haste to make a profit. This will be a good day for those who wish to gain inside information from colleagues at your work place. You have established a good rapport for those in the higher echelons of the management team. Your superiors may ask you to stay on for a time after regular hours. Bonus payments might result if you do.

3. SATURDAY. Rewarding. You should have no difficulty in meeting whatever challenges come your way today. You have plenty of energy, some to spare. In fact, you enjoy yourself when you are forced to do your utmost just to keep ahead of the game. It's like being tested and having to prove yourself. It would seem that you are out-stripping all opposition and are putting yourself in line for a promotion. That would also entail an increase in salary, at the precise time of year when it would be most beneficial. Telephone calls and/or correspondence can be just as effective today as face-to-face meetings. This will save you having to make any trips during the weekend. It will be a fortunate day for romance; marriage proposals will be acceptable.

4. SUNDAY. Inactive. This will probably be an easygoing kind of day. It is unlikely that you will find new problems cropping up. Try to get some rest and relaxation, forgetting your business troubles. You seem to have been pushing yourself quite hard of late. You and your mate or partner will probably enjoy some sort of quiet and intimate entertainment more than any kind of a crowded scene. Big, social parties mean co-mingling with large groups, probably out for boisterous fun. It might be fun to visit a special place you haunted in your childhood. If the weather is warm and clear, it would be ideal for a beach picnic or a visit to a park. Whatever you do, try to keep it simple and uncomplicated, requiring as few decisions as possible.

5. MONDAY. Mixed. The morning is favorable for putting property on the market. You may have been contemplating putting a business up for sale or even your own home. If so, you should get a very favorable response. Real estate transactions should go through without a hitch. The help of professional people will be invaluable if you need it. You may be having difficulty with a legal document like a contract or lease. Just make sure that you are not too rigid or grasping in enforcing your requirements and price. They could necessarily restrict or even negate the possibilities of a sale. That would defeat your purpose, as well as waste your time. Those who helped you might not do so again.

6. TUESDAY. Good. Employers may allow or even encourage the Ram to do more work from home. This will suit you, especially in the mornings. It will give you a chance to catch up with chores on the home front. You will also be able to do errands you were unable to do last weekend. The business arrangement may not last for long, but you can make use of it while it does. The work load will be the determining factor. Today should begin and end on a calm and uneventful note. It should be good for making plans for any parties or other entertaining you expect to do in your home. Romantic partners will be more inclined to go along with whatever you have planned in the way of entertainment. All in all, you have nothing to complain about today.

7. WEDNESDAY. Mixed. Take the lead if and when you are attempting to launch new creative ventures. Your ideas for making money from your artistic proposals should be right on target. You are sure to make a good impression on certain influential people. They may be ready to give you some financial backing, even though this may be limited. Aries artists and entertainers, among you, can afford to bid higher for their services, provided they have had experience. Make certain that your agent, or whoever else represents you, does not sell you short. This will be a favorable day for establishing closer rapport with your loved ones. But it might be wise to steer clear of sensitive subjects on the home front.

8. THURSDAY. Easygoing. Take advantage of the peaceful conditions existing now to push ahead with all routine matters. Catch up with any odd jobs that may have been piling up. If you can spare the time, get a headstart with household shopping chores. It could save you a lot of time later on when the shops get busy. It will also be a good time for associating with children. Their company can often help you place things in their true perspective. Don't neglect your hobbies and other interests that give you special satisfaction when you have spare time. Aries people must not allow their work to dominate their lives. It is important to allow time for pleasure and recreation.

9. FRIDAY. Worrisome. Aries may have little inclination today to take work seriously. This is regrettable because your competitors surely will! You could lose a lot of the respect that has been building up for you on the part of your superiors. You really must try to concentrate and show your usual enthusiasm for your work. Routine may be a bore, but the alternative of not having any job would be considerably worse. Do not allow friends who have too much spare time on their hands to influence you. You could be held responsible for broken contacts or commitments unless you do the job you are supposed to do. Later in the day, you may find some bargains around the shops.

10. SATURDAY. Rewarding. You are motivated to exhibit an energetic push on the job on the last day of the week. All's well that ends well will apply to your performance. The routine jobs that seemed to be dragging on forever are suddenly completed in record time. Even your superiors may be surprised at the speed with which you will round things off. The results will be above reproach and your value to your employers proven beyond any doubt. One ever-present incentive is the wish to improve your economic security. Letting your work drag on and taking little interest are not the means to this end. The morning favors research of any kind. Your willingness to work overtime will win praise.

11. SUNDAY. Demanding. It would appear that this will be a rather upsetting day for Aries-born people. It may turn out that you will not be able to follow through with the plans you had made for seeking pleasure and entertainment. Friends, or even relatives, may let you down at the last moment. In fact, you could find yourself stranded, left high and dry, and alone. It might be the best solution to spend more time at home, attending to family affairs. Older relatives may require your attention, perhaps as a result of chronic ailments that have reappeared with a vengeance. But some recent past developments in employment affairs may contain hidden advantages of which the Ram is not yet aware.

12. MONDAY. Difficult. Today would not be good for making any business moves on sudden impulse. Some lucrative-sounding proposals may be offered to you by unreliable people. But through careful examination, you may quickly discover that these are not what they are trumped up to be. Spouses and other loved ones may give Aries the kind of emotional support that only they can provide. It should be favorable for entering into new partnership associations. This, of course, is contingent on your having eliminated all areas of possible misunderstandings first. This will also be a happy and fortunate day for romance. You must take the iniative with regard to your love life unless you want it to stand still.

13. TUESDAY. Important. Leave no stone unturned when investigating the future potential of business partnerships. All options should be thoroughly explored as the promise for future development can be considerable. It is essential that you give as much time as you possibly can to career matters. You should be grateful that loved ones are showing complete understanding of what you are trying to achieve. You will be very pleased and flattered at the way your mate or partner sticks by you. This should be a favorable day for signing legal documents and also for obtaining information relevant to legal affairs. Romance must not be overlooked if you hope to continue good relationships. Go out of your way to show someone you love a token of your esteem.

14. WEDNESDAY. Inactive. You may be able to solve some problem that has been a nagging worry to you lately. You should plumb the depths to get to the bottom of whatever is the mystery. Friends and family members will be more helpful to you today.

Any information that you are provided with today is quite likely to be correct. You may find that influential people are pleased with your progress. Impress your boss by showing him that you are a live wire. Prove to whoever it is that you have the necessary strength and determination to stick to routine matters until they are completed. And not only that, but also that you have done the job satisfactorily. Check out any insurance policies you have. It may be time for their renewals.

15. THURSDAY. Satisfactory.   Any proceedings you may be involved in regarding inheritances or legacies can reach a critical stage today. Aries-born should try to be on tap so they will not risk missing something crucial. If that is not possible, you should be legally represented to protect your interests. It certainly should be someone you can trust to act on your behalf, as well as be familiar with the facts. Some creative work that you recently completed will win high praise for you. This might be one of your hobbies that you enjoy working on in your spare time. Romantic partners are likely to be especially compatible, and will gladly go along with your plans. It should be a happy evening, making arrangements for the future.

16. FRIDAY. Exciting.   This will be a real down-to-earth day for you. You will be eager to get going, champing at the bit. Excellent opportunities will be opening up and will make your adrenaline race. You seem to be on the threshold of achieving your ambitions and are feeling far more confident now about the future. This is a good time for older Aries to discuss retirement programs with the proper authorities at your work place. It's also a propitious day for gaining official clearance for business deals with large firms or corporations. The evening will be favorable for romance, with members of the opposite sex finding you extremely attractive.

17. SATURDAY. Mixed.   The Aries-born may find that in-laws or prospective ones may be offended by their behavior. They will often take offense at overly casual manners and customs. For the sake of your mate or partner, try to be on guard a bit against arousing the ire of such people. You must recognize that they have and live by a different set of values from your own. Keeping the peace is as important as doing your own thing. Lack of careful attention to details can render plans you had made for the future worthless. This could prove extremely frustrating, as well as be a complete waste of time. Be neat and careful when filing forms or dealing with legal matters.

18. SUNDAY. Upsetting. You will very probably awaken in a glum mood. Worse, it will be hard to put your finger on exactly what is bothering you. It could be that you are just tired and feeling the strain of the past week. You had some fairly rough days in a short period of time. Discuss the future with your beloved. This might help you to find your way out of a current impasse. But you will have to make a real effort to think in an optimistic vein, rather than anticipating the worst. Influential people will probably not be willing to release Aries from a binding contract. You will just have to work out some alternate plan for side-stepping this setback. Get to bed at a reasonable hour.

19. MONDAY. Difficult. This would be a good time to take a really long, hard look at some of your creative projects. Be more of a realist. Perhaps you have been spending too much money on ventures that will have little chance of winning approval from influential people. You had hoped to make some extra money, but you may only be blowing it away. It would probably be best to stop throwing good money after bad right now. You have to cut your losses quickly. Aries business persons could make some major miscalculations and these might then have an adverse effect on reputations. Smart operators are likely to discover that the Ram is easy prey.

20. TUESDAY. Tricky. Certain business transactions may well fall through, much to the delight of your competitors. You just do not seem able to make the right moves at this time. Try as you may, it will not be an easy matter to win the support of those people whose backing you need. Their help is essential if you are to succeed in making the progress you're aiming for. This is not the right time to sign important or binding documents. But do not lose heart if the odds appear stacked against you at the moment. Aries are advised not to initiate witch-hunts, however disgusted you may be with the corruption you see around you. Just take care to stay out of any entanglements with those responsible for it.

21. WEDNESDAY. Rewarding. You should be quite happy with the way events will turn out for you today. This will renew your good spirits after what has been a truly disappointing start to the week. A letter or telephone call you receive quite early will probably put you in a much better and happier frame of mind. Good news of a relative about whom you have been worried should set your mind at rest. It will be favorable for clearing up all routine matters early in the day. Aries could well be offered the pick of the jobs if they are first in at their place of employment.

Even though that may not be the case, getting in early is a smart move. It shows you are eager to work, and that's a start.

22. THURSDAY. Difficult. This is definitely not a day for speculation. In fact, you must be extremely careful with the way you handle money all around. Do not allow friends to tell you how to invest your money. If you feel you need advice, approach people who have excellent credentials and reputations in the field of finance. Loved ones may try making demands on you which you deem unfair to you. Do not go along with them just for the sake of peace. Handle irritable family members gently because they may be in a highly emotional state. Advice offered to you could be taken as personal criticism, but do not let it get under your skin. It would be better ignored than cause you distress.

23. FRIDAY. Disconcerting. To date, this does not seem to have been a very fortunate week for the Aries-born. With the exception of one bright spot in midweek, it has been mainly one, long uphill struggle. And this will be another day similar to those others. You will find it extremely difficult to pay attention to routine jobs. Those in authority will be demanding and not terribly forgiving. Nor are there likely to be many opportunities for increasing earnings at this time. You may be champing at the bit, but this is not the time to consider changing your job. You will have to keep a tight rein on your patience. People may make promises they have no intention of keeping.

24. SATURDAY. Inactive. You should take it easy today. It looks as though you may be feeling the strain of what you have been going through in the past few days. Do not take on any extra jobs or responsibilities. Slow down the tempo of your life, at least for a short time. Loved ones will be sympathetic and understanding, wanting to help you. The more time you can find to stay at home, the better it will be for you. If you feel up to it, the time is favorable for caring for the sick and helping the underprivileged. This evening should be a good time for getting in touch with old friends and/or acquaintances. You could entertain a small group in your home.

25. SUNDAY. Sensitive. You will have to fall back on your own resources today and make your own entertainment. It is not a good time, anyhow, to spend on business affairs or speculation. Attempts to get new projects off the ground are quite likely to be thwarted. Public officials may be at their most dogmatic worst. Do not get in touch with business associates whom you will be seeing in the coming week to discuss a work situation. Devote your thoughts and time on giving loved ones some sort of special treat. Pay more attention than usual to the needs and wishes of close members of your family.

26. MONDAY. Pleasant. This will be a good day for channeling your energy into mindful endeavors. You should be able to think more straightforwardly about the future now. Any work that you can carry out on your own, without relying on another's assistance, will be the most satisfying. You will also find it a great deal easier to concentrate for long spells at a time. Children and young people will respond to being treated with love and affection. Try to keep in close touch with members of the younger generation for whom you have some responsibility. Today is starred for Aries who make their living as artists or entertainers. Their theatrical abilities can win them appreciation and praise.

27. TUESDAY. Sensitive. Perhaps you feel you have not been having much fun during your leisure hours recently. You may now be feeling that you are missing out on the good things in life. It is pointless to try and force the issue, however. Do not waste your money on expensive pleasure and entertainment just to get away from the home environment. When you have to confront the authorities for one reason or another, you may feel that you are banging your head against a stone wall. You will feel annoyed with government officials today, as they seem to be making life particularly difficult for you. Unusually out-of-the-way business propositions can prove to be especially lucrative, much to your surprise.

28. WEDNESDAY. Important. This would be a useful day for looking after financial affairs. Check over your bank statements and your savings in other accounts to be sure interest is up to date. Pay any bills that are due now. Try to get a line on just how much cash you have on deposit, and how available it would be in an emergency. Your loved ones will be more reasonable about their spending. They are likely to show a greater willingness to go along with your ideas for increasing reserves. It should be possible to reach an agreement with those in authority on matters that have been a source of contention. You are likely to win legal disputes as judges can be especially tolerant and understanding.

29. THURSDAY. Good. Correspondence is favored as it can produce good results. If there is some special show you wish to see, a play, a concert or sporting event, you had better send for tickets now. If you wait until the last moment, you will probably be disappointed. Or, if you can get tickets, you will have to pay a premium price for your seats. The atmosphere at your work place will be friendly today. Associates will be willing to lend you a helping hand. They might even offer to replace Aries people who have some important personal plans to fulfill. Dealing with troublemakers and other difficult people today will prove more effective than usual. It will also be easier to handle them.

30. FRIDAY. Tricky. This can be a useful day for traveling around. Those who earn their living as salespeople, and work on a commission basis, should be able to increase their take-home pay considerably. Your charm and easygoing manner will make an excellent impression on those you are trying to win over. Shopping expeditions can be largely successful. You could find something you have been looking for over a long period of time. Loyal spouses or partners are apt to assume that Aries people know more than they actually do. As a result, embarrassing situations can develop, leaving in their wake resentment and disillusion. Do not attribute qualities to others that they may not possess.

OCTOBER

1. SATURDAY. Sensitive. If you feel that certain specific problems on your home front are getting you down, you might ask a trusted relative to come over and lend you a hand. If others have not offered to lend a helping hand before, it may be that they did not want to risk being accused of interference. You will be glad to know that parents and other family members are willing to help. It makes you more aware of the fact they have your best interests at heart. A short trip could be very effective in furthering partnership affairs and teamwork efforts. It will be a favorable day for Aries who are getting married or becoming engaged. More attention should be paid to existing in-laws.

2. SUNDAY. Upsetting. It will be difficult to get to the root of your problems. A family member may be hiding something from you, or may even attempt emotional blackmail. Do not allow yourself to be scared off or threatened into agreeing to any demands. Stand up for what you know is right. Feelings about the past may be misleading. Do not try to get in touch with an old flame just because you are hit by a wave of emotional memories. It would definitely be a bad idea to try to rekindle the spark that was extinguished a very long time ago. Memories play odd tricks and people tend to forget the heartaches, while recalling only the romance and good times.

3. MONDAY. Disquieting. This will be an unsettled day. There appear to have been many problems that you had hoped to straighten out over the weekend. But they seem to have been left hanging in midair. There will be an uneasy atmosphere at home for reasons unknown to you. So you will be quite pleased to get away from the domestic environment. Correspondence or telephone messages may go astray. Check to be sure that mail you posted some days ago has arrived safely. This is a time when you should leave nothing to chance. Bring old work up to date with the latest information and news that is available to you. This will involve research to make certain you have current information.

4. TUESDAY. Exciting. Expect this to be the best day of the month, so far. You will have more energy and drive than usual. You will now be able to throw yourself wholeheartedly into tasks that you have been staying away from. It will be favorable, too, for all artistic and creative work. Make the most of your natural talents. Show samples of your work to influential people for their approval. You are not likely to be disappointed with their reactions. You will be able to express your feelings and your ideas through the mediums of art or music. Results could be spectacular. This reaction should show you clearly that you should concentrate efforts on developing your talent.

5. WEDNESDAY. Easygoing. This will be a good period for quiet reflection. Review events of the past few weeks and try to determine where and why you made whatever mistakes you did. Only then can you take preventive measures against their repetition. Go over all accounts in detail. Find ways to cut back on unnecessary and wasteful spending. This will not be an important day from a money-making angle. You can still achieve a great deal, however, if you are prepared to deal with jobs that require a lot of attention to detail. Relax and take things easy in your leisure time. You may have become absorbed in a speculative proposition earlier on. But conditions are not favorable for taking action.

6. THURSDAY. Exciting. You will find yourself raring to go right from the start. The day will be favorable for distant travel.

You will enjoy yourself most if you can keep on the move. Romance will be uppermost in your mind. Love affairs are likely to take on a more serious overtone quite unexpectedly. The Ram may feel that now is the right time to consider making a close relationship permanent. Long-term, practical considerations point to marriage rather than keeping involvements on a purely casual basis. Your love of adventure and your curiosity could lead you to some interesting, unique places of entertainment. Be on guard against smart operators who may see you as an easy mark.

7. FRIDAY. Successful. You could find that routine affairs are not as boring today as they usually are. There may be more leeway to use your imagination and to be more original in the handling of your daily jobs. The atmosphere in your work environment will be pleasant and free of discord. This aura of pleasant relationships will be conducive to your giving free rein to natural talents. You can find new ways to streamline jobs that have begun to pall from tedium. You enjoy the challenge of this as well as the relief from boredom. This is a banner day for all work that calls for some degree of expertise and imagination.

8. SATURDAY. Productive. No particularly exciting or even difficult developments are likely to arise today. It will be unnecessary for you to take any important action as far as your career is concerned. It should be an opportune day for dropping in to visit with neighbors. But do not bother to travel very far out of your immediate vicinity. The results of any long trips you might take will probably be more than disappointing. Those who find themselves facing housework and such dull chores should try to catch up with them today. At least their completion will give you a sense of satisfaction. You can always make efforts to find ways to improve your health without going to extremes or taking a crash course in exercise.

9. SUNDAY. Demanding. Play it straight with loved ones right from the start. Aries people must be very careful about getting involved in secret love affairs. They could easily jeopardize everything that you have worked so hard to achieve. Pay more attention to the needs of your mate or partner. Youngsters will also require more than routine attention. Arguments may flare up within the home that will not be easy to resolve. You may feel that you are being pulled in two different directions at the moment. It will not be easy or satisfactory for you to cope. But harsh words can be quickly forgotten if forgiveness is asked and granted. Compromise is usually the key to fights and disagreements.

10. MONDAY. Fortunate. Start this working week as you mean to finish it. Go all-out to make a good impression on your boss. Now is the time to use all the energy at your disposal to persuade superiors to give your original ideas a fair hearing. Professional people who are experts can provide you with valuable legal advice. You may need it in regard to the drawing up of contracts. These could relate to a proposal you made some weeks ago. Today will be helpful for trying new approaches in teamwork and all co-operative endeavors. You should get the full support of your associates and superiors. Loved ones will be more understanding of the practical needs and basic requirements of Aries people. This will create harmony on the home front.

11. TUESDAY. Successful. Professional people and experts can provide valuable legal advice, if needed. Someone may be threatening to take you to court. It would be a good idea to check out just where you stand in this matter. You might find that you have nothing to fear. Those people may have been bluffing and talking so much hot air. It will be a favorable day for striking up partnerships with people at or from a distance. New starts that you embark on today are likely to turn out to be wholly successful. They could well bring you in handsome profits in the future. Discussions can be particularly valuable for clarifying difficult matters that have been unsettled for too long.

12. WEDNESDAY. Fair. A partnership's financial affairs may become critical if Aries allow their spending to get out of hand. You must try harder to keep control of the extravagant side of you nature. All will be well today, as long as you do not dip into savings to support pleasure-seeking. Don't allow so-called friends to sponge off you. Remember that you have worked hard for your money and you don't want to act foolishly now. It will be a good day for career affairs. Large companies and corporations will respond favorably to unusual and imaginative propositions. This positive sign will bring encouragement and relief to you.

13. THURSDAY. Easygoing. Self-employed Aries should find this a particularly pleasant and enjoyable day. You will not have to deal with a whole lot of jobs just to earn good money. Your services will probably be in great demand so that you will be able to pick and choose the kind of job you want. It will be an important day for the Ram who earns a living as a writer. Serious interruptions will be few and far between. All in all, this will not be a particularly active or demanding day. You can go over accounts and get caught up on any backlog of correspondence. Review recent spending. You may find ways you had not thought of for cutting costs. Confer with family members for their ideas.

14. FRIDAY. Mixed. Long journeys that you undertake today are unlikely to produce the results you wish. Trips made in an effort to improve business affairs will probably turn out to have been a complete waste of time. It would really be best for you to stick to your regular place of employment. The best way to gain information from people in other cities or towns is to write letters and to make more use of the telephone. The Aries person will find it hard to concentrate. He or she may also start to lose interest in studying and self-improvement programs. You should try to stay with such interests for your own sake. It will be a favorable day for deepening romantic ties.

15. SATURDAY. Special. This will be one of the best days that you have experienced in quite a few weeks. You will be in a much more optimistic frame of mind. Problems you have been fretting about will no longer get you down. Your approach now to difficult situations will be more dynamic. You should be able to find ways to boost your income to make up for any losses you have recently incurred. You will also find it possible to rise above any petty emotional and practical issues that have tended to cramp your style. Those of you who are prepared to paint on a broader canvas will find that this will be a banner day. Just make up your mind that you can do anything you really want to!

16. SUNDAY. Frustrating. The well-being of people who live at a distance from you is likely to be a cause of much concern. Someone for whom you care very deeply may be in some sort of trouble. This will tend to make the day extremely frustrating for you. You will feel powerless to do anything to help a friend whose interests and welfare you hold close to your heart. Various study courses you are taking seem to make quite unreasonable demands on the spare time of the Ram. You will find that concentration for very long periods is rather difficult. Impetuous or erratic actions can endanger good names. Think carefully before you speak unkindly about anyone. Are you in a position to know the facts?

17. MONDAY. Uncertain. It might be a little difficult to get into high gear early in the day. But by midafternoon, you should find that you have caught up with most of the jobs you had wished to handle. This would be a good time to do some background research into current business transactions. Find out exactly what has led up to the present stages. Rapport with your associates may not be particularly effective. It will be best to rely on yourself as much as possible now. Your associates appear to be vague and difficult to pin down. Misunderstandings can easily flare up. The Ram will not be above resorting to flattery and charm when the possibility of promotion or a pay hike arises.

18. TUESDAY. Upsetting. Influential people may decide or some business deal in favor of the opposition. This will cause you great disappointment. It looks as though your competitors have the upper hand over the Aries-born, at least for the time being. You will just have to bide your time and see what develops in coming weeks. There seems to be little you can do to change the minds of those who have some authority over you. Friends will easily be won over to your side by the infectious enthusiasm of the Ram. Their encouragement and support will go a long way toward restoring faith in yourself. Some conventional people may turn out to have surprisingly unconventional interests.

19. WEDNESDAY. Productive. It will be a good day fo getting on with important business matters. See what you can do to upgrade profits. Perhaps you have been getting into too much of a rut lately. You should be on the lookout to see how newer methods could be employed. You will find that superiors will be more amenable to your plans for change and progress. Valuable new agreements could be obtained. But bankers may not be willing to loan you sufficient funds to enable you to progress with your own projects. Influential people will not be as helpful as you may have thought they would be. Do not allow friends to try to influence you, even if they have your best interests at heart.

20. THURSDAY. Special. Influential people in good standing are likely to side with Aries in legal matters. You will be pleased to realize you can rely on the support of superiors. There seems to have been a problem that has been hanging over your head for some time. It concerns a matter that could take you into court. But you feel now that this contretemps could probably be settled privately, and at a lesser cost. It will be easier to concentrate on your work today. Interruptions will be few and far between. Friend and acquaintances may provide valuable contacts and introductions. It should be favorable for taking decisive action to assure th repayment of debts.

21. FRIDAY. Important. This should be an excellent day fo coming to grips with the kinds of jobs that stimulate you. They al low you the opportunity to give free rein to your natural, inbor talents. It will be better for working away from the public today. Close scrutiny by others can hamper your style. It is also favorable for appealing to the true emotions of superiors. You may be able to make an important breakthrough in your career. Opinions can easily be swayed with the correct logic. Your powers of persuasion will be at a high pitch which will carry great influence. Swearing associates to complete secrecy may be the best way to handle even the most routine of business matters.

22. SATURDAY. Worrisome. Aries people may be having misgivings about the future. Perhaps you are unsure about your prospects in staying on in your present employ. Superiors may have made promises about promotion that you do not feel sure they can or will fulfill. But it would be best for you to take your time before making any life-changing decisions. Your perspective may be out of whack today just because you are feeling down-in-the-mouth. Unexpected and promising developments may be just around the corner. Today would be good for tracking down people who are always virtually unavailable. Do not keep feelings of anger and resentment bottled up inside you at any time. They can get out of hand too quickly and you will suffer.

23. SUNDAY. Confusing. Young Aries-born people may grossly miscalculate the impression they make on others. If you are invited to some social affair where there will be many strangers, try to restrain your natural boisterousness. Don't be too pushy, either, especially with people older than yourself. Your sense of humor may not be appreciated as much as you like to think. Causing embarrassment for family and friends will hurt them and yourself. In the area of business matters, inaccurate appraisals of public opinion can result in a considerable amount of wasted time. But set aside a large portion of this day for some special entertainment. You should get away from anything connected with business and enjoy yourself.

24. MONDAY. Mixed. Don't hold back; get right into high gear. Make every effort to catch up with routine matters that were left over from last week, right at the start. Once you settle down into the regular routine, you should not find it too difficult to make fast progress. The Aries-born should now be able to assess business conditions reasonably far enough ahead to make long-term plans. On the other hand, superiors will be rather difficult. You may even feel that your boss is being obstructive and you will find it hard to figure out why. Those even higher up may impose severe restrictions with regard to absences and lateness. This would be a good period to try and do some serious reading, either for pleasure or a course you're taking. If it's for a course, find a quiet nook.

25. TUESDAY. Variable. A mixture of diplomacy and round-about methods can be the best way to make routine business dealings more lucrative. It will be a good time for having discussions with people behind the scenes. You may be able to find out some-how what your competitors intend to charge for their products in the future. If you succeed, you should then find a way to undercut those so that you will get more orders. This is a better day for the self-employed Ram than it is for those who have to take orders from above. Keeping your plans for future moves secret can be a major key to their success. Wrangling with partners over joint financial ventures is a pointless waste of time, money and energy.

26. WEDNESDAY. Fortunate. This should be a happy and en-joyable day. If you can work in more flexibility in handling routine work and normal business affairs, you will see increased earnings as a result. Do not limit yourself to the old ways of performing your work. It is also quite likely that changes will be forced upon you, and you should not try to block them. Monies earned by your spouse or other family members can help swell the financial cof-fers. Be sure that whatever savings accounts you have are earning the best possible interest. But you might have to go about recov-ering bad debts by the threat of legal action, or even by resorting to it. But try to avoid that if you possibly can.

27. THURSDAY. Quiet. This will be a useful day for pausing and assessing your personal affairs. You could try to get caught up with any backlog of correspondence, for instance. Keeping in touch with good friends is very important, especially if you are now separated by great distances. The telephone is another way of keeping in touch without having to resort to making a trip. And there are probably other areas of your life that require attention from time to time. There could be income tax matters, either a car registration or your driver's license to renew, and the inevitable bills to pay. Or you may just want to wander around the neighbor-hood and catch up on the gossip.

28. FRIDAY. Worrisome. Your spouse or loved ones may try to coerce you into taking on extra responsibilities and certain com-mitments. You will have to take a firm stand with the people who seem bent on throwing your money around. Arguments may de-velop, naturally, but you must take a stand and stick to your guns. You do not want to see your future security jeopardized for the want of determined action on your part. The quarrelsome behavior of romantic partners is probably only temporary. It may be due to simple fatigue or to ill-health. Disconcerting news may arrive from people who live at a distance later in the day. It might force you into taking an unexpected trip.

29. SATURDAY. Mixed. Some form of official permission that you have been waiting for might finally come through today. This may have to do with some household repairs that you cannot make without proper clearance because of building regulations. Or you may perhaps be adding onto an existing building. Whatever it is, you must adhere to building codes. You would be wise to seek professional help with the actual building which must be planned carefully down to the last detail. You don't want to find yourself spending more than is necessary for its construction. Romantic affairs can take on the state of a tug-of-war. Arguments and general friction may make the Aries-born doubt themselves.

30. SUNDAY. Sensitive. Aries and their mates or spouses may find themselves in bitter disputes over domestic and/or property affairs. The arguments not only will heat up but they will get you nowhere. The only way to take the wind out of your partner's sails is to stick to facts alone. Do not let yourself get drawn into a shouting match. It may be that the only way you can settle disputes is to declare a truce. Then, at least, you can get some rest and relaxation on this so-called day of rest. You may wish to give your favorite charity a helping hand by getting in touch with friends and persuading them to help out. Try to do something you cannot on work days, even if it's only a picnic or a long walk.

31. MONDAY. Important. Today will be a most fortunate ending to the month. Many of the worst problems that have been plaguing you, causing you sleepless nights frequently, can be resolved. You and your family will be able to come to decisions on the best ways to launch a new budget. This is an excellent time of year to try and increase your savings. The bills in winter are normally heavier than summer's, and there will be extra expenses over the holidays. Summon your inner resources of strength and determination. Help your associates to improve their work output. In doing so, you will doubtlessly improve your own. This will be a much happier day for romance than you have known for some time. Make the most of it and enjoy yourself.

NOVEMBER

1. TUESDAY. Manageable. Do not try to lay down the law with loved ones. If you try to be too bossy, serious fights could erupt within your home. Take a more relaxed form of live-and-let-live attitude toward your loved ones. You should be able to solve your own problems rather than attacking others. Using forcefulness will only produce even stronger opposition. It is not a day for taking speculative risks. If and when you have any money to spare, you should put it aside for use in paying bills. This should be a starred day for romance. It will also be lucky for engagement and marriage plans.

2. WEDNESDAY. Exciting. This will be an important day for you. Challenges should be met head-on. Aries people will have more confidence than usual and will be in the mood to take on exciting new ventures. Your superiors will be helpful and will encourage you to go further. Talk over vacation plans with loved ones later. You may be planning or hoping to go away over Christmas. If so, you had better start making some reservations. Resorts and transportation are extremely popular and in demand for holiday travelers. This is a good period for reaching a better understanding with your spouse or partner over the best way to handle children of mixed age groups.

3. THURSDAY. Mixed-up. An overly casual or disrespectful attitude at work could seriously jeopardize your relationship with your boss. Do not take people in authority for granted. Just because they may have been friendly toward you recently does not indicate that you are buddies. Be sure that you do not neglect your routine duties. No matter how dull they may seem, they must be completed. Dawdling and gossiping on the job will get you nowhere, fast. Aries people should keep in mind that any promises or commitments they make today must be lived up to at a later time. If you remember that, you may be less likely to go overboard when you commit to something.

4. FRIDAY. Difficult. A personal problem you had thought you solved is likely to come up again today. You may not be able to give the amount of time and attention to your work that you were hoping for. It will be quite difficult for you not to fall behind schedule. You might even have to work overtime to get it finished. Bankers or local officials may force Aries people into a difficult situation. Tensions and disagreements that have remained beneath the surface may come bubbling to a head. Alimony settlements could be particularly unfavorable. Some may be forced to pay out far more than they can afford.

5. SATURDAY. Mixed. It would be unrealistic to be pleased with the start made so far this month. It has not been easy for you to get along with other people. This is true both at home and at your place of employment. This will be a better day for dealing on your own with any jobs that arise unexpectedly. But you should guard against fatigue which can lead eventually to ill-health. Be alert to the danger of accidents, especially if you sometimes work in an unsafe area. Falls or a blow could lead to serious injury. But your partner or spouse will be helpful, cheerful and optimistic, without any complaints or nagging. This will brighten up your whole outlook.

6. SUNDAY. Enjoyable. This will be a pleasant and peaceful day for you and your immediate family. The more time that you can spend with them, the more likely you will be able to solve any irritating problems you have been unable to shake off during the week past. You might also try to make some hard and fast decisions about money. First, you want to increase savings meaningfully. It almost goes without saying that expenses will rise rapidly with the approach of several big holidays. You do not want to be caught short at such a crucial time. But take some time out just to relax and forget your troubles for a few hours.

7. MONDAY. Rewarding. Those Aries people who live alone may sometimes feel a bit lonely. They should actively seek others with interests similar to their own and share their knowledge. If you take a positive outlook on life you will get much more out of it. If you are someone whose career has suddenly come to a standstill, it will be very much up to you to alter the situation. The day will be favorable for all partnership ventures and transactions. Teamwork can assure lasting and lucrative results for deals it helped to get launched. Cooperative efforts usually pay off in the long run. Loved ones may come up with some sound, sensible ideas about the future.

8. TUESDAY. Good. This will be a first-class day. You should now be able to visualize the very real prospect of turning your hobby into an ongoing business concern. You have always tended to consider it as little more than a side interest. An influential person may take some special interest in your natural talents. You will feel encouraged to try some experimenting. Routine jobs will present no problems for you today. You are in the right frame of mind to race through them at top speed. If you have any interest in the occult, this would be a good time for investigations. Or some special sale might lure you to do shopping, instead.

9. WEDNESDAY. Fortunate. This is the third in a cycle of especially good days. Take all the opportunities that are open to you to increase your earnings. At the same time, try to improve your position before the year comes to an end. People with influence at your work place will be impressed if they see you are going all-out to get ahead. They are likely to give you a helping hand and encourage you to greater efforts. You should review your pension and retirement plans to be sure they are up to date. You must be on the alert to guard your future economic security. You might find reason to revise your thinking in certain areas.

10. THURSDAY. Changeable. Try to plan ahead as much as possible. This should be a good period for attempts to implement plans made earlier. You may have been considering forming new business partnerships. If so, you should arrange for meetings to see what would be the most propitious way to raise capital. You will need that if you hope to launch projects in the future. Aries people should also ponder ways in which they could speed up schedules. Time wasted is money lost, plus the risk of losing future orders. It may become necessary for you to travel for a face-to-face meeting with someone at a distance. Correspondence is time-consuming and frequently misleading.

11. FRIDAY. Good. This will be a very important day. Professional advice should be obtained in connection with marital affairs. Your relationship with your opposite number may be going through a very rough period. Try as you may, you are unable to come up with any solutions to these difficulties. So it would be a good idea to get in touch with a person who has marriage counseling experience. He or she can look at the situation more objectively than those directly involved. The day is good for healing rifts with in-laws. It should also be favorable for commencing study or self-improvement programs together with a loved one. You might want to arrange for a party for tomorrow evening. You will have to provide food and drinks, as well as round up your friends.

12. SATURDAY. Disquieting. Any interruptions will be most irritating. You will have trouble dealing with desk jobs, especially if you are attempting to do so from your home base. Children will be something of a problem for the Aries parent. They are likely to demand a lot of attention. Unexpected developments can interfere with distant business interests. You may have great trouble in finding out precisely what is going on. The search for new horizons can take on an entirely new aspect. Major breakthroughs are possible. But the inability to control emotions can damage reputations. The person who cannot keep a check on his own is surely unable to boss others.

13. SUNDAY. Sensitive. You may be feeling very uptight after a hectic week. But do not resort to panic measures. On this so-called day of rest, you should try to slow down a bit and get extra rest. Do not mix with high-strung and emotional people. Try simply to relax; do nothing if that suits you. The morning will be a particularly helpful one for professional artistes. Aries, in general, are likely to realize that they can no longer afford to keep sitting on the fence. Shilly-shallying will only waste their own time, to say nothing of that of others. Have confidence in yourself and your creative talents. The day will be favorable for visiting relatives.

14. MONDAY. Rewarding. People with a good deal of influence will be willing to put themselves out to help you. You should be able to make excellent progress with this assistance from authoritative figures. This will pertain especially if you have to deal with public or governmental departments. Large transactions can be satisfactorily closed. Bonus payments may be offered in return for extra hours of work. This financial reward will make it well worth your while to spend additional time working. But later on, financial discussions may result in Aries having to take on other commitments. And these will come at a time when you least want them. You will have to make up your mind to compromise.

15. TUESDAY. Mixed. Your personal affairs will require more attention than usual. You must devote more time and energy to them, at least for now. Loved ones may be feeling neglected. As they see it, you seem to be giving more time to your work and less to your home and family life. The irony is that what you are achieving in your career is for the good of all in the long run. However, you must not ignore the emotional needs of your family. The

Aries-born will find it easier to express themselves at this time. Also, they will do so with greater clarity and decisiveness than usual. But you must leave your work at the office and not bring it home with you.

16. WEDNESDAY. Uncertain. Any attempt to address a large group of crowds could prove disastrous today. Aries people may have made an error in judging public opinion. It would therefore be best to keep your opinions to yourself. Today is favorable for reaching an amicable understanding with associates. You can settle matters relating to business financial affairs and division of profits. You might even come up with a fairer way of distributing dividends. People of influence may stand in the way of your realizing a secret hope or dream. Tax experts and accountants could increase their fees. They might consider taking payments in installments if you are short of money.

17. THURSDAY. Encouraging. The week looks as if it is starting to improve in many ways and will from here on. You should be very pleased at the way an artistic venture is going. You will receive every kind of praise. This may make you feel that you are on the verge of an extremely important breakthrough. It will be a good day for attending auditions and interviews. Secret maneuvering can prove to be the key to success in career and public transactions. Aries business people should not think themselves above beating others at their own game. Retired people can be especially helpful with the advice they can give you. Listen carefully; their experience is priceless. They could even help you avoid making mistakes they may have made.

18. FRIDAY. Good. This should be an even better day than yesterday for all creative jobs. You should be able to increase your income by making more of your specialist talents. It will also be favorable for attempts to settle legal disputes out of court. A mutually acceptable agreement can probably be reached. This is a good time for gaining sponsorship and public support for worthwhile charitable causes. Among other things, it will also be good for conducting negotiations behind closed doors. It is also the right time for signing secret or confidential documents. Later on, you may be able to catch influential people in a relaxed and informal mood. If so, that would give you a good chance to propose your latest ideas for marketing or selling.

19. SATURDAY. Useful. You may be feeling somewhat jaded this morning as a result of your late-night partying. But this must not stop you from making good use of any excellent business opportunities that may arise. Some good news may come in through the mails this morning. This might be money that has been owed to you for special work you completed some time ago. Aries-born people may have found others willing to sponsor their personal projects. This could be of great help as it is not easy to come up with large amounts of cash on short notice. But Aries must guard against being excessively outspoken. This can win enemies quickly and make it difficult to negotiate a loan.

20. SUNDAY. Easygoing. Any action on the business front is going to be decidedly limited. This is as it should be on the one day you have to rest up. Instead of concentrating on your career, try devoting more time to your home and family. There are lots of ways you can show them how fond you are of them all. A heart-to-heart talk with loved ones would go a long way to clearing the air. Understanding another's problems is half the battle. And knowing that someone is listening, and caring, will bring you closer together. They, too, have personal desires and goals. Make time to work on your favorite hobby or catch up with reading.

21. MONDAY. Important. The morning is probably going to be the best period of the day. In the first place, you will have a clearer idea of what you want. You should be able to go a long way toward getting this if you make the right approach to influential people. Debts that have been owed to you for some time should be repaid. You may even have to remind friends of the money they borrowed from you. It would appear they have conveniently forgotten about their debt. Long-term schemes, that were expected to yield profits over a considerable period of time, can start producing quicker returns than were hoped for. Generous gifts and gestures of esteem given to others will be remembered.

22. TUESDAY. Promising. Take care of your minor financial matters first. Get your accounts in good order and review them. Consult with accountants on matters you feel unsure of. You may not have any idea of what you should do to make more interest on money you have stashed away. They may come up with ideas that you know nothing of. Romantic and marital affairs will take a sudden turn for the better. In fact, the future looks decidedly more promising in all areas having to do with someone who means a great deal to you. Influential people may not be available for interviews at just the time you most want to talk with them.

23. WEDNESDAY. Satisfactory. Publicity drives and advertising campaigns can yield substantial profits. Those of you involved in commercial affairs such as these will not have any complaints. You will find yourself treated fairly by the people in authority. The firm you work for may be offered an extremely lucrative contract, despite its having faced some very stiff competition. You will find some ideal ways for expanding operations faster than planned. Place any spare cash you may have in good, solid investments that will bring you high profits. Speculation sometimes works to your advantage, but it is risky.

24. THURSDAY. Important. There will be nothing that will be too much trouble for you today. You will possess qualities that will naturally draw others to you. Show off those of leadership. If you are involved in a business involving buying and selling, the new contracts you land could lead to a promotion. But be careful that you do not neglect your loved ones in your zeal to get to the top of the heap. It will be a favorable period for romantic involvements with people in age groups different from your own. But such relationships will tend not to be meaningfully emotional. They could be compared with ships that pass in the night.

25. FRIDAY. Upsetting. Self-employed Aries may become alarmed to realize that new contracts are not coming in as fast as you would like. This is the time of year when business usually picks up, not drops off. Your cash flow could be jeopardized, leading to serious shortages. This would not be a good day for requesting a loan from a bank official. It would be better to wait a bit if you can. You should not have much trouble in dealing with day-to-day affairs, however. You might find them fairly dreary and unchallenging, of course. Travel is not recommended as far as business is concerned. It is not likely to produce any out-of-the-way results.

26. SATURDAY. Important. You will find that this is just the kind of day you were hoping for! The first part, including midday, should be devoted to business affairs. Try your best to wind up the loose ends of work contracts and agreements. After that, the time will be very much your own. It will be a kind of helpful day all around for you. You can concentrate on future planning without interruption. People of influence will respond with enthusiasm to Aries' proposals. They may even offer valuable assistance and full support. On the home front, this would be a good time to plan how to increase its value. Confer with your spouse or partner.

27. SUNDAY. Enjoyable. This would appear to be another good day for you. Combining its better aspects with yesterday's will result in an excellent weekend for you. There will be next to no pressures to contend with. Your loved ones will be especially happy if you can devote the major part of your day to them. There is much to be straightened out in the way of home and family affairs. Acting as a team, you and your mate will find it easier to work out any differences. Your hobbies and other creative endeavors should receive some attention. In fact, you may be able to solve some problem that has blocked your progress up till now. Young children and teenagers will enjoy any outing.

28. MONDAY. Sensitive. Today may be largely taken up with disciplining children. You cannot afford to let them walk all over you, so it is up to you to show who is boss. When they realize this, their attitude will become more respectful. Your business affairs will probably not give you much cause for worry. You might even be able to finish your work early and use the time off for yourself. If you are taking any courses, it might be an opportune time for some extra study. Or you might feel more like spending an hour in the gym exercising moderately. It's not too early to think about Christmas and whatever shopping you have to do, to say nothing of writing Christmas cards.

29. TUESDAY. Uneventful. There will be no need for Aries to put themselves out today any more than absolutely necessary. This may be just as well because they are probably feeling rather drained after yesterday. Straightening out emotional problems for others always takes a lot out of one. Superiors at your work place will undoubtedly be willing to allow you to attend just to routine matters. They will not appear to want to burden you with anything extra. You will appreciate this and realize that they are considerate. Later on, you might want to continue roughing out holiday plans and making notes of gift ideas.

30. WEDNESDAY. Productive. There will be plenty going on today to keep you fully occupied. Unfortunately, the only jobs you will have to contend with are unlikely to be creatively stimulating. This will not apply to your personal plans. Study and other self-improvement programs will be better than ever for you. At home, you will probably find that proposed vacations have been made final. So the time has come for making firm reservations for travel and hotels. Otherwise, you will stand a good chance of being turned away. Your advance planning for daring projects will win the cooperation and support of others. This is no time for idle gossip. Even though someone else starts it, you need not reply.

DECEMBER

1. THURSDAY. Important. This should be an important and active month for the Ram. Start it off well by pushing as hard as you can to reach your objectives. And your goal to do so is before the end of the year. Greater concern over your future economic security may provide the necessary incentive. Another ingredient is the added exertion you must put into routine work and other business matters. Take a fresh look at the old, familiar problems that have not been solved by using regular methods. There have to be other ways of doing almost anything. It's up to you to figure them out. Just use your usual ingenuity and common sense.

2. FRIDAY. Changeable. Do not let the pressures of work and personal affairs make you forgetful. Check your appointment book daily so as not to miss important engagements. If you fail to keep a date with someone, whether they are important or not, you will be in the doghouse. If the appointment was a business one, you may lose out on a contract. This is a good time to buy pets. An animal can become the focus of love and affection, especially if there are children. But they should be taught how to give it proper care and not tease it. If you happen to be an Aries boss, this would be a good time to give your staff a pay raise.

3. SATURDAY. Difficult. You may think that you have more time to take care of your regular job than you actually do. You may try goofing off during the morning, so that you will run into great difficulty in keeping up to your schedule. Take greater pains in trying to resolve problems that have sprung up in the relationship between you and your partner. Control your urge to justify yourself and try to prove that you are right all the time. If you can't adopt a give-and-take attitude, you may doom your relationship. Do something special this evening to show your affection and sincerity. Try asking your partner what they prefer to do.

4. SUNDAY. Sensitive. Tread softly today. One word of criticism could really cause a major blowup within your household.

You may be feeling the strain of the past week and be overly critical. Take your mind off problems by concentrating on hobbies and other creative pursuits. Or get out of the house and take a long walk to calm yourself. Later, you may find you can show interest in family affairs and become part of the group again. You could even offer to help out with some of the routine chores. Find ways of enjoying yourselves as a group, even if it's only looking at old family albums. Don't spoil the only day you have to forget about business by worrying about matters you cannot control.

5. MONDAY. Lucky. Your work and other employment affairs must take priority over personal ones. For one thing, you need to increase your income insofar as possible. There will be more than the normal number of bills coming due by the end of the year. And the holidays always mean extra spending for entertainment and presents. Long-term research projects can be advanced, particularly those involving large numbers of statistics and other data. Older people, probably relatives of yours, will be particularly cooperative. And don't stop experimenting with new ideas. You can never tell when you might just hit the jackpot.

6. TUESDAY. Demanding. Joint resources could become the cause of extra concern and anxiety. Loved ones have ideas of their own about how to handle these. They may be unwilling, too, to try and reach a compromise solution. Your health may require attention. You should see your doctor at the first sign of a bad cold and nip it in the bud. If you let it get really bad, you could be sick over the holidays and ruin your fun. Aries should learn to tone down their tendency to speak to others in an abrupt way. They should show the same respect toward them as they expect to get themselves. Otherwise, you will find yourself being left out of get-togethers and other social affairs.

7. WEDNESDAY. Upsetting. If you go over your accounts, you may discover that you are not as well off as you thought you were. Aries may invite the wrath of partners by their excessive spending and extravagance. Just plain carelessness in handling financial matters could lead to unnecessary expenses. Be on guard against letting your bank balance get into the red. That would be bad news indeed, especially at this time of year. If you handle tools or machinery today, be extra careful. Safety guards should be used at all times. They are there to protect you, not annoy you. Do not dramatize a personal crisis or try to get sympathy.

8. THURSDAY. Buoyant. This will be a tip-top day, the opposite of yesterday. Superiors may drop hints of a pay raise and promotion in the coming year. This will wipe out the dismal events of yesterday and give you a charge. Use your initiative in drawing up plans for the future. You have a vivid imagination and you should not let it go idle. You can afford to strike out against well-known precedents and set your own guidelines. If you have difficult people to deal with, take a no-nonsense attitude toward them. Otherwise, you will find your authority jeopardized. It is not too early to go on a shopping expedition, with Christmas drawing near.

9. FRIDAY. Important. If you are a gambler, this is quite likely to be your lucky day. You may very well receive a financial windfall. A project that you invested in a long time ago, and had just about written off as a dud, may suddenly show profits. This would be an excellent time to get together all information you can about courses in higher education. You might have to enroll quite early in the most useful ones. If you're aiming for a higher niche, you could probably improve your chances by learning about its makeup. You might also get help from experts in the field who could advise you what to study. This is the kind of exciting challenge you enjoy.

10. SATURDAY. Disconcerting. Do not jump to hasty conclusions about your associates at your place of business. People may have been spreading rumors that are totally unjustified. Wait until you can get all the facts together before pointing any fingers. Some Aries have a tendency for deception in the field of public affairs. Still others may deliberately conceal their motives. But nobody should be reprimanded for being allowed to have their say unless they are lying. Since this is the start of a weekend, make plans for fun and entertainment in advance. Put all thoughts of business affairs right out of your mind. Worry doesn't help, anyway.

11. SUNDAY. Good. Today should be favorable for deepening your existing romantic involvements. Most relationships can be made more secure. Loved ones will be willing to lend you a hand in your business and career affairs. Much progress can be made in discussions about your financial affairs with a spouse or partner. Your thoughts may also turn to Christmas and whatever plans you are making. If you are preparing to go away for several days, you might have to confirm certain reservations. You could probably do some shopping today since many large stores are open at this time of year, even though it is Sunday. It's getting late, too, for Christmas cards.

12. MONDAY. Special. Go all-out today to try and earn more money, even if it means you must work overtime. Expenses are always higher than anticipated, especially at this season. The day will be good for business transactions as a whole and for financial affairs. You might be able to make use of group or club functions to air your personal views and ideas. Your audience will be comprised of many with your sort of background and tastes. This will ensure rapport and understanding of some people, even if they are not in total agreement. Friends may also be actively helpful which will give you a boost both with the job and your morale.

13. TUESDAY. Mixed. An important letter or telephone call you were hoping to receive will not arrive. This will be upsetting because the matter is one of money that is owed to you. But today would be good for getting in touch with government officials or similarly influential types in connection with affairs overseas. They are frequently able to cut red tape in connection with business dealings. This might be a good day for you to join a club or a society with interests that you wish to study. Loved ones may disturb Aries by making financial demands that you will find excessive and unreasonable. But you will still find it difficult to know where to draw the line.

14. WEDNESDAY. Productive. Today will be somewhat mixed, but not a total waste. It would be well to get rid of any routine jobs that you always find boring early in the day. You might not have enough determination later on. It will be favorable for pinning down people who are usually evasive and even somewhat devious. Get them into a situation they can't back out of, for once. You might even be able to extract a firm commitment for something. Behind-the-scenes actions can be especially helpful in furthering your career and business affairs. Original and unusual business propositions may prove to be particularly worthwhile. Be thankful you did not turn them down earlier.

15. THURSDAY. Successful. Any dispute in which you are involved, whether legal or personal, would be best settled as quickly as possible. Taking such cases to court can be an unnecessary waste of time and money. There are only ten days left till Christmas which means it is now or never for mailing your cards. Aries should practice using tact and diplomacy in their dealings, rather than their normal aggressive tactics. As the old saying goes, honey catches more flies than vinegar. You might want to find out some rather personal information about someone you are thinking of employing. If so, private investigations are favored over the more usual telephone calls or word of mouth. Be subtle, though.

16. FRIDAY. Sensitive. New financial propositions you receive from peculiar or unlikely sources can turn out to be especially lucrative. Your secret contacts, as well as those who work away from usual business setups, can bring Aries good luck. Your personal likes and dislikes can sometimes interfere with your good judgment. This is a failing many Aries have, one which should be suppressed. Your words should be chosen carefully, especially if you have negative feelings. If children have come back into your household for the Christmas holidays, do not lose your temper with them. They have naturally high spirits and should be allowed some freedom from restrictions.

17. SATURDAY. Tricky. Any shopping you try to do today will probably be made more difficult than usual by crowds of Christmas shoppers. Almost any other day or evening would be less frantic. The day could be useful for Aries who want to get new projects started. If you need the help of others, however, you must be very careful of the danger of stepping on people's toes. Your directness is sometimes considered rude or even offensive. You are apt to make others feel threatened in some way. Trying too hard will often produce negative results rather than those you were aiming for. Save some of your energy for having fun this evening.

18. SUNDAY. Fortunate. An undercurrent of excitement will be felt by all in the household. Everyone will be getting into the spirit of the holidays. Young people do not have to worry about school for the next two weeks and can enjoy themselves. You may find that in-laws can provide you with valuable introductions to certain key people in positions of authority. The upshot might be a boost for your career or access to even more influential officials. Learning as much as you can about your profession can be extremely beneficial. Try to get some advice from an expert as to what courses of study would be the most useful to you. Most people feel flattered to realize someone is seeking their guidance.

19. MONDAY. Upsetting. This will not be a good day for your financial affairs in general. You may get word of higher taxes in the coming year, as well as a rise in insurance fees. The cost of borrowing money could also be in for an increase, as well as the charges made by your accountants. All of these will have a direct effect on your personal funds for daily expenses, as well as your reserves. You may have to work out a new budget before the end of the year. Don't let such worries affect the quality of your work. You have established yourself as a steady, dependable person, with good rapport with those in authority.

20. TUESDAY. Mixed. This should be an auspicious day for financial transactions. Fresh proposals made by your colleagues could be especially worthwhile. Great care must be exercised when contracts and agreements are being drawn up for business deals. Be on guard against loopholes and ambiguities which could cause financial losses to Aries people in the future. You may receive some money today without having had to work for it. It might be a commission due to you for some time that you had forgotten about. As an unexpected windfall, it could not have come at a better time. Understandably, your spending at this time of year climbs rapidly.

21. WEDNESDAY. Enjoyable. You will find that business affairs and pleasure will mix well today. If the office party takes place some time, you will have a chance to socialize at all levels. This would also be a good opportunity to take a more active role in your community affairs. There are usually many opportunities to volunteer your help for. Fund-raising is an important role, to say nothing of talking neighbors into helping out. If you don't have time to talk face-to-face with someone, you could telephone or write a brief outline of what is needed. The day will also be favorable for putting more exertion into your creative projects, or catching up with reading.

22. THURSDAY. Difficult. You are going to have to keep a tight rein on your feelings today. For some obscure reason, you seem to want to alienate those with whom you hope to work closely in the future. You appear to be in an argumentative mood, willing to get into any kind of heated discussion with almost everybody. People in authority may opt for radical changes or unconventional ideas. If the changes favor Aries, they will last for only a short time. You must make every effort to keep your extravagant tendencies in check. A major upheaval in your business career could necessitate similar changes in your home and family life. These could be the cause for some outspoken resentment.

23. FRIDAY. Tricky. Regular business affairs may turn out to be confusing and potentially deceptive today. Do not assume anything, no matter how normal it might seen, nor should you take anything for granted. At the same time, the day will be good for signing contracts or agreements with large firms. You could find that prior discussions with a bank official are enormously helpful in clearing up any misconceptions. If you feel that someone in your firm is withholding information that could help you, bypass the person and go straight to the top. Assistants sometimes assume they know more than their superiors and could mislead you.

24. SATURDAY. Sensitive. You may be feeling the need for some good advice today. So do not ignore what people in authority tell you about the future of your career. Try to exercise greater tolerance when dealing with others. Any personal criticism of yourself may contain more than a grain of truth; think about it carefully before dismissing it. You are not always able to judge the effect that your attitude sometimes has on others. Even short trips will prove ineffective if Aries tries to cover too many bases in too little time. The generosity of family members is quite exceptional. This is your absolute last chance to buy Christmas presents! It is now or never!

25. MERRY CHRISTMAS! There should be no pressures on you to mar the day. You can relax and enjoy some good times, and forget your worries. There may be some family reunions with those who live in other parts of the country. It might also be possible to patch up an old feud with a family member. Forget the past differences and start building a new and happier future. Even if there is little excitement or activity within the household, you can still enjoy the best part of the day at home.

26. MONDAY. Satisfactory. This may feel like the lull after the storm, or perhaps a bit of a letdown following the excitement. Certainly today will be more dynamic than yesterday, with plenty of action. You might want to give children some special treat. But you will have to watch your budget carefully, with entertainment costs on the rise. The same goes for any special ideas you might have connected with romance. You may find yourself planning ahead for possible moves you will make in your career early in the coming year. That is a mere five days away, so it is not a bit too early to give it thought. Keep clear of any influential business people, however; they will be unreceptive.

27. TUESDAY. Mixed. This is definitely not the day to gamble. Follow this piece of advice and you won't have to worry on that score. You certainly have paid out a lot of money during the Christmas season, but it would be stupid to think you could win it back. Children may become overly excited and tend to break their possessions or those of other people. But far worse will be the tendency of your romantic partner to break his or her word. The person you probably felt very sure of has probably just been playing with your emotions. Turn to your creative or artistic pursuits. Your originality and inventiveness will occupy your mind and keep you happy.

28. WEDNESDAY. Manageable. Some of you may be returning to work for the first time since last week. If so, you could be faced with completing the routine sort of work you should have done before the holiday. You could enhance your business reputation by handling unusual and out-of-the-way matters. Craftsmanship and technical skills can earn anyone the respect of other workers and employers. Unfortunately, your work could conflict with romance today which will cause quarrels. But you must realize that your work has to come before pleasure now and stick to it. A loved one may be trying to coerce you into changing your job, without any regard as to your feelings.

29. THURSDAY. Challenging. Today will be favorable for getting new contracts signed. The agreements you are able to consummate today should make you feel far more secure about your future. Be sure you get the best possible terms without sacrificing anything. Making allowances for inflation rates should have been taken into consideration. The Aries alertness and quick thinking will attract the attention of those who have some measure of control over you. Not only could a promotion result, but you may also earn a substantial end-of-the-year bonus. Even a self-employed Aries can secure a valuable contract by keeping an ear to the ground and beating another to the punch.

30. FRIDAY. Demanding. Even though you may have worked out a busy schedule for today, you might have to rearrange and streamline it. Your health could be the deciding factor, requiring you to concentrate on personal matters. At the same time, loved ones may nag you to take on more responsibility for domestic problems. Legal proceedings may take a disconcerting turn with unexpected developments. You simply cannot count on a favorable outcome now. Quarrels between partners could lead to sudden separations and then to breakups. And it will undoubtedly be the Aries people who have to pick up the pieces and bear the burden. On top of that, influential people could turn out to be difficult.

31. SATURDAY. Mixed. New information that has been provided will prove particularly helpful to you. It will enable you to formulate your business plans that you are so keen to launch in the

New Year. Aries may find ways to increase their net incomes, but it is important to keep receipts for spending outlays. They will enable you to take tax deductions on certain items. It would be a good idea to review all your personal financial affairs at this time. You might have to make adjustments in your spending. You find that certain people in positions of authority are unreliable and unlikely to keep their word. Forget them and concentrate on having a happy New Year's Eve!

October–December 1987

OCTOBER

1. THURSDAY. Mixed. Sleep may have been something of a problem for you recently. The chances are you have had one or two sleepless nights. This is all the more possible for young Aries parents. You may well have been kept awake by the demands of youngsters. One of your greatest problems at the moment would appear to be a low energy level. You should not take on any chores that would take a great deal out of you physically. The day will be good for career affairs, though. Better results can be obtained by paying more attention to routine matters. But overconfidence could spell danger in your relationships with superiors. You could antagonize them if you appear to be taking over. Don't overstep your authority.

2. FRIDAY. Useful. Friends can be helpful to you socially. They may be able to provide useful introductions. This is one of those pleasant days when you should be able to mix business with pleasure in order to advance your interests. Partnership affairs can be improved. This is an ideal period for getting anything that would require team effort launched. Distant people or affairs can be solidly helpful in connection with business profits. Try to pick the brains of people older and more experienced than yourself. Take note of the mistakes of others in order to avoid such pitfalls yourself. You can learn a great deal by such efforts. It is vital to stay alert and not to fall into a robotlike pattern.

3. SATURDAY. Exciting. This morning would be an excellent period for getting in touch with friends. This pertains especially if there are any particular social activities you wish to involve them in. It will also be good for the sports-minded Aries person. You will enjoy participating in your favorite sporting activity. It is also a good day for travel in connection with outdoor pastimes. One of the more pleasant aspects about today is that you should not need to spend too much money in order to get the best and the most out of it. News received from someone far away may mean the realization of some of your most treasured hopes and wishes. This will be enough to ensure that your weekend will be a banner one. You can revel in anticipation of things to come.

4. SUNDAY. Good. Coupled with what took place yesterday, this would appear to be one of the most pleasant weekends that you have spent in quite a while. Although this is normally a day of rest, it would seem that lines of communication will be busy while you attempt to set up some important deal. Behind-the-scenes maneuvering may enable you to make some agreement with an influential person. It would not ordinarily be easy to contact such a person under regular workaday conditions. It will be favorable for tête-à-tête conversations with partners in connection with joint finances and resources. You will be able to establish guidelines far more easily, and without hassle, in a quiet, home environment.

5. MONDAY. Challenging. This will perhaps not be quite the rip-roaring start to the working week that you had been hoping for. It might be best to keep your more ambitious tendencies in check. The more unconventional academic interests of the Ram are likely to meet with some opposition behind the scenes. Aries readers who are involved in the teaching profession would do best to stick to the dictates of department heads, rather than attempting to introduce more revolutionary ideas. Too much physical or mental exertion must be avoided at all costs. Pleasant and unexpected news may be received from loved ones at a distance. It could entail a visit from someone you have not seen for many years. Or there may be an invitation in it for you.

6. TUESDAY. Deceptive. This is a tricky day for dealing with associates at your place of employment. Career and business affairs must be handled with a great deal more care than has been the case lately. You must not take any chances that could put the future happiness and security of you and yours at risk. Aries people cannot afford to take anything for granted at the office or factory. Be sure that you do not take any action that could lead to gossip or put you in the bad books of your boss. If involved in cooperative ventures, there is a risk of Aries people losing their money. Compromising with partners may be the only solution to deadlocks. You must be prepared to give a little ground.

7. WEDNESDAY. Satisfactory. This has not been a very stimulating working week so far. Perhaps you have been aiming too high. This will be a pleasant enough day, however. Also, there is a good chance that Aries people will be able to make an important breakthrough with their academic endeavors. An element of good luck is likely to assist readers who are giving attention to overseas affairs. A letter that arrives is likely to make you more sure of which direction you should be headed. In the evening, pleasant experiences can develop into tugs of war with loved ones. It is important to be more sensitive to the feelings of others. Aries can find it difficult to admit they might be wrong.

8. THURSDAY. Sensitive. Your hunches should be followed up as they are more likely to pay off. This is especially true when you are dealing with business matters. More money can be made today if you are prepared to be a little more daring. The older Aries person should give more thought to the ideas of younger co-workers. They are eager to try their ideas for streamlining the way routine affairs are handled at their place of employment. Imaginative schemes or approaches should pay off. If financial gains are made, extra care and thought must be given to the matter of taxes. Make sure that you put enough money to one side to meet such debts. You may have to adopt a more formal method of budgeting so that you always have some reserve.

9. FRIDAY. Worrisome. An uneasy feeling has come over you about the promises of support that were made to you recently. It looks as if they are not likely to be lived up to. Influential people may be vague when you approach them about matters connected with salary increases and promotion. You are likely to find that most of your working day centers around routine matters. There will not be the anticipated opportunities to add money to your take-home pay. Financial affairs contain an element of misunderstanding. It is important to maintain clear lines of demarcation between personal and shared resources. Aries who handle money on behalf of other people must be careful what they say to clients. Thoughtless words can lead to lost business or ill-will.

10. SATURDAY. Good. Get out and about at the start of this weekend. The energetically inclined Aries will be pleased to have more opportunity to take the lead. Do what you can to get in touch with people in faraway places who can be helpful to your long-term ambitions and objectives. Spouses or loved ones will back you and will not try to put any barriers in your way. It is a favorable period for pursuing partnership agreements. Do what you can to get them drawn up and signed before you take a weekend break. Influential people will more than likely give the 'go-ahead to teamwork activities that involve travel. This will greatly increase the credibility of your proposals. It will also lessen the weight of total responsibility. Romance is happy tonight.

11. SUNDAY. Demanding. Work out a schedule in advance for today and stick to it. This is a period when a lot of time and energy could be wasted unnecessarily. One of the problems that develops this Sunday is that friends and family alike will be in a confused mood. They will be unable to make up their minds as to how they wish to spend their leisure time. If you hang around waiting for others to take the lead, you will begin to feel very frustrated and edgy. Outings and trips may have to be canceled due to ill health. You may find that you are spending more time at home than you had anticipated. Concentration on academic or self-improvement attempts is likely to be difficult. This will not be a Sunday you will remember with pleasure.

12. MONDAY. Disconcerting. It will be difficult for you to get into high gear. This is a particularly troublesome day for Aries people who are attempting to round off routine matters that were under way last week. Daily chores and activities that center around home and family affairs are likely to be delayed because of disagreements with loved ones. During the morning, traveling conditions may be bad and this could result in delays and missed appointments. Allow yourself more time for any journey that you have to make to faraway places. This is not an easy day for dealing with publishers, printers and the like. The evening is the best period for handling your personal affairs. You will undoubtedly be free of interruption, so can concentrate better.

13. TUESDAY. Fair. This will be another day that starts off on the wrong foot. The chances are you will be delayed leaving home and this could result in missed connections. You may arrive at your place of employment well after you should have. Influential people will not be interested in your personal problems. You will have to put a good deal of effort into your job in order to catch up. Aries people may be feeling hopelessly undecided about important career issues. Family members whom you turn to for guidance may not be very helpful or supportive. But later on it will be more favorable for terminating affairs successfully, especially financial ones.

14. WEDNESDAY. Disturbing. Too much haste will definitely mean less speed. One thing that you must avoid is cutting corners and resorting to panic measures just because you have gotten far behind with your duties. The pressure on domestic affairs or family members may make it impossible to give the necessary attention to teamwork endeavors. Aries people cannot afford to be too independent. Listen to the advice of older people. Stubbornness on your part would only get you on the wrong side of authorities. Influential people will demand some compromise from you if you wish to gain their support. This could take the form of a reciprocal service such as the endorsement of their pet project. You should not expect something for nothing.

15. THURSDAY. Useful. Fortunes seem to be very topsy-turvy at the moment. Try to level out today. Do not take on anything which might entail risk to your savings. Speculation would not be a good idea. The best way to build up your reserves is by steady and diligent effort at your place of regular employment. Aries people will find that they have the opportunity to take some time off from work later in the day. Spouses or loved ones will probably take care of all plans for amusement and entertainment. It looks as though it could be a promising day for romance. Seize whatever opportunity presents itself, especially if you are attracted to someone and the feeling is mutual.

16. FRIDAY. Sensitive. In marital affairs, romance and finance must be kept apart. Do not allow emotional feelings to influence the way you handle your money. Loved ones may be making demands on you that you must not succumb to. Feelings must not be allowed to intrude into discussions about mutual resources. If you feel that members of your family have been extravagant lately, you must take this opportunity to speak up. This applies even if you run the risk of making yourself unpopular. People of greater professional experience can be particularly helpful to the creative and artistic endeavors of the Ram. You will welcome this assistance and be eager to absorb all they can do for you.

17. SATURDAY. Sensitive. Influential people will be more willing than usual to listen to you air your grievances. If you feel that you have been treated shabbily at your place of employment, talk the matter over with your boss. Any reasonable grounds for complaint that you have are likely to be dealt with fairly and impartially. Try to clear the air now so that you can carry on feeling happy and contented on the job. You may get the go-ahead from superiors for cooperative endeavors involving an element of risk. It should be a good day for attempts to boost your pay. Taking or planning for vacations or holidays is recommended. But due to possible misunderstandings, business associates may say it's the wrong time for vacations. You will have to stand your ground.

18. SUNDAY. Variable. The morning period will be useful for reflecting on work and career affairs. Go over recent events in your mind. Where mistakes have been made, make a mental note and do all that you can to ensure that you do not repeat errors.

Learn from your past experiences. Aries people may come up with some bright ideas for improving efficiency. But they should not start by themselves on any new ventures. These definitely require the consent and the approval of superiors. There may be fundamental problems over finances between you and your loved ones that you will have to try to resolve today. The longer they remain unsettled, the wider the chasm between you will grow. And that will only make your differences harder to settle.

19. MONDAY. Difficult. Take this day at a nice and steady pace. If you allow yourself to get confused you will undoubtedly make serious errors on the job. Particular attention must be paid to accounts. Check and double-check figures. Take every precaution against making any errors that could prove to be costly at a later date. Trying to get too much done in the morning could leave you feeling frustrated and bad tempered. Pay more attention to your diet. Be sure that you eat proper meals. Snacks or junk food, eaten on the run, will not provide necessary nutrition. It will be difficult to make any headway with projects related to distant affairs. Inability to concentrate on academic endeavors must not be allowed to create depression.

20. TUESDAY. Deceptive. Business partners are now likely to come to you with all sorts of exciting ideas. Associates will be full of enthusiasm and will think that they are onto something good. For your part, you should investigate the background of all speculative ventures very closely. Be sure to do so before you invest your hard-earned money. Risks and the taking of chances are not likely to reap you the much-promised dividends. Today will be good for attempts to straighten out joint financial problems with loved ones. But later on, in the evening, mates or spouses can be rather temperamental. Whatever else, they should by no means be provoked or angered. Try to steer conversation into safe waters by discussing plans for a holiday or party.

21. WEDNESDAY. Important. At last things seem to be looking up for the Ram. You appear to have had to mark time with important new projects for quite a while now. Today should see you with the opportunity to make an important breakthrough. It is good for attending to legal formalities connected with distant affairs. You should be able to make considerable progress with a property matter that seems to have been hanging fire for quite some time. In-laws can be valuable business partners or assistants due to their greater knowledge or experience. Your spouse or loved ones may impress you with their profound understanding of religion or philosophy. The chances are you have never discussed such matters with them in depth before now.

22. THURSDAY. Good. Make the most of this rather promising period. More time should be given to money-making endeavors than to the search for pleasure and entertainment. An early start will be important. Rush jobs are likely to come up later on. You should therefore make an effort to get on top of routine affairs. You do not want to have these hanging over your head during the early morning period. The day will become calmer as it progresses. You should be able to discover a new confidence in yourself. Helping mates or business associates today will reap rewards later on. More of your spare time should be given to matrimonial affairs. You can't expect a relationship to carry on without a great deal of persuasion and help.

23. FRIDAY. Demanding. This will be a vitally important day for your financial affairs. Before you contemplate making any big expenditures you should look into your accounts. Be sure that you have ample cash on hand to cover all regular bills. Do this before you start buying anything new for the home or for your personal wear. Any moves that you make now will be irrevocable, so you must be very sure you are fully aware of what you are doing. Transactions relating to banks, insurance, and taxation have to be handled with extreme care. Aries people involved in research work may make an extraordinary breakthrough. This could involve anything from fame to winning a monetary award, depending on the field of research.

24. SATURDAY. Important. Carry on with any specialized activities that you have been working on recently. Do all that you can to promote your natural talents. You will be pleased at the support you get from your loved ones. This is a propitious day for those Aries who are trying to break with the past and move on to greener pastures. Long-distance travel can be particularly important with regard to exchanges of stimulating ideas with colleagues in faraway places. Academic or self-improvement endeavors can be assisted by a stroke of good luck. The day will be good for all matters requiring analysis and careful investigation. Much can be accomplished on any one of many different fronts. It will be up to you to seize the opportunity and make the best possible use of it.

25. SUNDAY. Exciting. This will be one of the most pleasant Sundays that you are likely to have spent so far this month. Loved ones will be easygoing and will be amenable to following your suggestions as to the best way to spend your leisure hours. You will also be provided with encouragement and moral support from your opposite number to pursue any academic interests that are of importance to you. Study activities will go well. You are going to find it easier to retain knowledge that will be valuable to your career prospects. Your mate may be even more willing than you are to rise above petty emotional and practical difficulties. But your temperament is not as easygoing, perhaps. Aries are inclined to be stubborn and opinionated. You may have to modify your views.

26. MONDAY. Satisfactory.   This can be a rather unsettling day for distant affairs. It might be best not to make any journeys unless you have definite appointments to see people in other towns or cities. You are likely to find it hard going if you are trying to sell new ideas or new machinery or other consumer goods. It would be best to stick to routine activities as much as possible. Even bold Aries will be horrified at the problems that will be encountered if they take on too much. But your usual buoyancy and self-confidence are likely to reassert themselves. You will thus be able to recognize any favorable propositions if they are presented to you. This gives you a decided advantage over others not so quick to recognize an opportunity that has merit. Make the most of such good fortune.

27. TUESDAY. Difficult.   It will be a tricky day when you should not take any chances in your public or your private life. Aries people must be careful about getting involved in flirtations that could affect long-term happiness. Someone with whom you have already made your life or are intending to could be upset. Routine business affairs can be helped by a visit to your bank manager. Seek advice if you are considering expansion some time in the future. Discuss taxation and investment matters with knowledgeable people. You cannot afford to daydream or indulge in impractical schemes. Don't pay too much attention to people with vivid imaginations if they try to give you advice.

28. WEDNESDAY. Calm.   Loved ones may offer to make some readjustments in the handling of marital resources. This will give Aries a freer hand for career affairs. This midweek day will offer you valuable breathing space. It will afford better opportunities to take stock of your overall situation. Influential people will try to give you a free hand to use your imagination on the job. But you must be doubly sure that you fulfill any additional responsibility that is entrusted to you. Now should be a good time for contacting your boss to discuss the possibility of time off later in the week. There are undoubtedly some personal matters that you are going to have to resolve during office or company hours. You may have a claim to settle or perhaps have to arrange for the care of an older family member.

29. THURSDAY. Mixed. Money and friendship will not mix. People may come to you trying to borrow cash. But frequently, they will not be able to give you a definite date as to when they will be able to pay you back. Be very cautious about visitors from overseas who ask you to make them a loan. They will probably promise to pay you back as soon as they get home to their own country. However, you must make every effort to get cast-iron guarantees before you dig into your own reserves to support them. Bankers and other influential people may be willing to sponsor the more imaginative schemes of Aries. But this is not a good day for making any direct effort to increase business profits or stock turnover. There are too many negative factors involved at this time.

30. FRIDAY. Fair. It's time to get moving. There will be a lot for you to accomplish today. Time must not be wasted on secondary matters. Aries people must have the necessary academic qualifications and knowledge to be able to render genuine service to others. These people are helping to make the world a better place to live in. Friends will be more than usually sympathetic to your forward-looking schemes. Loved ones will be easier to influence today. You will be able to get your own way in areas where you have recently been held back. Contacting in-laws is something that should work out well just now. You will find that you are able to get on with older people more easily than has been the case in prior years. Some mellowing may be taking place on both sides.

31. SATURDAY. Good. The month of October is likely to end on a happy note for you Aries people. You have had more than your fair share of setbacks over the past few weeks. Nevertheless, you seem to have been able to draw on hidden reserves and sort out quite a few of your problems. These included emotional as well as financial problems. You should be prepared to give free rein to your imagination. Follow on all your hunches. These will undoubtedly lead to greater success in career as well as in public affairs. Superiors will be impressed by your ability to buckle down to your chores on your own. Your independent spirit will be much admired. Those of you who are interested in depth psychology and psychoanalysis should try to contact people in the know.

NOVEMBER

1. SUNDAY. Disturbing. Secret fears and anxieties are likely to arise. You may not be sure of just how much someone who you greatly care for really feels about you. It will be difficult for you to rise above your emotional problems. It would be a good idea to bury yourself in any work that you can accomplish from your home base sometime during the day. Try to catch up with your letter writing. Settle bills that were due and should have been paid before the month of October came to an end. Aries people may find that the pressure still remaining from past events does not allow them enough freedom to be more forward-looking. It could result in restlessness and a sense of having been cheated.

2. MONDAY. Deceptive. If you are in a too easygoing mood, it would be a risky attitude. Take no one and nothing for granted. Do not be late for work or slacken off in performance this Monday. People with any sort of authority over you may be keeping a closer eye on your progress than you were aware of. Aries must avoid being absentminded. Check your engagement book to make sure that you do not miss out on any important appointments. You may have made some last week, but forgotten them. This is not a good day for contacting influential people or trying to have any special favors granted. Joint financial ventures that you are trying to launch are likely to be delayed due to reasons beyond your control. Try to find out the reason behind the holdup and see if you can rectify it.

3. TUESDAY. Productive. Partnership affairs must be handled with kid gloves. Cooperation is the key to helping you deal with your chores. Do not do or say anything that would upset your mate or partner. Be more aware of the needs and desires of others. Don't put your foot in it by bringing up past disagreements that should be dead and buried by now. Spouses and business associates can be temperamental. This is a good day for study and self-improvement endeavors. Aries who will shortly be taking examinations will find it easier to concentrate. The evening can be lucky. People and events are more than likely to fit in with your personal plans and desires. This will create harmony and ensure a pleasant gathering.

4. WEDNESDAY. Tricky. The morning could contain some unexpected problems for you. A letter or telephone call that you receive could cause you to change your plans at the last moment. You will, in all likelihood, find that you have quite a lot of traveling to do It will probably be connected with your work and not all of it will bear fruit. Spouses or loved ones will continue to be somewhat difficult. The intentions of the Ram could easily have been misunderstood. Make sure you explain yourself clearly if you are talking over emotional and other personal problems. Sometimes even the slightest suggestion of criticism can be blown out of all proportion.

5. THURSDAY. Worrisome.   You Aries people could easily give in to sudden bouts of depression. Your resistance is likely to be low. You have been trying to cope with emotional problems all week. Perhaps they have been taking rather more out of you than you realized. Problems within the household will interfere with outside activities. This will be a highly sensitive day for finances. Aries cannot afford to take any risks. There can be some depressing news in connection with taxation or legacies. This is not a good day for seeking the assistance of influential people. Try to hold off for another week or more before you approach them.

6. FRIDAY. Quiet.   Take it easy. Slow down the tempo of your life somewhat. Do not take on more than you have to. It would also be a good idea to pay more attention to your health. Be sure that the diet you are on is beneficial to your needs. It should be giving you all the vitamins and minerals that your mind and body require. This will not be a particularly eventful day. You will therefore be able to get ahead with many of the little chores that you have been putting to one side for all too long. Go through your personal financial affairs and make sure that everything is up to date. It would be wise to get caught up on all fronts today. That will ensure your enjoying a weekend free of worries.

7. SATURDAY. Good.   There can be little doubt about the fact it will be the best day of the week! Many of the difficulties that have been weighing you down can now be overcome. Home life will be much more relaxed and settled and there will not be so much interference with your outdoor life. Probably you Aries will have a backlog of unresolved matters you have been unable to cope with during the last three weeks. This was partially due to your inability to contact people connected with your problems. This is a favorable day for getting out and about. Put all your drive into what is most important for making the future successful and happy. Also try to get some kind of entertainment lined up for later in the day and the evening. You must forget business and worries and have fun.

8. SUNDAY. Variable.   Nothing much is likely to take place this Sunday that will set your world on fire. However, this can be a pleasant enough weekend day. It will be even better if you are not too forceful with loved ones. Remember that they have the right to lead their own lifes as they wish. You must guard against showing that dominant streak in your nature. The morning could be a good time for staying at home. Try seeing more of the people you have been separated from earlier in the week. Aries people may receive a long-distance phone call that will cheer them up considerably. Later in the day, it will be good for getting out and about with loved ones. Listen to their ideas for having a fling and follow their lead.

9. MONDAY. Demanding. Things may not proceed according to plan. If you are waiting at home for repairmen, they may not be on time. There will be delays that you will not be able to do very much about. You will be at the mercy of people in authority at your place of employment. The sort of chores that you are required to handle are likely to be somewhat mundane. Try to concentrate if you have to deal with financial matters though. Mistakes made now could prove to be extremely costly at a later date. Domestic problems may arise at the worst possible time. Aries people may have to cancel or postpone important business appointments. The reason could be illness, or just an unexpected change of plans.

10. TUESDAY. Sensitive. Odd jobs in and around the home should not be neglected any longer. Be more of a handyman or become a do-it-yourselfer. Try to deal with little things that have gone wrong. Buckle down to complete repair and redecorating work that has been going on for long. Loved ones will be helpful. Home improvements that you yourself are able to make will help you to increase the value of your property. Bankers and other influential people will be more willing than usual to help you if you are attempting to raise a short-term loan. Later on though, domestic affairs are likely to be stormy. Devote a lot of time to trying to settle those in a fair way as soon as possible.

11. WEDNESDAY. Disconcerting. You will find that interruptions are likely. It will be difficult to concentrate for very long periods. It may not be possible to handle the sort of jobs that you had planned to complete. Don't be in too much of a rush. More haste would definitely mean less speed. Spouses can get into a muddle over domestic arrangements. Communications problems can have a disruptive effect on home and family affairs. People may be vague and forget to deliver important messages to you. There could be a certain inevitability about marriage disputes and arguments. But this should not be made an excuse for indulging them. In fact, it could be a challenge for everyone to prove the assumption wrong.

12. THURSDAY. Mixed.   Excessive spending on pleasure today would be inadvisable. Think more about the future and the welfare and security of you and yours. Cash may be reserved as payment long overdue, for jobs that you completed some time ago. This money should be plowed into savings funds and not frittered away. Romance must not be allowed to deplete your reserves even further. Meetings with loved ones could result in your having to dig deeply into your pocket. Make sure that you are not being taken for a ride. If the money side of your life can be kept under control, this can be an especially happy day for meetings with relatives or long-time friends who mean a great deal to you but no longer live near you.

13. FRIDAY. Uncertain.   Speculative activity today can produce good, long-range results. However, it must be based on a sound appraisal of the risks involved. You should listen more closely to the advice, though, of people who have provided you well with invaluable information in the past. Older professional people may be able to put you on the track of something unusually lucrative. However, there is also quite likely to be a considerable amount of paying out to do. Debts for household repairs should be met promptly. In business, Aries can be helped tremendously by some unexpected good luck. This will possibly come in the form of active assistance from business partners. However, there could be help from a totally unexpected source such as an inheritance.

14. SATURDAY. Important.   This will be the kind of day that should leave you feeling very well satisfied. There will be good opportunities for the Aries business person to tie up a lucrative contract. This should take place before he or she takes a weekend break. Certain people may have been difficult to get hold of earlier in the week. But now they will make themselves and their services available to you. It should be one of those days when you will be glad to knuckle down to some hard work. The results of your labors should be most lucrative. You will get a great deal of pleasure from dealing with anything that allows you to be artistic. Do all in your power to achieve financial security for you and yours. This entails good, sound planning ahead for the future.

15. SUNDAY. Disturbing.   You must be strong-willed today. If you have made plans for it as the day when you are going to start a new sort of diet or keep-fit course, you must exercise self-discipline. There are likely to be marital tiffs with which you will have problems coping. Your mate or partner may be complaining about the amount of time you have been giving lately to your outside activities. If you want to keep the peace at home, you will have to include your nearest and dearest in your entertainment ideas. Aries should try to get some work done even if this proposal meets with opposition. Remember that there is nothing to be gained by going to extremes.

16. MONDAY. Mixed. Routine occupational activities may not get off to a smooth start. This is the first day of the working week and you may find the going rough. It may be that you have some difficulty in getting into top gear after your weekend break. The situation will not be helped at your regular place of employment by the moodiness of those with whom you have to work. It may be difficult for you to keep your temper under control. Throughout the morning, concentration will be particularly demanding. Upsetting news from a distance may be the cause. Partners, however, can be especially effective when it comes to dealing with problems at a distance. They wield power and recognize the value of a firm hand at the helm.

17. TUESDAY. Encouraging. This will probably be one of the best days of the month of November, to date. It seems to have been an up-and-down month for you so far. You will be overjoyed to be able to bring many of the projects up to date that you had inadvertently fallen behind with. Loved ones will be helpful to distant affairs once again. This will not be a particularly pressing day at your place of work or business. You will not feel that you have to hurry tasks that require precision and attention to detail. It is a propitious opportunity for giving more time and understanding to marital partners. Don't ever pass up a chance to enhance relationships. No matter how solid you may think yours are, there is always room for reinforcement.

18. WEDNESDAY. Satisfactory. Boredom with routine could be your biggest enemy today. Do what you can to brighten up chores that you do not really want to handle. Try to impress your superiors. The best way is to show that you have the staying power to see that outstanding matters are brought to a successful conclusion. The morning can be useful for discussing future aims and activities seriously with business associates. However, Aries people may be required to make some definite kind of commitment that they would prefer to avoid. Loved ones may make some unexpectedly rapid progress in their self-improvement or academic endeavors. Encourage them further with praise you really mean. You might offer a special prize for continuing their good work.

19. THURSDAY. Productive. This can be an especially fortunate day for Aries whose profession involves them in any form of research or investigational work. You will enjoy probing and making new discoveries. You will probably find inspiration from the backing that you get from an important person you have long admired. The morning period will be the most inspiring. So this is the time you should concentrate on priorities insofar as possible. Taxation and insurance matters should be given great care. Get your financial affairs better organized. It might be a good time for channeling partnership finances into new sound business investments. But make very sure of your ground before you commit such finances since you are not dealing solely with your money.

20. FRIDAY. Demanding.   Slow down the tempo of your life somewhat. It would seem that you have been rushing around a good deal lately. You may have taken more out of yourself than you realize. This is an important day for shopping expeditions. You may be able to pick up goods at very reasonable prices. If you do so, you will add beauty to your surroundings. Be discriminatory in your choice and make sure that you purchase at the most competitive stores. Romantic affairs may encounter some heavy weather. Nevertheless the Aries optimism and cheerfulness will help to put matters to right. Turn on your charm and be at your most persuasive.

21. SATURDAY. Important.   Today will be good for pursuing academic interests and other activities relating to self-improvement. Get involved in subjects that have long held a great deal of interest for you. People will not be so pushy. You will be able to devote yourself to what you consider to be your priorities. The Aries resourcefulness should be valuable in converting apparent difficulties to good account. With an extra burst of enthusiasm, you can and will succeed. The chances are, you will find yourself at the top of the hill at long last. This is a favorable time for planning vacations if you are intending to go away this Christmas. Don't risk missing out on transportation or desirable accommodations. Make plans and reservations early.

22. SUNDAY. Sensitive.   Emotional problems may have to be faced up to. Perhaps you and your opposite number will have to discuss certain personal matters. You may have been avoiding doing so too long. Try to be adult and diplomatic. Avoid direct criticism as much as possible. Do not try to dictate to others as to how they should run their lives. Parents born under the sign of the Ram may have to deal with unruly youngsters in a rather strict way. Some of you may be breaking with the past and starting out in new directions. Loved ones will give you encouragement to help overcome difficulties. They may also give you tangible help in the form of money and introductions.

23. MONDAY. Disconcerting. This is a tricky period for routine business activities and public affairs. You will be hard pushed to keep up with your schedule. Colleagues will be making demands on your time. Future projects may have to be discussed in greater detail than you would have preferred to do. Aries cannot afford to be too glib, as competitors will be actively plotting against them. Watch out for gossip and rumormongering at your place of employment. Keep your relationship with influential people strictly on the up-and-up. The evening can be good for following up investment hunches. But don't act impulsively. Track various indicators for a time before making your decisions.

24. TUESDAY. Important. Friends can provide you with valuable introductions. These can be very helpful in career affairs. This is especially true for Aries who are involved in the arts and in cultural activities as a means for making a living. Do what you can to be seen in the right places socially. Career activities can be advanced by doing a bit of research. Libraries and government buildings are good sources for such activity. But Aries should not be too hasty in interpreting the information they find. They may fail to appreciate its full significance. Expenditure on humanitarian projects must be kept within the bounds of reason. After all, charity must begin at home. You must first take care of your own future.

25. WEDNESDAY. Variable. Social activities will be useful if your work involves overseas governmental officials. You will be able to get on extremely well with foreign visitors. But you must be able to mix business with pleasure during your meetings with them. Get out and about as much as possible. You can use that Aries charm to excellent effect. Some useful knowledge may be supplied to you that would not have come your way in the normal run of things. Loved ones may saddle you with some awkward problems. You may be unable to come up with any immediate solutions for them. Take time to think them through from every angle. Sooner or later, you'll be able to decide what to do.

26. THURSDAY. Sensitive. Discussing partnership affairs with friends and acquaintances is not advisable. Your present domestic problems must be sorted out by you and you alone. Other people's advice is likely to be way off the mark. You will have some difficulty in expressing your feelings. Perhaps you will feel insecure because someone you are fond of seems cold and distant. Aries people should find this a lucky day for business. Moves can be made with the guidance and advice of influential people. The end results will turn out to be extremely lucrative. The mutual friends of partners can be helpful in overcoming future business planning problems. It may be that this is their particular area of expertise.

27. FRIDAY. Rewarding. This is probably the best day of the month. Get off to an early start. What you have to attend to today is likely to be very stimulating. Get on top of your duties early in the day so that you can feel free to turn your attention to artistic pursuits. Do not stifle your creative talents. It may be possible to get an influential person to give financial aid to a project that is very close to your heart. It will be a fine time for those Aries who are attending interviews for new jobs. They would very much like to be chosen for such. Some behind-the-scenes maneuvering can be helpful to your joint financial affairs. This might involve requesting a tip on a new commercial venture or property investment.

28. SATURDAY. Confusing. Always be direct when dealing with officials. There may be income-tax problems that you have not been tackling in the right way. Get together with your accountant and talk over the best and fastest way to get your affairs in better order. Aries are likely to be feeling rather antisocial today. The basic reason for this is probably that they have been socializing a great deal earlier in the week. They would now like to have a little more time to themselves. Just as long as you avoid offending others, this tendency can be very beneficial. Much good work can be done in privacy, free from distractions. There is no real cause for despondency, so don't let the blues get you down.

29. SUNDAY. Upsetting. It will not be easy for you to relax today. Perhaps you are suffering from nervous tension. It would be a good idea for you to get out and about, though. Try to unwind by doing some light exercise. Perhaps a change of environment would do you a world of good. The morning stretch, in particular, can be the most unsettling time frame. There is probably not any concrete reason, at least not one that you can put your finger on. There will probably be a vague feeling of dissatisfaction. It is important to share any problems with loved ones. It is far better than trying to pretend that your problems do not exist. Ignoring them will assure that they will remain with you. Face them squarely and find a solution.

30. MONDAY. Quiet. The month comes to an end on a peaceful note. You will not be required to make any moves of great significance. Although this is the beginning of a new working week, you will have to focus on winding up outstanding jobs. That will prove more beneficial than making any new starts. There will be less emotional disturbance. All in all, you will find it easier to cope today.

Aries persons will find it easier to appreciate the smaller things in life. Walking some of the way to work may provide a pleasant change. You should not always be in so much of a hurry. Take things steadily and slowly this evening. Give yourself time to enjoy a good dinner and a relaxing evening.

DECEMBER

1. TUESDAY. Exciting. The last month of the year gets underway with you apparently in fine fettle. You will feel more sure of yourself and of the direction in which you wish to go. This is an especially favorable time for giving attention to personal matters. You may have had some problems lately coping with them. Loved ones are likely to be more responsive to your romantic overtures. Aries people may experience a boost to the ego as a result of the verdicts on their work by professional experts. Those Aries who are involved with the publishing world may soon experience a lucky breakthrough. It could be connected with a long-awaited project that has finally come through. Or it may be that you have been offered a better position with increased responsibility.

2. WEDNESDAY. Fair. As the day progresses, so financial affairs are likely to pick up. You should push hard to increase your income. Any extra cash that is earned should be put into your bank or your savings account. You must remember that you have a particularly costly time of the year approaching. Peculiar business propositions should be examined closely. They could turn out to be very lucrative. People at your place of work or business will be generally helpful. But personal gains may have to be paid, however reluctantly, into joint savings accounts. Aries cannot rely on having any extra spending money! Romance can be exciting and passionate.

3. THURSDAY. Demanding. This is one of those tricky days when you should take no one and nothing for granted. Be wary about making flippant remarks when out socially with people you do not know very well. Your meaning could easily be taken the wrong way and cause bad feelings and resentment. You may have some trouble explaining to loved ones just how you feel they rate in their career and in public affairs. But the effort will be worthwhile. This is a good time for catching up with paperwork, bookkeeping, and accounts. You will find it easier to work on your own today. You would have a hard time in getting cooperative ventures launched. It is far better to do a job well than to fight the odds and perhaps be unsuccessful. Wait for a more opportune time.

4. FRIDAY. Troubled. The mental endeavors of Aries-born people may be doomed to failure. It looks as if you are trying to achieve too much in too short a time. It will be very difficult for you to stop your mind from wandering. Your personal life appears to be going through many changes at this point. And even you may be a little unsure about what direction you are going in. Do not try to push people who mean a great deal to you into making definite decisions. Communication difficulties may lead to messages from distant places being garbled in transmission. Rather than try to act on what might be misinformation, hold off until you have a clear signal.

5. SATURDAY. Changeable. Mixed trends are indicated for today. Concentration will once again be difficult to attain and maintain. You will be better equipped to work in short bursts, rather than with any sustained effort. Do what you can to stop your mind wandering while at your place of employment. If you are hoping to gain promotion in the coming year, you must make a very concentrated effort to impress those who have any sort of authority over you. In the morning, Aries people should try to avoid being in the wrong place at the wrong time. Superiors may be anxious to get in touch with them. If you are feeling drained, an early night is strongly recommended. On the other hand, a night out on the town should probably be good for you. You need a change of pace.

6. SUNDAY. Good. The chances are that this will be just the sort of Sunday that you relish. You are unlikely to be placed under any pressure. You might feel like staying put in bed or spending a longer time with the oversized papers. Aries people will derive pleasure from pottering around the house and attending to odds and ends. It might be a good idea to aim for more involvement in neighborhood and community affairs. You should discover just what has been going on in your district that might affect you or the value of your property. Loved ones may be able to assist you with a business or financial problem. Whatever you do, don't start to worry again. Life is too short. Let tomorrow take care of itself.

7. MONDAY. Sensitive. Aries people, for whom the buying or selling of property has been dragging on, should pull themselves together and get in touch with professional real estate people. You must find out what can be done to hurry matters up. It would seem that some constructive progress could be made in this area of your life. This is especially true if you are hoping to exchange contracts before Christmas. The day is favorable for investing in collections of antiques and other such precious items like rare stamps and old coins. Browse around the secondhand stores. You may well be able to pick up some bargains. Mates or spouses who are restricted to the home may be difficult to reason with. You will have to show great patience and be calm and kind.

8. TUESDAY. Quiet. Much of this day can be given over to placating loved ones. They may be feeling they have been left out of things. Try to spend more of your spare time that you have not allocated to a specific project at home. Do not give in to the temptation of being extravagant. Current property transactions should be pursued diligently. This is an excellent day for house hunting. You might be able to find the home of your dreams at a very reasonable price. However, definite promises of purchase or down payments should not be made. Aries people should neither hasten things nor delay them unnecessarily. Take events in your stride. Do not rush in blindly, forgetting to show caution.

9. WEDNESDAY. Enjoyable. Today will be good for sporting activities. It will also favor having a good time in general and letting your hair down. People will enjoy your company as usual. You will most likely find yourself very much in demand socially. There may be one or two things that you feel need to be said. But you can probably let off steam without hurting the feelings of loved ones. Try to straighten out the domestic budget. It is essential that more money must be put to one side. The minds of Aries people can be particularly astute and perceptive. This is an excellent time for study and academic pursuits. But romance can cause problems. Spend time and thought on how best to resolve them.

10. THURSDAY. Good. An interesting and constructive day would appear to be ahead of you. It will be favorable for discussing plans for the forthcoming festive season. You may be planning a holiday with a different theme this year. Loved ones are likely to be in complete agreement with your exciting schemes. Superiors will be willing to listen to reason if you need a little extra time off to attend to a personal matter. You may find that at last you have the feeling that the holiday period will soon be upon you. The evening can be good for Aries sportsmen or women who are anxious to try their mettle in competition with others. This could mean card or board games, or even an impromptu dance contest.

11. FRIDAY. Disconcerting. After what appears to have been a relatively successful week so far, it looks as if some of your hopes and desires are likely to be dashed today. In all probability, you are feeling below par and do not have your usual resilience. Do not allow yourself to be consigned to the dumps by negative-thinking people. Routine employment affairs may be rather a bore. But they at least are not likely to be subject to interruption. This is not a day when you should take risks with partnership finances. Neither would it be wise to do any meddling with taxation affairs. Stick to your usual routine and don't go out on a limb. Just bide your time and this phase will pass. Travel could be tricky tonight; relax at home.

12. SATURDAY. Useful. Put your house in order. Deal with chores on the domestic front that may have been piling up throughout the week. You can do a good deal toward improving your future economic security by paying more attention to budgetary matters. Loved ones will be willing to help you in any practical way that they can. More money must be set aside to meet additional Christmas expenditures. They will soon be a fact of your lives. Be cautious about introducing new methods of working. This is especially true if you are attending to matters connected with your regular employment affairs. These new ideas are not likely to be too well received by superiors. There is something about change that causes resentment and even fear.

13. SUNDAY. Sensitive. It might be in your best interests not to attempt to make contact with influential people. They could somehow have some sort of control over your future job security this Sunday. Such matters might best be left to regular office hours. Trying to thrash them out under social conditions would be very ill advised. The morning period is especially sensitive for meetings with people who have any sort of authority over you. Attempts to make money through second-string jobs could prove to be a waste of time. Such efforts may be dismissed out of hand by those from whom you are seeking support. Be sure not to let loved ones down. They will not be likely to forgive you in a hurry. Hurt feelings are hard to heal.

14. MONDAY. Demanding. Partners, whether of a marital or business kind, may seem to be doing their utmost to bring out the worst in Aries people. You may well wonder about the motives of people who have been known to you for a long time. They certaiinly do not seem to be trying to make your life any easier. Perhaps others are so motivated by self-interest that they do not realize the mistakes they are making. These have to do with valuable relationships of the future. It might help to have a serious and calm talk with the more reasonable people. Try to point out the irresponsible and weak side in their natures without giving offense. This may be a waste of time, but it would be better to try than to do nothing.

15. TUESDAY. Satisfactory. The advice of partners can be particularly helpful in connection with distant affairs. You may be planning trips to countries overseas in the not-too-distant future. If so, talk to people who are close to you and who are familiar with such areas. They will be able to tell you what to take and what to avoid when you are over there. Loved ones will also be willing to come to your aid where academic interests are concerned. Perhaps you are considering applying for further educational courses soon. It also seems that members of the family will be more interested in being helpful in a practical way than by being affectionate. It could be that they are merely distracted by having so much on their minds.

16. WEDNESDAY. Good. This will be an important midweek day. Progress can be made at your place of employment. Aries people will benefit from conferring with professional people. They can offer Aries good financial advice in the banking and investment areas. People skilled in business management will have good ideas on how you can put your skills to the best possible use. Listen to the advice of influential people. You know, from past experience, that they have only your best interests at heart. Some private investigation can help to iron out ambiguities and confusion. Aries people who are involved in public relations will find this is the right moment to launch new and exciting publicity campaigns.

17. THURSDAY. Unsettling. Aries-born people may be in for a shock in connection with taxation and insurance matters. Perhaps you will discover that you have a larger payment to make than you had anticipated. Officials that you have to deal with will not be as understanding as you might have hoped. It will not be possible to get any additional time to pay. You may possibly have to dip into cash reserves that you had hoped to keep to one side for pleasurable activities. It will be particularly hard for you if you have failed to keep up payments. This is not a day when you should be too ambitious regarding future investments. It might be best just to sit tight for now and observe market trends.

18. FRIDAY. Variable. Aries business people should be able to improve their reputations. As a start, they should try to adopt a more deliberately pleasing public image. On occasions, you have been known to put your foot in it. This is a time when it is important for you to keep some of your more firmly held opinions to yourself. This is for the sake of maintaining good working relations with people that you must rely upon in some way or another. Bringing a smile into routine business transactions can make them both more pleasant and more productive. Perseverance is needed in mental and academic endeavors. Keep working hard at it and you should win through in the end. You may be trying to work in surroundings not conducive to concentration. Find a quiet area.

19. SATURDAY. Productive. Get your last-minute Christmas shopping done before the rush really gets into full swing. Go over your list of people that you have planned to buy for. Be sure that you have not inadvertently left out anyone who always remembers you at this time of the year. You will probably find yourself doing quite a lot of rushing hither and thither. But you will be happy to keep yourself meaningfully occupied. Stock up with food and drinks you will be consuming during the festive season. Be sure that you do not leave yourself short of anything, including money. The morning will favor those who are prepared to get out and about and try something completely new. Aries people recognize a challenge when they see one.

20. SUNDAY. Important. Distant affairs are likely to keep Aries people on their toes. It looks as if you might be doing a lot of running around and about. You might be invited to visit a friend or a member of the family. You will not otherwise be able to see this person over the Christmas season. You will also have quite a lot of preparations to make within the home. There may be last-minute Christmas cards to get off and lots of presents to wrap. Important job decisions may have to be made with regard to employment activities in the New Year. Those of you involved in self-improvement or academic pursuits should go all-out in your efforts to succeed. The more you know, the more likely you are to advance to higher positions.

21. MONDAY. Rewarding. You will be feeling fairly confident and sure of yourself today. This feeling of well-being would appear to be well placed. You appear to be on the verge of an important breakthrough. Because you have worked hard for this, it is very well deserved. Business affairs are likely to be looking up. There may be a chance to strike a really good deal that will bring you in some much-needed cash. This would come in very handy over Christmas. Career prospects will be best for those Aries who are not too lazy to do all the necessary groundwork. They are also prepared to do their own research. Try to overcome obstacles in connection with alimony, inheritances or taxation problems. If you can work out solutions now, you will be able to put them out of your mind for good.

22. TUESDAY. Happy. No additional problems are likely to appear on the horizon to bother you or to upset your plans too badly. Loved ones will probably make this a day for you to remember. Someone who really matters to you is likely to demonstrate, in no uncertain terms, how much they really do care for you. It will be the little things that count the most. This is an especially favorable day for love and romance. For the Aries woman, it is a reassuring period. Those who desire marriage may find that wedding bells will not be as far away as they had surmised. Once the holiday season has passed, events may speed up considerably.

23. WEDNESDAY. Difficult.   Aries people should try to keep a close watch on business profits. More money seems to have been going out on unnecessary expenditures than you may have bargained for. The financial affairs of your business could be heading straight for taxation problems in the future. It is essential that you do adopt a much more cautious attitude. You realize that this is a time of the year when you like to enjoy yourself. But that does not mean you should not take all the necessary precautions in your workplace. Information may come up about a friend or acquaintance which you find particularly disturbing. It is wise, however, not to trust hearsay, nor to judge anyone too harshly. Until all the facts are known, the person in question should be regarded as above reproach.

24. THURSDAY. Good.   There will be plenty going on around you, both at home and at work, if you are at the office today, that is. Office and factory parties will be pleasant occasions. You may have the chance to get to know someone much better whom you have always fancied. Aries people will also have a strong desire to spend some time today discussing serious issues with close friends. Philosophy and religion can be natural topics. Behind-the-scenes contacts may enable the Ram to get on the right side of some highly influential people. Career prospects are likely to look up as a result. Cultivate the friendship extended by those who are in a position to assist you with your career.

25. FRIDAY. Merry Christmas!   Aries may feel strangely detached from the festivities going on today. It will not be at all easy for you to get into the spirit of things. Nor can you seem to get onto the same wavelength as those people with whom you are spending your time. However, it does not mean that you won't derive a lot of enjoyment in your own way. You may appear to be in a more subdued mood than usual. Loved ones will be loyally affectionate. They will not try to push you to do anything that would go against the grain. It may be possible for you to glimpse a deeper side to people than is usually apparent. People you remember from the past may cause feelings of nostalgia and perhaps a tinge of sadness.

26. SATURDAY. Upsetting. Today could be something of an anticlimax for you. You may be feeling a little below par physically and this could mean that you become more easily depressed. Perhaps it will not be as easy as usual for you to get on top of your feelings. Try not to take it out on others. Avoid taking on tasks for which you feel a natural revulsion. Spending more time alone could possibly be helpful. Settle down with a good book to take your mind off gloomy thoughts. The health of in-laws may leave much to be desired. Visits to hospitals or institutions may be necessary. Charity work can run into trouble. Do not be responsible for cash belonging to others. Why take on another burden?

27. SUNDAY. Promising. A much happier and more positive day is at hand for your personal affairs. You seem to have shrugged off your recent doldrums. It may be that you did not really enjoy the festive season as much as you usually do. But it should be possible now to ease any tensions that may have built up within the home. Matters of the heart will take a turn for the better. Your love life seems to be entering a much more steady and rewarding phase. Single Aries may meet compatible partners at the homes of friends. Or friends themselves may become lovers. But this is not a day for mixing with the kind of company that might endanger reputations.

28. MONDAY. Encouraging. The Ram will be feeling far more confident today. It will be a pleasure to get back to work. It looks as if there is much that will be exciting on the agenda. People will be paying you compliments and admiring your abilities, rightly so. Superiors could be doing more than just talking about promotion for you in the coming year. The evening is particularly favorable for self-improvement activities. You may be able to make an enduring mark in your chosen field of endeavor. Distant business affairs that had been put to one side over the holiday period can now be attended to. Someone in another town can finally be reached. Gradually, you will find the routine of your job will return to normal.

29. TUESDAY. Deceptive. Influential business people cannot be relied upon. They may say one thing and then go ahead and do another. The more you can deal with work on your own and in your own way, the better you are likely to fare. Promises have been made may well be broken. People may be talking big. But when the crunch comes, they will not be prepared to put their money where their mouth is. Associates may be hiding their true intentions and sympathies. As long as you can set your own pace, financial gains can be considerable. A clear understanding must be reached with loved ones and friends over money matters. Actually, it will be easier for everyone when they know where they stand.

30. WEDNESDAY. Quiet.   This will be a useful day for paying bills and for getting your affairs in some kind of order. You may also be able to contact a builder or electrician now. There is some work to be done in your home that has required attention since well before Christmas. Aries people should pick up the threads of their personal finances and get things back into order again. Some attempt should be made to reorganize savings programs. This is a good time for making New Year's resolutions to cut down on spending in the future. Any financial moves must be discussed with other parties before being implemented. This applies to domestic and business affairs.

31. THURSDAY. Disquieting.   For most Aries-born, bread-and-butter issues are likely to come at the top of the list. Money problems will be very much on your mind. It seems unlikely that you will be in the mood to go along with the extravagant ideas of friends for having a good time. You will prefer to do your own celebrating in a quiet way. You cannot afford to take financial matters for granted. Try not to end the year on a sour note by depleting your joint resources. End-of-the-year extravaganzas should be kept within the bounds of moderation. It might not be long after midnight that you decide to stop celebrating and go to bed. You have saluted the start of the New Year and now it's time to rest.